KIPLINGER'S REVISED & UPDATED

WORKING FOR YOURSELF

FULL TIME

·

PART TIME

·

ANY-TIME

JOSEPH A. ANTHONY

KIPLINGER
TIMES BUSINESS

KIPLINGER BOOKS, WASHINGTON, D.C.
TIMES BUSINESS, NEW YORK, N.Y.

KIPLINGER
BOOKS

Published by
The Kiplinger Washington Editors, Inc.
1729 H Street, N.W.
Washington, D.C. 20006

Library of Congress Cataloging-in-Publication Data

Anthony, Joseph, 1960–
    Kiplinger's Working for yourself : full time, part time, anytime /
by Joseph Anthony. — 2nd rev. ed.
        p.   cm.
    Includes bibliographical references and index.
    ISBN 0–8129–2645–5
    1. Self-employed–United States. 2. Small business–United States–Management. I. Title.
HD8037.U5A58   1995   95–35617
658'.041–dc20   CIP

This publication is intended to provide guidance in regard to the subject matter covered. It is sold with the understanding that the author and publisher are not herein engaged in rendering legal, accounting, tax or other professional services. If such services are required, professional assistance should be sought.

Second edition, first printing. Printed in the United States of America.

Book designed by S. Laird Jenkins Corp.

Acknowledgements

One of the benefits of writing this book for Kiplinger was being able to draw on the recollections of subscribers to *The Kiplinger Washington Letter* who shared their experiences good and bad of working for themselves. Many friends and associates also gave freely of their time to tell me their self-employment tales. Although only some of these people actually appear in the book, I'm thankful for the time and thoughts shared by all.

Their efforts add up to a tasty combination of real-life stories and recipes for self-employment success. Many of these people have started businesses that are food-related. That is not part of any gustatory design; it merely reflects my love of food and of the people who dedicate themselves to its preparation. Working for yourself is a little like preparing a great meal: It's easier if you're starting with the right ingredients.

Many other people helped make this book possible. David Harrison and Patricia Mertz Esswein worried about what people starting businesses really care about and helped shape and improve the final product. Dianne Olsufka and Karmela Lejarde provided plenty of all-around editorial assistance, Judy Marcus took on the burden of factchecking the book, and Rosemary Neff smoothed out rough edges. Special thanks to Max Fallek, Kris Davis, Melynda Dovel Wilcox, Kevin McCormally, and Ronaleen Roha for their input. Jonathan Kirsch is a gentleman and a scholar, and I am grateful for his legal representation.

Finally, some personal thanks go to: my parents, Barbara and Joseph Harb; Heidi Yorkshire, who told me to write this book; John Wasik, Jack Langguth and the much-missed Andrea Eagan; and the people who helped make my first self-employment venture a success when they hired me to mow their lawns and shovel snow from their sidewalks.

Joseph Anthony

Table of Contents

CONTENTS

Introduction

By Knight A. Kiplinger
Co-Editor, *The Kiplinger Letters*
Editor in Chief, *Kiplinger's Personal Finance Magazine*

We at the Kiplinger organization have a special affection and respect for small-business owners, who are legion among the subscribers to our business Letters and personal-finance magazine. The hundreds of letters and calls we receive each month from small-business owners give us a detailed view of the challenges and opportunities they grapple with each day. They tell us of their headaches with marketing, personnel management, credit problems and more. And they share with us their stories of triumph.

The yen for self-employment is age-old. My grandfather, W.M. Kiplinger, felt this impulse back in 1920, when he resigned a secure wire-service reporting job with the Associated Press to found his own Washington information agency for banking clients. The interest in working for oneself has accelerated recently, amid downsizing turmoil in corporate America. Thousands of security-conscious managers are discovering, ironically, that putting trust in one's own ability may lead to a more-secure future than trusting a giant corporate employer. Increasingly our reader mail reflects this growing interest in striking out on one's own, and many of the letters ask for our advice on getting started. That's what gave us the idea for this Kiplinger book.

When we surveyed the field, we found many fine books on single aspects of the self-employment subject: retail, consulting, part-time business, franchises, buying an existing business, and so on. But we were surprised by the lack of a single book with an overview of all these subjects. Moreover, we found that most books on starting a business assumed that the decision had already been made. But before getting to "how to," many prospective entrepreneurs need counsel on *"whether* to." That's why this book starts out leading the reader through an analysis of the motivations and aspirations behind the work-for-yourself dream.

After conceiving the idea of a new kind of self-employment guide, we went looking for an experienced business journalist to put it all together. We were fortunate to find Joseph Anthony, who is not only a talented reporter and writer but who is also a self-employed freelancer whose personal experiences enrich this book. Mr. Anthony had at his disposal the staff expertise of *Kiplinger's Personal Finance Magazine,* which writes often about self-employment. Working closely with the author was our very talented managing editor of Kiplinger Books, Patricia Mertz Esswein.

There's no one way to start working for yourself, simply no sure-fire formulas, and the search for that "one and only" is something that stops many people in their tracks. But the good news is that there are actually *many* ways you can start working for yourself. You can start part time, or you can plunge in cold turkey. You can start with an idea for a new product or service, or an idea for improving an existing one. You can go it alone or in partnership with others.

Similarly, you can start your search for help at more than one place in this book. It's designed to help you no matter what stage you're at in the process. Whether you just decided today that you would like to be your own boss, or whether you've been plotting your path to self-employment for months or years, this book can help get you to your first day of business.

Different sections of this book will be of varying interest to different readers. If you're curious about franchises or buying an existing business, skip ahead to chapters on those subjects. No matter where you start, you'll probably find that the issues you have questions about relate to other issues that must be considered when working for yourself.

We hope this book is valuable in helping you decide whether and how to start working for yourself. Wherever your quest leads, you have our best wishes for financial success and self-fulfillment.

Knight Kiplinger

Washington, D.C.

Who Are the Self-Employed? (And How You Can Be One of Them)

CHAPTER 1

"A journey of a thousand miles must begin with a single step." Lao-tzu, 604 531 B.C.

Notice that this chapter isn't called "Who Starts a Business?" There's good reason for that. While this book will, in fact, help you do just that, it also recognizes that in the '90s more and more people are breaking away from careers where they've worked for others. They're doing so more to work for themselves than to "start a business" in the traditional sense of that phrase. Maybe they desire a simpler lifestyle and decide to turn a hobby into income. Or they're new parents who want to continue their careers to some degree while they take care of their child. Perhaps they're victims of corporate downsizing and have decided to strike out on their own as consultants. Few of these people think of themselves as starting a business. But that is exactly what they are doing.

The very fact that you've picked up this book says

you're probably thinking of a change in your own work life. This book will help you if:

- you've been thinking of working for yourself and haven't yet overcome your own inertia.

- circumstances, personal and/or professional, make starting and running your own business your best career move.

- you've already set out on your own and are seeking additional information and advice.

Jusp, Cartoonists & Writers Syndicate

Whatever stage you're in and however you hope to define yourself—entrepreneur, self-employed person, independent contractor, proprietor, free-lancer, small-business owner, consultant, one-woman or one-man band—this book is your map to working for yourself. It will help you "organize, manage and assume the risks of a business or enterprise," to quote from Webster's definition of an entrepreneur.

You may not need all the information you find here. A one-person operation won't be concerned about staffing up, for example. But regardless of the size of the intended business, it doesn't hurt to be aware of all the factors involved in starting a standard business. You may encounter things you otherwise wouldn't have thought of but should have. And, you never know what will happen to that intended small, just-doing-it-to-make-ends-meet operation. You could well become successful beyond what you plan—or perhaps want.

Potential Entrepreneur or Self-Employed Person?

Don't get hung up on any notions of what it means to be an entrepreneur. In the '80s, that word conjured up notions of the new American hero who created a company, jobs and wealth. And that may be exactly how you envision yourself and your future. But in the '90s, even *Inc.* magazine, the bible of Entrepreneurship with a capital E, recognizes that growth-oriented start-ups don't represent the universe of entrepreneurs. Author John Case identified four types of entrepreneurs who will create businesses in the '90s in his article entitled "How to Survive Without a Job" (*Inc.,* June 1992). He describes the types as:

"The traditionalists."

We all know these people. These are the folks who sell goods and services to consumers, buy family-owned manufacturers or distributors, or buy a franchise. They expect to hire and fire their fair share of employees over time. Traditionalists have to be good at a little bit of everything and they plan to *keep* things "pretty much the way they've always been," says *Inc.*

"The job creators."

These people want to *grow* their own businesses and their payrolls. They don't just want to be their own boss, they want to be other people's, too. They tend to be creative managers of money because the rapid growth of their businesses demands ever more cash.

"The soloists."

They *are* their businesses. Their product is themselves—their knowledge, experience and contacts. The revolution in information and technology has infinitely expanded their markets, but growth per se isn't the point. Soloists want—and have—lots of control over what they do, they accept the ultimate responsibility for it, too. They don't hire employees; they network with other soloists to get clients' jobs done.

An entrepreneur? "Someone willing to work 16 hours a day for himself so he can avoid working eight hours a day for someone else."

"The minimalists."

They're a hybrid of all of the above. They're building businesses that may provide goods, services or expertise; they're doing it with a few key employees, little cash and low overhead; and they're deliberately staying small so they can continue to *enjoy* their businesses. Like soloists, they network, but typically with other businesses, sometimes very big ones, and often for purposes of marketing.

It's Your Choice

While there are different "types" of people, the goals of these entrepreneurs tend to be similar: to create a more manageable work life, a more fulfilling career or a more satisfying personal life; to work and live where they want; or to use their skills to become more financially secure and self-sufficient.

Those rewards don't come easy. Another definition of entrepreneur—one of the more whimsical, but not the least accurate—is "someone willing to work 16 hours a day for himself so he can avoid working eight hours a day for someone else."

That captures the essence of life for many people who become self-employed. But even so, working for yourself doesn't have to be as draining as running a marathon, nor as risky as crossing the Pacific in a canoe, nor as challenging as climbing Mount Everest. In short, working for yourself can be an invigorating adventure.

My Own Adventure

I've been working for myself, in one form or another, for more than a decade. I've held down full-time jobs while running a business on the side; I've also worked for myself full-time. I've found I'm a very demanding boss but also one who is willing to let his key employee—that's me, of course—take a vacation as a reward for a job well done.

My work has always been linked to the publishing industry, and as the years have passed I've seen some integral aspects of my business change. When I started, writers typically pounded out their assignments on typewriters and either mailed or hand-delivered printed text to their editors and clients. Today, word processors, high-quality printers, and modems for telecommunicating copy to publishers, ad agencies or corporate clients are the rule. The facsimile machine has become a standard piece of office—and home-office—equipment. The "fax" and express delivery services have shrunk the distance between my clients here and overseas. Sending a 500-word letter by fax can be as speedy as and far cheaper than engaging in a 500-word conversation by telephone. Sending a 500-word e-mail message can be faster and cheaper than both.

The rapidly evolving ways of sending, retrieving and massaging information are also changing fundamental aspects of my business and millions more. On-line services, for instance, make it possible for me to gain nearly instant access to literally hundreds of newspapers and magazines useful to my needs. The convergence of all sorts of information tools—including televisions, computers, telephones, cable systems and satellites—is creating a world in which any "data"—including music, articles, books, movies, television programs, advertisements and conversations, and anything else that can be converted into a stream of ones and zeros, the common language of computers—may be transferred from anyplace to anyplace by a variety of means. Information, as it turns out, is a very liquid asset.

All this has decreased the importance of where my business is located. Earlier in my career, I lived in Washington, D.C., and, because I had many local clients, felt I needed to remain there. But over time, I've become more confident in my work, and technology has enabled me to carry on long-distance relationships with my clients as I've moved from the East Coast to the West Coast.

While writing this book, I moved from Los Angeles to Oregon. My publisher is in Washington, D.C., and I'm maintaining relationships with clients and other professionals around the country. We not only communicate by letters, but we also work and converse with the help of telephone, computer disk, computer scanner, fax, modem and several choices of express delivery. Obviously, not all self-employed people can work in the location of their choice.

The electronic and communications revolution has decreased the importance of where my business is located.

But this becomes an option for more and more people as communications progress. (And I consider it a communications progression, not a revolution—the means and convenience of communications change, but what needs to be communicated remains the same.)

If it means that more of us can live and work in the places most satisfying to us, so much the better. After all, working for yourself—whether full-time or part-time, whether you'll be a company of one employee (yourself) or head of an organization with dozens of employees—is · an opportunity to have more control over your life.

Why People Do It

The reasons people think about starting their own businesses are as varied as the businesses they eventually run. Some examples:

Cooking small, but beautifully

Caprial Pence is one of the most highly regarded chefs in the Pacific Northwest. In the early 1990s she decided to leave her job with a large hotel in Seattle and open her own restaurant. She wasn't interested in starting a large, expensive restaurant that would require borrowing money, getting investments from limited partners or working 16 hours a day overseeing an operation that would have 250 customers a night. Instead, she and her husband, John, decided to open a small bistro in Portland, Ore., that seats fewer than 25 people. Their restaurant, Westmoreland Bistro & Wines, doubles as a wine shop from which dinner guests can select their favorite vintage. "We could have gone for a big place," says Caprial. "But we didn't want that, any more than we wanted to spend all our time working for a corporation. We just wanted a small business that would support us and that would allow us to have a *life*, not just a job."

Taking charge of mere circumstances

John and Patricia Trotta were living comfortably in Greensboro, N.C., where they both worked for a company that sold steel grating supplies. "Then the company we worked for was sold in 1986, and the new owners wanted to transfer us to New Jersey," remembers Patricia. "But the cost of housing was a lot higher there, and we would have had to take a cut in our standard of living to stay with the company."

So the Trottas took another path: They started their own business, Hidek Supply, which fabricates and sells steel grating products, handrails and spiral staircases to corporations, other steel fabricators and some general contractors. "We started as a representative of another manufacturer, and then began producing products on our own," says John, who lists his title with Hidek as "Proprietor."

Although they hadn't set out to run their own business, the Trottas have made a success of Hidek. "We weren't looking to get rich," says Patricia. "We were just responding to being victims of circumstance."

Leaping out of middle-management

Charles J. Dervarics had often thought about being in business for himself as he worked his way up the publishing ladder. "I'd seen friends go off on their own and succeed, and it looked kind of attractive; they looked like they had pretty good lives," says the Alexandria, Va., resident. "But I tend to be fairly careful and didn't want to try something like that on a whim."

Dervarics made the jump when he found himself in what looked like a middle-management crunch at the publishing firm where he worked as an editor. "I'd gone about as far as I could go with the job I was in," he remembers. "I'd been promoted to middle management, and I'd worked hard to get to that position, but once there I realized there really was no higher place for me to go."

While he knew he wasn't in danger of losing his job, Dervarics felt he would stagnate if he didn't instigate a ca-

"So, I said to myself, Dave, you can keep doing dog shows all your life or you can move on to something bigger."

Steiner, Cartoonists & Writers Syndicate

reer shift. But he didn't want to simply quit and start a new business cold. His solution was to negotiate with a company for a contract to produce two of its newsletters. The contract gave him a revenue base that allowed him to leave his job and support himself while getting his editorial and publications consulting business off the launching pad.

The initial going was a little rough, especially when he was working out of the small rented apartment where he lived. But Dervarics's cash flow soon increased, and today he runs his business out of his house. "I always liked the idea of working out of my home, not having to deal with a commute every day," he says. "The whole thing has really worked out very well."

Who better to work for?

Bruce Burns didn't even think of himself as an entrepreneur—still doesn't, in fact, even though he's had his own business for more than a decade. "In a lot of ways I'm not adventuresome; I kind of surprised myself when I went off on my own," says Burns, whose GXI Graphics Exhibits Interiors Inc. designs and builds trade show exhibits, custom interiors, and other display and office spaces for corporations.

Burns had experience in similar businesses but had begun to feel trapped and wanted greater control over his life and his work. "I think I'd just reached a point where I wanted to have very high regard for whomever I worked

Who Is Most Likely to Break Away?

• •

The **Center for Entrepreneurial Management**, a nonprofit consulting organization founded and directed by author Joe Mancuso (180 Varick St., New York, NY 10014; 212–633–0060), says that folks who launch themselves in businesses are most likely to be:

- Offspring of self-employed parents.
- Previously fired from more than one job.
- Immigrants or the children of immigrants.
- Previously employed in businesses of fewer than 100 employees.
- The oldest child in the family.
- College graduates.
- Willing to rely on outside management experts.
- Realistic risk-takers, not high-risk takers.
- Well-organized and good at organizing others.

Many people have found that the best way to cope with upheavals in the corporate world is to leave it and construct their own company and career.

for, and I realized that finding someone with exactly the same values I have would be unrealistic."

The Motivation They Share

The Penses, the Trottas, Dervarics and Burns are typical of many small-business owners. Among the more common reasons people start working for themselves:

- **They want to feel good** about what they're doing.
- **They have what they think is a great idea** for a business.
- **They want to control** their own business futures.
- **They want to make the major decisions** affecting their financial lives.
- **They feel they're stagnating** in their present jobs.
- **They feel bored, unappreciated, underpaid, underutilized or buried** under a mountain of bureaucracy in their current jobs.
- **They're frustrated** with corporate life.
- **They're anticipating a second career** or a "postretirement" career and they want to lay the groundwork for it.
- **They've reached the top** or are nearing the bottom in their present career paths.

Many people have found that the best way to cope with upheavals in the corporate world is to leave it and construct their own company and career. Numerous middle managers have taken this path after finding that their opportunities have dwindled, not because they are unqualified for advancement but because the number of upper-management openings pales in comparison to the volumes of qualified executives competing for those positions.

You may have been in this boat; you may even have headed off already and begun your own business. In that case—or if you've already considered your desires and needs, your personal finances, and the type of business that's right for you—the first five chapters of this book will cover some familiar terrain. You may want to dive right into Chapter 6, our introduction to developing and carrying out a plan of action for self-employment.

What About More Time and Money?

When you imagine the self-employed, do you think of people who start work when they feel like it, stop when they want to, take time off whenever they need it and make a lot of money?

Suffice it to say, the fantasy is far more attractive than the reality, as most people who've started their own businesses know. It's common for individuals to put in 12-hour days for six or even seven days a week when they're getting a business off the ground. When you're your own boss, you can drive yourself far harder than someone else could or would, because you know how much you're capable of and because you're doing something that you see ultimately benefiting *yourself*—not an impersonal corporation.

Surprisingly, surveys indicate that the chance to make a lot of money doesn't rank high among the reasons people start their own businesses. In one survey by a major accounting firm, for example, less than one-fifth of small-business owners strongly agreed that financial reward was the main reason they owned their own businesses. By comparison, nearly three-quarters strongly agreed that being able to act on their own ideas was a major source of satisfaction.

Personal pride and satisfaction, autonomy, and control of one's own destiny all carry great weight with those who are their own bosses. Increasingly, people are working for themselves not because they want to make a lot of money but because they want to do something they enjoy. They want to feel they have some control over a part of their lives that consumes a majority of their waking hours. They simply want to do something that doesn't alienate them and instead makes them feel good about the person they see in the mirror every morning.

Increasingly, people are working for themselves not because they want to make a lot of money but because they want to do something they enjoy.

A survey of 198 business owners by Cicco & Associates Inc., a Murrysville, Pa., consulting firm, revealed that small-business owners got their satisfaction from (in descending order):

1. Pride in product or service

2. Control

3. Freedom

4. Flexibility

5. Self-reliance

6. Customer contact

7. Income

8. Employee contact

9. Recognition

10. Privacy

11. Security

12. Status

Who Starts Down the Road?

There's a big difference between wanting to work for yourself and actually doing it, and there's no formula to predict who will follow through on their ideas and visions.

Certainly, having as a role model (and near-at-hand consultant) a parent who was self-employed can be a big asset for a budding businessperson. But you don't have to come from a long line of entrepreneurs to succeed in your own business. Nor do you have to have any of the other "typical" backgrounds or personality traits of a business founder. In real life, there's no Central Casting source of business operators. The truth is, many people who've spent their lives in 9-to-5 jobs—people like you—have what it takes to run their own businesses.

Desire, Tenacity and Other Intangibles

There are, however, a few traits that many of the self-employed seem to share. You don't need to possess all these characteristics, but you're more likely to be drawn toward working for yourself if you have a few of them, including:

Self-confidence

We won't pull any punches—starting a business can mean getting rejected or slapped down a few times. You may have the skill and talent to produce a product or service, but you may never have had to "sell yourself" before. Making cold calls to prospective clients may be the hardest and least enjoyable thing you've ever had to do, and on top of that, you will have to learn to take no for an answer. Initial costs may be higher than you anticipated, and the market for your product may be slow to develop. The clients you thought you could count on may bail out. Lenders may turn you down. Even those closest to you may, with all good intentions, express doubts about the wisdom of your new enterprise.

But successful entrepreneurs keep believing in themselves during the tough times and when confronted by doubts. This is an essential quality. You have to believe in yourself if you expect others to believe in you.

A sense of timing

This relates to your self-confidence. Good timing (or business intuition) is the ability to perceive the value of a product or service just before a market develops for it. It doesn't pay to be too prescient: You can't make money if you have a great idea that people won't want for another five years.

Recognizing "security" as a state of mind

Not long ago, it wasn't unusual for a person to spend his or her entire professional life with one corporation. There was an implied social contract in the work world: A company would nurture and protect (and not fire) its employees, and employees in turn would be loyal and dedicated to the company.

In many places, though, those days are fast disappearing or long gone. While there are still many people who have worked for one corporation for their entire careers, job-switching has become the norm. Today businesses downsize, eliminate divisions or sell off units, all at the drop of a quarterly report. Even such rock-solid and established corporations as IBM, long known for its generous benefits packages and policy of never laying people off, have let employees go.

In some industries (high technology, for example), people expect to move up the career ladder only by moving from one company to another. Corporations may cushion the blow of layoffs, downsizings and outright firings with termination packages, but such packages don't change the basic truth that, for many workers, "job security" is more realistically measured in months than in years. Corporate loyalty to workers is, in short, increasingly a thing of the past.

This new work world treats blue- and white-collar workers alike. At one time, layoffs of white-collar, middle-manager types were rare, and those managers who were temporarily unemployed hid their "affliction" out of embarrassment. Today, management layoffs are so common

The basic truth is that, for many workers, "job security" is more realistically measured in months than in years.

You have to have the equanimity and confidence to persist when the week draws to a close and you have little, financially speaking, to show for your efforts.

that those caught in restructurings and other corporate squeezes have formed support groups and networking organizations to exchange thoughts and information. And there is no shame in being laid off. One upper-level manager started her own consulting business and announced the venture to friends and associates with a letter that said, in part, "Due to business decisions, my position...was terminated. I will not hide the fact that this news hit me hard. Nor will I deny that the support of family and friends was the most valuable shoulder at a low time. I leave...without rancor and with memories of happy times and wonderful people." The time has passed when people had to hide that they were, as some liked to say, "between assignments."

Willingness to invest your savings

As you'll see in Chapter 17, it's possible to get money—if you need it—for a start-up business, but most lenders or investors will want you to put your own money at risk before they pitch in. And why not? After all, if you're not confident enough about your business idea to invest your own money, other potential investors are unlikely to be confident in you and your commitment. This may be a blessing in disguise: Individuals can often start small businesses with their own savings and resources. By putting your own money into your career and doing without outside investors, you can retain total financial control over your new enterprise—and reap all the rewards when it becomes a success.

Comfort with not receiving a regular paycheck

Call this the "No visible means of support" phenomenon. Especially in the early stages of a business, it's not unusual to have money coming in only sporadically, if at all. You have to be concerned with cash flow, of course, but you also have to have the equanimity and (here's that word again) confidence to persist when the week draws to a close and you have little, financially speaking, to show for your efforts. This is a mighty incentive to remain employed by someone else while setting up your own business during evenings and weekends.

Ability to plan for and live with irregular checks

Confidence is a great thing to have, but a good attitude alone won't produce a successful business venture. Simply put, the self-employed have to expect periods of weak, or even non-existent, cash flow. That kind of planning is part of an overall business strategy, an integral part of a successful start-up and the focus of much of this book.

Competitiveness

Entrepreneurs like a challenge and view life as a series of games they can win. You might succeed on your own without being competitive, but entrepreneurial winners tend to see a way of succeeding where others have failed, of doing something in a new or better way than they've seen it done before.

Note that we're talking in general terms here, discussing qualities of entrepreneurs rather than specific requirements. That's because there is no such thing as a "standard" self-employed individual. Indeed, that's why entrepreneurs are something special—they see the world, or at least some portion of the world, a little differently from those around them. Where others see problems or even disasters, they see opportunities. They're the people who, for example:

- **love to be in charge of organizing events,** have seen the tremendous problems couples have trying to handle all the details of their weddings...and become wedding planners.

- **understand programming languages,** see how small businesses are using only a fraction of the power offered by desktop computers...and become computer consultants.

- **have worked in all aspects of the hospitality industry** and know that a restaurant needs not only a good chef but also manageable overhead, reliable suppliers and dedicated staff...and become restaurant owners.

Where others see problems or even disasters, entrepreneurs see opportunities.

- **have a knack for sales** and see how corporations are befuddled when trying to choose a telephone system, lease office space or purchase supplies...and become a specialist in selling or helping businesses buy those products and services.

- **enjoy making money at what they do,** but would rather make money doing what they enjoy.

They're the folks who, quite often, have seen or learned something in their own personal or business experience and who know that they can meet a demand for a good or service—and meet it as well as or better than the existing players.

They're the people who have taken a long look at their likes and dislikes, their present lives and goals, and decided that at the end of the path to personal satisfaction lies a business of their own.

Why You Want to Work for Yourself

"To thine own self be true."   *Shakespeare*

Before co-founding her wedding-flowers business, Marcia Lipsenthal did the most basic—and perhaps most telling—analysis of her wants and desires. "I thought about how much I needed to make each week and whether it was possible to do that selling flowers," says Lipsenthal. "The other part of the analysis I did for myself was taking the time to realize that I lived in beautiful surroundings and didn't like having to leave them to go to work, and I had a young child and didn't want to leave her during the day, either. So what I needed, for my personal and professional satisfaction, was a business that would pay enough to support my family, keep me close to home and allow me to be with my daughter. I knew I could tolerate all the stress of having a business in exchange for getting those benefits."

Her analysis led to Flower Ladies, which produces more than 100 varieties of organically raised flowers and arranges them for weddings in the Santa Cruz, Cal., market. The business allowed Lipsenthal to spend a lot of time with her daughter, Ruby; it's paid the family's bills; and it's permitted Lipsenthal to stay close to home—she started the business on the rich acreage around her house.

Sometimes we forget the obvious: You'll be happier—and probably more successful—if in starting a business you satisfy your personal goals.

Taking Stock

Before you can start working for yourself, you, like Marcia Lipsenthal, have to identify what your personal objectives are in starting a business. This process can yield more tangible benefits than any cookie-cutter "analysis" of character.

Among the statements that Lipsenthal found were part of her self-inventory were:

- I want to be with my young daughter during the day.

- I want to make enough money to live on.

- I want to enjoy the surroundings of my home.

- I enjoy growing flowers.

- I can tolerate the stress of running a business in exchange for these benefits.

Those sentences just scratch the surface of what can go into a self-inventory. We won't pretend to know all the questions that you'll ask yourself as you consider working for yourself, but we can give you a group of statements—a list of *wants*—that will prompt your own thinking and help you organize and crystallize your thoughts and desires. You'll "want" to add your own "wants" to this list, of course.

Your list is important because it can put and keep you on the right track in starting a business. You're more likely to succeed at something that satisfies your wants. In other words, you'll be happier—and probably more successful—if in starting a business you are going to satisfy your personal goals, take on a work routine that suits your lifestyle, and embark on the kind of work you like to do and are good at doing. Obvious? Sure. But it's something that people can lose sight of. Keeping an eye on your list of wants will help you properly choose and define your business. Let's face it: There's no sense in working for yourself if you're not going to be happy. I mean, who would you complain to?

Myth & Reality

At this point, it's worth mentioning three myths that are common among people who *don't* work for themselves.

Myth No. 1: You don't have to answer to anyone when you run your own business.

Autonomy? Ha! Being self-employed can mean

A Self-Inventory

Here's a starting point for brainstorming about your own business. Check off any of the following that apply to you and add your own statements in the space allowed. Remember, these items aren't mutually exclusive; you can check off more than one in any group.

For more intensive exercises in assessing your interests and desires, take a look at *What Color Is Your Parachute?* by Richard Bolles (Tenspeed Press, P.O. Box 7123, Berkeley, CA 94707; 510–559–1600; $14.95 plus $3.50 for shipping and handling) or consider career counseling and vocational testing offered by colleges, universities and private counseling firms.

Career strategy

❑ do what I do now, for myself.

❑ do something completely different, for myself.

❑ go back to school or take more training.

❑ occupy my spare time.

❑ turn my hobby or avocation into my job.

❑ create an outlet for nontraditional skills and talents.

❑ create my own "first job" without entering the corporate world of work.

❑ create an intermediate career while I'm raising my family.

❑ resume a career after raising a family.

❑ create a second career for myself before or after retirement.

❑ create a business I can pass on to my family.

Financial goals

❑ supplement my current income from other employment or sources.

❑ generate my own income and purchase and manage my own "benefits."

❑ make enough money to support myself and my family.

❑ achieve the financial freedom to pursue other activities I care about.

❑ make enough money to not have to work within a certain number of years.

(continued on page 20)

having to answer to any combination of partners, clients, customers, landlords, suppliers, trade groups, consumer organizations and employees, as well as local, state and federal tax collectors and licensing entities. (Dealing with various outside interests is discussed more fully in several other sections, including Chapters 16 and 21.)

A Self-Inventory (cont'd.)

Personal relationships

❑ be closer to my: children/spouse/parents/siblings/extended family.

❑ spend more time with friends.

Schedule

❑ work part-time.

❑ work full-time.

❑ work regular/flexible hours.

❑ start work at___A.M./___P.M.

❑ finish work at ___A.M./___P.M.

❑ work/not work evenings/weekends.

❑ take vacations when I choose to.

❑ be available to travel with my spouse/partner/friend/family.

Location

❑ do work that allows me to stay where I am now.

❑ do work that allows me to move anyplace in the U.S. or abroad.

❑ live in the big city/a small town.

❑ live in my ideal location/my hometown/my college town.

❑ live closer to places where I go for recreation (mountains, seashore, lakes, other).

❑ work close to/somewhere other than/in my home.

❑ eliminate my commute.

❑ travel occasionally/regularly as part of my work.

Nature of work

❑ work with ideas.

❑ work with things.

❑ work with people.

❑ work with animals.

❑ work with plants.

Nature of output

❑ produce and sell tangible products—things I can see and feel.

❑ produce and sell information and advice.

❑ produce and sell other services.

❑ sell products/services that others make/provide.

Myth No. 2: Nothing's easier than working for yourself.

In fact, many entrepreneurs have never worked so hard—they find they are their own worst slavedrivers. "I certainly wouldn't work until all hours if I had a regular job and paycheck," an East Coast business owner told me as he

Doing good

- ❏ help people.
- ❏ help the environment.
- ❏ foster other concerns and causes.

Work relationships

- ❏ work alone.
- ❏ work with a partner or partners (spouse/ friend/family members/a former co- worker/other).
- ❏ work with the close help of a staff.
- ❏ work with my former employer/former clients/new clients in a new, self-employed capacity.
- ❏ work with other self-employed people.
- ❏ work with consumers.
- ❏ work with children or young adults.
- ❏ work with women/men.
- ❏ work with parents.
- ❏ work with retirees.
- ❏ work with older people.

Customer relationships

- ❏ work one-on-one with clients.
- ❏ avoid working closely with clients.
- ❏ eliminate middlemen.

Work style

- ❏ do work that is more creative.
- ❏ do work that is less dependent on cre- ative tension or stress.
- ❏ do work that is more/less technical.
- ❏ be more/less of an administrator.
- ❏ be more/less of a craftsperson.
- ❏ be more/less "hands-on."
- ❏ do manual work.

Scope of work

- ❏ do work that requires me to do many dif- ferent tasks or allows me to work on more than one project at a time.
- ❏ do work that is more defined in scope.

Work space

- ❏ work indoors/outdoors.
- ❏ create my own personalized work space.
- ❏ work in leased office space.
- ❏ work at client sites.
- ❏ operate a storefront location.
- ❏ operate a nontraditional "store," such as a street vendor, flea-market or shopping- mall stand.

worked at his computer late one night. "But for the clients of my business, I do whatever has to be done."

Myth No. 3: Whether to go into business for yourself is a simple "yes or no" question.

The factors and questions involved in starting a business are rarely black-and-white. As we've indicated, deciding you want to start a business is not a matter of answering just one question but of addressing literally dozens. And once you do decide to start in, you'll have to handle more

Information Resources

- **The U.S. Small Business Administration.** The SBA has a host of publications, available for $1 or less, on financial management, business planning and marketing. They're listed in the SBA's *Resource Directory for Small Business Management,* available free from your local SBA office. The SBA can accept mail-orders only.

- **The Service Corps of Retired Executives (SCORE;** district offices listed in the blue government listings in your phone book). Affiliated with the SBA, this is an organization of 13,000 retired businesspeople who volunteer to sit down and talk, free of charge, with individuals interested in starting their own businesses. (For more information on SCORE, see Chapter 14.)

- **The Office of Women's Business Ownership** (202–205–6673). This SBA division offers several programs geared to helping women in business.

- **The Minority Business Development Agency** (U.S. Department of Commerce, 14th and Constitution Ave., N.W., Washington, DC 20230; 202–482–5741). This agency is responsible for helping develop the country's minority-owned businesses and providing management and technical assistance (but no direct financial assistance).

- **The American Management Association** (135 W. 50th St., New York, NY 10020; 212–586–8100). The AMA presents thousands of seminars and courses on management issues annually in major U.S. and Canadian cities. One division is geared to small-business concerns. Membership in the organization costs $160 for individuals and $850 for corporations; one of the benefits for the association's more than 65,000 members is a discount of 10% to 15% for seminars, which can cost several hundred dollars each.

questions—a lot more. That's why the rest of this book is here—to help you identify and answer all the other questions you're going to have.

Would You Hire Yourself?

Acknowledging your reasons for wanting to go into business is all well and good, but somewhere along the line you'll have to ask yourself, "Can I deliver?" One way to answer the question is to imagine yourself as the first in line

- **The National Association of Women Business Owners** (1413 K St., N.W., Suite 637, Washington, DC 20005; 301–608–2590). Forty-nine chapters nationwide with more than 5,000 members address issues of concern to women running their own businesses.

- **The Latin American Management Association** (419 New Jersey Ave., S.E., Washington, DC 20003; 202–546–3803). About 500 businesses belong to this association, which offers members help with marketing, networking and education.

- **Colleges and universities.** Many schools now offer extension programs or non-degree courses for people interested in starting or running a business. Classes for "nontraditional" students—that is, people who aren't straight out of high school—have in recent years become an increasingly important source of students and revenue for institutions of higher education. The schools have re-sponded by going out of their way to make returning students feel at home. Courses are often at night and conducted on once-a-week schedules to accommodate adults who have full-time jobs and commitments. Contact colleges and universities in your area for specific information.

- **The National Foundation for Teaching Entrepreneurship** (64 Fulton St., Suite 700, New York, NY 10038; 212–233–1777). In partnership with other organizations that work with disabled and disadvantaged youths, this foundation sponsors entrepreneurial training programs around the country. Contact the foundation for information on programs in your area.

Ultimately, however, you'll have to ask yourself, "How much do I want it?" The body and the family may be willing, but how's the spirit?

for a job interview at your new business. Just as every applicant has strengths and weaknesses, so does every prospective new owner of a small business have strong suits and blind spots. Starting a business isn't exactly like interviewing for a job—for example, you don't have to answer someone else's (potentially embarrassing) questions about why you're leaving your old job, or, for that matter, what kind of animal you would be if you were an animal.

Instead, *you* have to ask the questions—questions about your professional skills, your experience, your accomplishments, and how they may help you in your business venture. Use the process to reaffirm that *you* would hire *you.*

The Personal Questions

There's one other "want" that's implicit in everything above: what your family wants. It's probably impossible to overestimate the importance of emotional support from your spouse or immediate family when it comes to a new business, whether or not they're actually running the cash register or helping put together widgets. Because of that, your list of wants should effectively be doubled—not just "I want..." but also "My family want..." The more those two lists overlap, the more likely you are to get the kind of support that can make your venture a success.

Ultimately, however, you'll have to ask yourself, "How *much* do I want it?" The body and the family may be willing, but how's the spirit? Take it from an expert: "More important than your financial resources, than your willingness to take risks, than any standard formulas is your appropriateness to the business—how much you want to do this thing," says New York management consultant Darlene Orlov. "You've got a lot better chance of succeeding if you want to put your heart and soul into it. If you're not totally committed, you're not going to make it."

Remember, it's up to you as the prospective business owner to put all the pieces together and decide that this—whatever *this* is—is the thing for you. No matter what anyone else may say, you and only you can make the

Five Sources of Support and Affirmation

No man or woman is an island, and no one should feel he or she has to shoulder alone the burden of deciding whether to start a business. You can turn to others for information, help and support in this tentative stage. Among those worth talking to:

Your family, friends and associates

Who better to serve as sounding boards, sources of leads and suppliers of positive reinforcement? You can be sure that they'll care about you enough to lend encouragement and provide moral support as you wrestle with your decisions. Ironically, you can also hope they'll overcome any fear of bursting your bubble and be honest enough to tell you if your ideas are stinkers.

People already working for themselves

Businesspeople probably won't mind talking with you, so long as the venture you're considering won't be in direct competition with their own. To get information about a specific type of business you're considering, you can even talk to someone with the same business—especially if that someone is outside your prospective market area. This can be the best way of getting a realistic perspective on the hours you'll have to put into your business, the potential financial rewards, the pitfalls to beware of, and so on.

Trade associations

There is an association representing the interests of virtually every type of business in the U.S. Associations can guide you to trade papers and newsletters and can provide information about the health of their industry and its outlook. You can find out which trade associations are relevant to your business ideas by getting a copy of the *Encyclopedia of American Associations,* published by the Gale Research Company or *National Trade and Professional Associations,* published by Columbia Books Inc. Many libraries carry these books in their reference department.

Professional helpers

Four types of professionals—lawyers, accountants, marketing consultants and bankers—can be a big help to small businesses. These people work with business owners every day, and they often have valuable insights and stories to share, plus the nitty-gritty on taxes, licensing, finances, typical cash flows, recordkeeping requirements, advertising and selling techniques, general market conditions, and other factors. Most professionals will offer an initial consultation of between 20 minutes and one hour free of charge to prospective clients. (Getting the most from these professionals when you're paying for their time and help is discussed more fully in Chapter 14.)

Other professionals and business owners in your community

Don't forget service groups, such as the Chamber of Commerce or Kiwanis International; fraternal organizations, such as the Knights of Columbus or the Elks; college organizations; merchant groups; networking groups—in short, anyone who might be able to give you another perspective on your desires.

commitment. It's sort of like a marriage. If you're at the altar thinking, "Oh, well, I'll bail out of this if it doesn't look good after a couple of months," you're probably not going to put a 100% effort into the marriage, and you're in serious danger of becoming a divorce statistic in a very short time.

Same thing with starting a business. You're more likely to succeed if you have thought about it long and hard, have acknowledged the risks and benefits, approach it with conviction and are *psyched up* for the adventure to begin.

Can You Afford to Work for Yourself?

"If the creator had a purpose in equipping us with a neck, he surely would have meant for us to stick it out."
                                                    Arthur Koestler

"I have enough money to last me the rest of my life, unless I buy something."
                                                    Jackie Mason

Like most people thinking of starting their own businesses, management consultant Darlene Orlov had plenty of unanswered questions. She wasn't sure exactly what aspect of her background as a corporate manager for such firms as International Playtex and Gulf & Western would appeal to her clients. Nor did she know how much to charge or how many clients she would get. But she *was* sure of one thing: She was going to slash all nonessentials from her personal expenses. "I cut way back—I didn't want to have an exceptional financial burden on top of the burden of starting the business," Orlov says. Her advice to others? "If someone has the drive it takes, they'll sacrifice."

A Question of Degree

Just how much you may have to sacrifice will depend on your specific situation:

- **the kind of business** you're looking forward to creating and how much up-front money, if any, you will need;

- **and where you can get that money,** possibly from your own salary, a spouse's salary, savings and other resources.

Perhaps most important, many of your choices will depend on whether you anticipate developing your business:

- **on the side** while maintaining your current full-time employment,

- **part-time,** with other part-time employment (your old job or a new job) to keep body and soul together,

- **full-time,** because you've quit your old job, retired, or been fired or laid off,

- **or some combination** of the above.

The Essential Questions

What you're trying to anticipate at this point is not so much financing a business, as we discuss in Chapter 17, but financing your personal transition from employed to self-employed. This is an opportunity to take a reality check of your personal and family financial resources and to analyze your risk-taking ability accordingly. This is key in determining your initial approach to your business.

This section will help you lay to rest that haunting question, "When or how could I afford to quit my present job?" If you've already been laid off or fired, the decision has been made for you, and you can assess the damage and plan accordingly.

Key questions that you'll have to answer are:

- **How much money do I have coming in?**

- **Where's the money coming from?** What's my income, my spouse's income, unemployment benefits, severance pay, "golden parachute," investment earnings?

- **How much is going out,** and where, exactly, is it going?

- **How much of my spending is non-discretionary,** for such essentials as food and shelter, and how much is discretionary—I could reduce or eliminate those expenses if I needed to?

- **Am I partially or fully vested in my retirement plan?** How much of the accumulated funds could I take with me if I leave my current employer? Could I borrow from or against those funds?

- **What are my current assets?**

- **What are my "quickly liquid" assets,** such as checking accounts, savings accounts and money market funds—sources of cash that can be tapped easily?

- **What are my "not-so-liquid" assets,** things like a house, other real estate or long-term bonds, that could be used as collateral for a loan? Which of these would I be willing to use as collateral for a loan? (Remember, anything put up as collateral—including your house—can be taken over by a lender if you don't repay the loan.)

- **What are the limits on my credit cards?**

- **What are my other sources of money?** What do I have that I could sell to raise cash if I had to? Which antiques or family heirlooms would I be willing to sell?

- **What are my longer-term financial commitments?** How soon will my children be ready for college? Am I planning to have another child? How does my retirement fund look?

- **Do I have adequate insurance?** How will I pay for an illness if I leave my current job? Where's the money going to come from for a child's illness, or a message from the orthodontist that Billy needs braces?

- **How long am I willing and able to make sacrifices** in my current standard of living in order to pursue a new business?

In short, how far out can I stick my neck? What can I do to stick it out farther?

The stronger your resources, the greater your confidence that you can weather any unpleasant surprises.

Getting the Answers

The following exercise will help you create your personal financial profile. It will also be good practice for the sort of financial assessment that you'll eventually have to do for your business. What you're going to do is calculate your net cash flow (or discretionary income) and your net worth. (See the work sheets on the following pages.)

Determining your net cash flow will give you some idea of how much income you need—either from your current job, your new business, your savings and investments, or a combination of those—to keep body, soul and family together. It will also tell you how much you have left over that you can channel into your business, now or later. Alternatively, you'll discover how much you may need to change your lifestyle so you can get your business going.

Determining your net worth will give you some idea of the strength of your current financial resources. The stronger your resources, the greater your confidence that you can weather any unpleasant surprises—a slow start-up, heavy initial expenses, customers who pay late or not at all—when starting the business.

Also, you'll be able to get by with less financial help from outsiders, or none at all, if your existing financial situation is strong. (Ironically, the stronger your resources, the more help you'll be *able* to get from outsiders if you want—the old saw that everyone wants to lend money to people who don't need it has some truth to it.)

Your Net Cash Flow

This exercise is where you find out where your money is coming from and where it's going. Net cash flow is, simply, your income minus your expenses.

Income

For this, you'll need monthly and annual average totals for your earnings and expenses. Begin by recording your income. Wages and salary will be obvious. If you receive dividends or capital gains on a quarterly or annual basis that you could easily withdraw from your accounts, figure their monthly contribution to your income as well. The same goes for interest on any savings accounts or bonds. Look at the yearly total, and divide by 12 to get your monthly average.

You'll have to decide how to treat commissions and bonuses. If they're a regular part of your monthly income, you could average a year's worth and use that as your monthly figure. If you can count on receiving a bonus once a year, you could average three years' worth to get an annual figure. If a bonus is just a nice surprise, you may want to just throw it into the pot when you receive it.

Expenses

Expenses are a little trickier. Some expenses, like your mortgage payment, car loan and real estate taxes, are readily apparent. Others—food, clothing, entertainment—aren't paid for just once a year or on a regular monthly schedule. The best quick way to calculate annual spending on such items is to keep track of everything you spend for a few months (that's right, you and your spouse should save every receipt and every check stub; keep a little notebook with you so you can write down what you spend when you don't get a receipt) and then multiply to get an estimate of the year's total.

Positive cash flow

Hopefully, your total income will be larger than your expenditures. In that case, the difference between the two is your *discretionary income,* or *positive cash flow*—the amount that should be going into savings and investments. From the perspective of a business start-up, positive cash flow presents you with two opportunities: you can use the income for start-up expenses, or you can save it as a financial "cushion" for when the business is under way and, as often happens, your monthly income temporarily declines.

(continued on page 34)

How to Figure Your Net Cash Flow

Income	Total for Year	Monthly Average
Take-home pay	$ _____	$ _____
Dividends, capital gains, interest	_____	_____
Bonuses	_____	_____
Other	_____	_____
Total Income	$ _____	$ _____

Expenditures		
Mortgage or rent	$ _____	$ _____
Taxes not withheld	_____	_____
Food	_____	_____
Utilities and fuel	_____	_____
Insurance premiums	_____	_____
Household maintenance	_____	_____
Auto (gas, oil, maintenance, repairs)	_____	_____
Other transportation	_____	_____
Loans	_____	_____
Medical bills not covered by insurance		
Clothing purchases and care	_____	_____
Savings and investments	_____	_____
Charity	_____	_____
Recreation and entertainment	_____	_____
Miscellaneous	_____	_____
Total Expenditures	$ _____	$ _____

Summary		
Total Income	$ _____	$ _____
Minus Total Expenditures	– _____	– _____
Surplus (+) or Deficit (-)	$ _____	$ _____

How to Figure Your Net Worth

WHAT YOU OWN	$ Amount	WHAT YOU OWE	$ Amount
Cash		**Current Bills**	
Cash on hand	_____	Rent	_____
Checking accounts	_____	Utilities	_____
Savings accounts	_____	Charge-account balances	_____
Money-market accounts	_____	Credit-card balances	_____
Life insurance cash value	_____	Insurance premiums	_____
Money owed you	_____	Alimony or child support	_____
Marketable Securities		Other bills	_____
Stocks	_____	**Taxes**	
Bonds	_____	Federal	_____
Government securities	_____	State	_____
Mutual funds	_____	Local	_____
Other investments	_____	Taxes on investments	_____
Personal Property *(Resale Value)*		Other	_____
Automobiles	_____	**Mortgages**	
Household furnishings	_____	Homes	_____
Art, antiques and other		Home equity	_____
collectibles	_____	Other properties	_____
Clothing, furs	_____	**Debts to Individuals**	_____
Jewelry	_____	**Loans**	
Recreation and hobby		Auto	_____
equipment	_____	Education	_____
Other possessions	_____	Other	_____
Real Estate (*Appraised Value)*		**Total Liabilities**	$_____
Homes	_____		
Other properties	_____	**Total Assets**	$_____
Retirement Funds		**Minus Total Liabilities**	–_____
Vested portion of		**Your Net Worth**	$_____
company plans	_____		
Vested benefits	_____		
IRA or Keogh plans	_____		
Annuities (surrender value)	_____		
Other Assets			
Equity in business	_____		
Partnership interests	_____		
Total Assets	$_____		

Goodbye, theater tickets and goodbye, expensive candlelit dinners. Hello, entertainment at home and increased cash flow.

Negative cash flow

If you're spending more than you're earning, well, you have got a problem that has to be dealt with whether or not you ever start a business. You're either dipping into savings, borrowing money, living off your credit cards or drawing on some asset like the equity in your home. Short-term, a little deficit spending isn't necessarily bad. But long-term, individuals are not allowed to act like the federal government. Ultimately, you have to rein in your spending or increase your earnings.

Adjusting Your Cash Flow

You can use your expense breakdown to identify places where you could cut your spending if necessary. Goodbye, theater tickets and goodbye, expensive candlelit dinners. Hello, entertainment at home and increased cash flow.

There are other ways of adjusting your cash flow to help you start working for yourself:

- **It could make sense to move your savings from short-term accounts** paying low rates of interest to longer-term commitments at higher rates.

- **Do you have balances on credit cards charging 18% annual interest or more?** Pay them off with low-yielding savings or convert them into home-equity debt at tax-deductible interest rates of little more than half of what bank cards charge.

- **If you have a fixed-rate mortgage that you took when interest rates were higher than they are now,** you may be able to refinance it and, even after paying closing costs, save thousands of dollars in annual interest payments. (You can also add the closing costs into your new loan. If the new interest rate is substantially lower than the old one, you may still pay less each month.)

In fact, a few expenses could decline as a matter of course when you start a business:

- **If you operate out of your home,** or go from a profession in which you need to wear a coat and tie or a business dress every day to one in which jeans and a sweater are acceptable, your clothing and cleaning bills will shrink. My standard "business outfit" when not meeting clients is jeans, T-shirt and sneakers; the jeans are abandoned in favor of shorts or bicycle pants in the summertime.

- **Similarly, locating a business closer to (or even in) your home** will cut your commuting and automobile upkeep costs. It could even eliminate your need for a car or a second car.

- **If a portion of your house is used strictly for business purposes,** you could deduct part of your rent or mortgage payment from your taxable income. Talk with an accountant about current rules covering these and other deductions. (For more information about the costs of setting up your enterprise, see Chapter 16.)

Working from home can cut your expenses in ways you might not have anticipated.

Armed with a category-by-category breakdown of your total expenses—and your rough estimate of how much you could trim those expenses—you'll have a realistic view of when and how you can become self-employed. If the business you have in mind won't meet your estimated needs, then you'll have to think about another one that will, modify your idea to boost your bottom line, or decide to remain a salaried employee or seek regular employment for now.

The Self-Employment Tax

When you're someone else's employee, it's easy to take for granted that your employer must pay half of your social security tax. If you never thought about it as a benefit before, you probably will when you become self-employed.

If you earn $400 or more a year from your business, the tax—all 15.3% of it—will apply to your self-employment income. That's basically the net income that you will report on the Internal Revenue Service's Schedule C, "Profit (or Loss) From Business."

Here's how the tax works, based on 1995 rules: The full tax applies to the first $61,200 of income. For purposes of this cap, "income" includes self-employment income and any wages you earn on a job from which social security taxes are withheld. An employee who earns $40,000 from which the tax is withheld, for example, would owe the 15.3% tax on no more than $21,200 of self-employment income.

There's one twist, though. The self-employment tax has two parts: 12.4% pays for the retirement benefits, and 2.9% goes to pay for Medicare. The full 15.3% tax applies to only the first $61,200 of income in 1995, but the 2.9% applies to all of your net earnings.

Along with the tax come...*the deductions*

You'll get to reduce your self-employment income by 7.65% when figuring how much social security tax you owe. Say you make $50,000 in self-employment income. That's the amount you'll report on your Form 1040. But when figuring your social security tax on Schedule SE, "Self-Employment Tax," you'll reduce the $50,000 by $3,825 (7.65% of $50,000). Since the tax rate is 15.3%, the deduction saves you $585.

You get an income tax deduction for 50% of the self-employment social security tax you pay. For example, if you have $50,000 of self-employment income subject to the tax, the bill will be $7,065 ($50,000 x 15.3% – $585). You get to deduct half of that amount—$3,533—when you figure your income taxes. If you're in the 28% bracket, you'll save $989. When those savings are taken into account, the effective social security tax bill drops to

"The way I see it, Ferguson, I've got to be me... or somebody pretty much like me."

From the Wall Street Journal—Permission, Cartoon Features Syndicate

$6,076 ($7,065 – $989). And that makes the effective tax rate 12.15% rather than 15.3% ($6,076 ÷ $50,000). You'll get this benefit whether you itemize your deductions or not.

Why tax planning pays

Successful efforts to trim your taxable business income will produce double savings. In addition to cutting your income tax bill for the year, you may also save on social security taxes. Every $1,000 of extra business deductions would save $153 in social security taxes.

This is a good example of why, as a self-employed person, you will want to establish a great working relationship with an accountant. He or she will not only prepare your tax return each year but should also keep you apprised of the inevitable changes in tax law and offer year-round advice on ways to minimize the tax hit on your business.

Knowing Your Net Worth

This section is where you get answers to all the questions about the value of your possessions. What good is it to know your net worth? Here are a few reasons:

You can convert parts of it into cash if necessary.

As we'll discuss more fully in Chapter 17, many assets that make up your net worth—including company retirement funds, life insurance policies, equity in your home, and your own retirement accounts—can be converted into money to finance your transition from employed to self-employed.

It can just plain make you more confident.

If you have a lot of debts, you may feel your entire financial life is "in the red." (Ever notice how often people say, "I'm broke" and how infrequently they say, "I'm solvent"?) But it's likely that those debts are more than offset by assets—including your house, car, and other possessions—that you've accumulated over time. Computing your net worth may well make you feel a little better about what you have.

Many assets that make up your net worth can be converted into money to finance your transition from employed to self-employed.

It can make prospective lenders feel good.

If you need more money for your start-up than you can raise through your own resources, you'll find that one of the simplest outside sources is a personal loan. Banks and other lenders usually require that all but the smallest personal loans be *secured* by assets. Another term for this is *collateralizing* the loan. Both phrases are nice, polite, technical ways of saying the same thing: You agree that the lender can lay claim to (and even take away) something you own if you're not able to repay the loan.

Using your own financial resources and obtaining personal loans are just two ways of financing a business start-up; early sources of financing for your business are discussed in detail in Chapter 17.

Calculating Net Worth

Determining your net worth is a piece of cake. First, add up the value of everything you own—stocks, bonds, checking-account balances, retirement funds, jewelry, cars, houses, Van Gogh paintings, Caribbean islands...sorry, we got a little carried away there. Anyway, you get the idea.

From that total—your total assets—subtract everything you owe: your mortgage, car loans, personal loans, charge card balances, and so on.

The difference is your *net worth.* The table on page 33 lists everything you need for computing your net worth. A few pointers to help you with figuring your net worth:

Assets

The value for many of these categories—checking and savings accounts, for example—is obvious. Other values are not so obvious.

Savings bonds. If you have U.S. savings bonds, you can find their current interest rate by contacting an institution that sells them or by calling 800–US–BONDS (or 202–377–7715 in the Washington, D.C., area).

Your home. Ask a real estate agent for an estimate of the current market value of your home and other real estate, or check your local land-records office for a listing of how much similar properties in your area have sold for recently.

Retirement plans. For pension and profit-sharing plans, include only the amount you could withdraw in cash *now*, not what you may receive in the future. Your personnel office should be able to provide that figure.

Retirement accounts. Remember that you may be hit with a penalty and may have to pay taxes on any early withdrawals from your individual retirement accounts. For example, you would have to pay a 10% penalty if you took money from an IRA before you're 59½—unless the with-

Help With Your Finances

If you're considering working for yourself, this is a good time to find an accountant or financial planner who can help you with your personal money management. You could rely on this person in your business, too.

One rule to start practicing now: Keep your personal and business finances separate, especially your recordkeeping. This is true whether you're just earning supplemental income on the side or setting out to form a company employing many people. If the IRS comes calling, you won't want to have to disentangle years' worth of family and business paperwork.

Do-it-yourselfers can consult:

Books

- *Kiplinger's Make Your Money Grow,* by Theodore J. Miller (Kiplinger Books).

- *Making the Most of Your Money,* by Jane Bryant Quinn (Simon & Schuster).

- *The Consumer Reports Money Book,* by the editors of Consumer Reports Books.

Software

Personal computer software that can help you with recordkeeping and budget-ing (selling for under $100 unless stated) include:

- *Quicken,* by Intuit (for Windows & Macintosh).

- *Andrew Tobias's Managing Your Money,* by MECA (for Windows & Macintosh).

- *Financial Navigator,* by Financial Navigator International (for Windows, $495).

- *MacMoney,* by Survivor Software (for Macintosh, $120).

- *Kiplinger's Simply Money,* by 4Home Productions (for Windows, $69.95).

- *M.Y.O.B. Small Business Accounting,* by Best!-Ware Inc., (for Windows and Macintosh, $120).

For heavier-duty financial planning—if you need to take stock of your financial position and projecting where your saving and investing patterns will take you in the future—check out:

- *WealthBuilder,* by Reality Technologies and *Money* magazine (for Windows and Macintosh, $170).

*Anyone thinking
of starting a
business must
consider insurance.*

drawal is part of a series of roughly equal payments tied to your life expectancy. To use this loophole, you must stay with the lifetime payout schedule for at least five consecutive years *and* until you're at least 59½ . If you violate either of those requirements, the IRS would apply the 10% penalty retroactively to your pre-59 ½ withdrawals. If you have a substantial amount in your IRA accounts, this exception may permit you to withdraw thousands of dollars a year (see also the discussion in Chapter 17).

Your car. To get a good idea of how much your car is worth, check the local newspaper classifieds or consult a price guide such as *The National Auto Dealers' Association Official Used Car Guide,* available at banks and libraries, or *Edmund's Used Car Prices* and the *NADA Official Used Car Guide—Retail Consumer Edition,* available on newsstands.

Your other possessions. For household furnishings, be conservative: Estimate how much you think you could sell each piece of furniture for today, then slash all those estimates by 50%. (Few things depreciate faster—and are worth less than their owners think—than furniture.)

Liabilities

This calculation is a little easier, although certainly less pleasant. About the only debts you won't immediately know the size of are your home and other property loans. Those are easy to find out, though: an amortization schedule or loan payment summary, available from your lender, should tell you exactly the amount you still owe.

Protecting Your Neck, Even When You Stick It Out

There is one other area that may not show up on many individuals' current expenses but that anyone thinking of starting a business must consider: insurance.

Health Insurance

If you're married, taking advantage of your spouse's group medical coverage may be the most cost-effective way to insure yourself and your family.

If you're planning to become self-employed after you retire, check whether your company allows retirees to continue group coverage indefinitely. Some even pay part or all of their retirees' premiums. If you cannot remain on the group plan and are just a few months away from qualifying for medicare, a short-term individual policy (three months to a year) would see you through.

The COBRA back-up

If neither of these options fits your situation, then you're probably going to take advantage of interim coverage required under federal legislation called COBRA. In most circumstances COBRA entitles you to remain insured under your employer's group medical coverage for up to 18 months (29 months if you're disabled) after leaving the company, so long as you leave for reasons other than "gross misconduct." You have to pay the full amount of the premium your employer would ordinarily pay, plus another 2% to cover overhead costs. You can find out from your employer how much your current health insurance plan costs.

There are exceptions to COBRA coverage. You may not be covered if:

- **You work for a company** with fewer than 20 employees.

- **You work for a church.**

- **You work for the government of a U.S. territory or the District of Columbia**. (Federal employees receive COBRA-like protection under "Temporary Continuation of Coverage" rules.)

Shopping for an individual policy

Even if you will be covered under COBRA, it's smart to start looking for alternative coverage well before the 18 months runs out. Individual policies often require waiting periods of six months to a year or even two for coverage of *any* preexisting conditions (medical problems you've had prior to buying coverage). Depending on your circumstances, you may want to pay for double coverage for that

Even if you will be covered under COBRA, it's smart to start looking for alternative coverage well before the 18 months runs out.

period of time so that you can make a seamless transition to an individual policy. After COBRA runs out, you can often convert to a nongroup policy from the same company without a break in coverage. But if you are young and healthy, you might be able to find cheaper and more comprehensive insurance elsewhere. Conversion policies are often the last resort for people who can't get coverage elsewhere.

See the accompanying boxes for sources of information about purchasing medical coverage for yourself (and for your employees, when and if that becomes an issue). See also Chapter 11 for information on the tax deductibility of health insurance.

Disability Insurance

Disability insurance is by some measures more crucial even than life insurance: The odds are better than 50–50 that a 35-year-old will at some point before reaching age 65 be disabled for 90 days or more.

Comparison Shopping for Health Insurance

As the accompanying discussion shows, you may be able to continue your group coverage for up to 18 months. But well before that coverage runs out, you should investigate your longer-term options. Three sources of information that can help are listed below.

If, after shopping, you find that the cost of maintaining health insurance coverage is just too high, the sources in the box beginning on page 44 will offer some alternatives.

- **The Health Insurance Association of America** (555 13th St., N.W., #600 East, Washington, DC 20007; 202–824–1600). The association will provide information on companies that sell major medical policies to individuals.

- **Quotesmith Corp.** (Darien, Ill.; 800–556–9393). Quotesmith tracks rates, coverage and safety ratings of 400 insurance companies and Blue Cross and Blue Shield plans. Free insurance price comparison reports are available.

- **Wilkinson Benefit Consultants Inc.** (Towson, Md.; 410–832–7503) will scan its data base of 1,000 health-plan options to find the best ones for your business. The firm charges $250 for businesses with one to three employees, $300 for four to nine employees, and $400 for 10 to 19 employees. You'll receive detailed price, coverage and safety comparisons for the three lowest-cost plans suited to your needs, plus price comparisons of another dozen policies.

Most workers are provided some sort of disability insurance coverage in their present jobs. But employees cannot assume the payments for, and remain covered under, employer-provided disability insurance policies after leaving the company. This can leave people who are trying to become self-employed in a coverage bind. "A group disability policy cannot be transferred when you leave the company to start your own business," says Victoria Ross, an Arlington Heights, Ill. senior financial advisor with American Express Financial Advisors. "But you cannot purchase a new *individual* disability policy either, because you don't have a track record of earnings and profits in your new business that an insurance company could look at to determine what level of benefits you would qualify for."

Get it while you're employed

That means that, under most circumstances, you can't get a disability policy for at least two or three years after you start your business. There is one way around this, though, says Ross: If you purchase a disability policy while you're still employed, you can keep the policy after you set out on your own. You may already have purchased such a policy if the amount of earnings replaced by your employer's coverage and other sources (such as social security, workers' compensation, IRAs or other savings and investments) wouldn't meet your needs.

Costs of these policies depend on individuals' health, age, and other variables. One example: A policy for a 32-year-old male nonsmoker, paying $1,500 tax-free per month after a 60-day waiting period, would cost about $852 per year from one insurer.

The moral: If you're thinking of starting a business in a year or two, look into disability policies now.

Life Insurance

These policies appear on the monthly expense statements of many more people than other types of insurance. If you currently have your own life insurance policy, you should review it with your agent to make sure it's adequate for your family, and continue making payments on it. Your job status has no bearing on your eligibility to continue with a personal insurance policy that you already have. If you've been relying on employer-provided life insurance, now is the time to contact an insurance company about covering your family. Over the short haul, term insurance (which is renewed annually and has no "investment component" and pays only if you die) provides the most cover-

Getting Around the High Cost of Health Insurance

Once you've been shopping for health insurance, you may find that it's prohibitively expensive—for yourself or any employees. Keep in mind that if you purchase health insurance for yourself and deduct any of it as a business—as opposed to just a personal—expense, you'll have to provide coverage for any employees, too. (For more on the tax deductibility of employee benefits and other issues related to staffing up, see Chapters 11 and 15). With 25 or fewer employees, you'll find that you may have to pay half again as much as large companies, and like some business owners, you may see rate increases of 30% to 50% a year. That's because of higher administrative costs for the insurance companies and smaller pools of workers over which they can spread expensive claims.

Some relief may be found through the following sources:

AFFINITY GROUPS

With association coverage you can get an insurance package that's tailor-made for a group of similar businesses. Trade organizations also provide coverage for individuals who may be denied coverage because they work in industries that some insurers say tend to submit large numbers of claims—including florists, lawyers, doctors and restaurant workers.

The downside of affinity groups is the principle of "adverse selection." Association policies may start cheap to attract members, but if prices go up later healthy people will leave the plan and only the most ill members will remain, causing premiums to go up even more. Plus, there's no guarantee that a trade group's plan is a better buy than an individual policy or that you'll automatically be accepted. And policies sold by groups that cater to small businesses generally have more exclusions of coverage than other policies and stricter guidelines for accepting new applicants. They may also charge an application fee.

STATE AND CHAMBER OF COMMERCE PLANS

Many states have proposed or passed legislation that would allow small businesses and, in many cases, self-employed people to purchase "bare-bones" policies that exempt them from providing each worker with coverage for state-mandated services, such as psychiatric or chiropractic care.

Many states and several regional or state chambers of commerce offer insurance pools to small businesses.

The following is a list of state offices and chambers of commerce that provide some type of small business insurance program. Contact the groups directly to receive full information on eligibility requirements.

age for the least amount of money.

Be sure to factor the cost of these forms of coverage into your anticipated costs of becoming self-employed.

Looking Ahead

You'll note, undoubtedly, that a few personal finance questions may not get answered in these calculations.

Connecticut
Department of Insurance
203–297–3800
Greater Hartford Chamber of Commerce
203–527–6634

Delaware
Delaware State Chamber of Commerce
302–655–7221

Florida
Community Health Purchasing Alliances
   (state-run program)
904–921–8038

Georgia
Atlanta Chamber of Commerce
404–586–8455

Idaho
Department of Insurance
800–721–3272

Illinois
Illinois Department of Insurance
217–782–4515

Indiana
Indianapolis Chamber of Commerce
317–464–2277

Iowa
Department of Insurance
515–281–5705

Kansas
Department of Insurance
800–432–2484

Kentucky
Kentucky Chamber of Commerce
502–695–4700

Maine
Bureau of Insurance
207–624–8475

Maryland
Maryland State Chamber of Commerce
301–261–2858 (D.C. area)
410–269–0642 (Baltimore area)

Massachusetts
Division of Insurance
617–521–7794

Michigan
Local chambers of commerce
   Contact local office.

Minnesota
Department of Commerce
612–296–4026

Missouri
617–521–7794
All insurance carriers
   covering small employers
Independent agents

Montana
Tax credits available for
   small business owners
   through Department of
   Revenue:
Sole Proprietors:
406–444–3361
Corporations:
406–444–2441

Nebraska
Nebraska Chamber of Commerce
402–397–4800

New Hampshire
IBS Business Services
   (administers plans for
   local chambers of
   commerce)
800–487–4427

New Jersey
Small Employer Health Benefits Program
908–632–7408

(continued on page 46)

Some long-term financial questions—planning for tuition payments a decade down the road, for example—aren't answered if you haven't already embarked on a savings and investment program for those more distant expenses. If you have financial questions you haven't dealt with before, it's time to begin reading up on investment strategies or to

Getting Around the High Cost of Health Insurance (Cont'd.)

New Mexico
Los Alamos County and Santa Fe Chambers of Commerce (through Blue Cross and Blue Shield of New Mexico)
505–988–4425

New York
Syracuse Chamber of Commerce
800–427–1551

North Carolina
Department of Insurance
800–762–5547

Oklahoma
Oklahoma Basic Health Benefits Board
405–530–3475
Oklahoma State Chamber of Commerce (through Blue Cross and Blue Shield)
918–560–2300 (Tulsa)
405–841–9525 (Oklahoma City)

Oregon
Department of Consumer and Business Services
800–438–0842
Insurance Pool Governing Board
800–542–3104

Pennsylvania
Pennsylvania Chamber of Business and Industry
800–755–3021

Rhode Island
Insurance Department
401–277–2223

South Carolina
South Carolina Chamber of Commerce
800–951–2549

Tennessee
Insurance Department
800–861–1270
Nashville Area Chamber of Commerce
615–259–4723

Texas
Department of Insurance
800–252–3439

Utah
Salt Lake Area Chamber of Commerce
801–364–3631

Vermont
Vermont Chamber of Commerce
802–223–3443

Virginia
Metropolitan Richmond Chamber of Commerce
804–527–6418
Hampton Roads and Virginia Peninsula Chambers of Commerce
800–543–8919

Washington
Insurance Commission
800–562–6900
Local chambers of commerce
Contact directly.

Wisconsin
Department of Insurance
608–266–3585
Green Bay Area Chamber of Commerce
414–437–4722

Wyoming
Department of Insurance
800–438–5768

contact a financial planner who can advise you on meeting these unaddressed goals.

Of course, deciding to start your own business and figuring out what type of venture is right for you (the topic of the next chapter) are also part of those longer-term goals.

BUSINESS COALITIONS

The following business coalitions and associations offer various types of low-cost health insurance programs.

Alabama
Central Alabama Coalition for the Medically Uninsured
205–934–9300

Arizona
Healthcare Group of Arizona
602–253–9119

Arkansas
Blue Cross-Blue Shield of Arkansas
501–378–2000

California
Health Insurance Plan of California
800–447–2937

Colorado
Colorado Health Care Purchasing Alliance
303–333–6767

Connecticut
Connecticut Business & Industry Association
203–293–3800

Kansas
Wichita Independent Business Association
316–943–2565

Kentucky
Blue Cross and Blue Shield of Kentucky
502–426–9000
Humana
502–580–1000

Massachusetts
New England Business Association
617–332–7680

Minnesota
Employers Association Buyers' Coalition
612–644–9702

Missouri
Ozarks Area Business Group on Health
417–869–4411
Southeast Missouri Business Group on Health
314–651–4688

Nevada
Sierra Health & Life Insurance Co.
702–871–0999

North Dakota
Greater North Dakota Association
701–222–0929

Ohio
Council of Smaller Enterprises (COSE)
216–621–3300

Tennessee
Tennessee Primary Care Network
800–523–3112
Memphis Business Group on Health
Write to: 2675 Union Extended, Memphis, TN 38112.

Utah
Utah Community Health Plan
801–533–3780

Wisconsin
Health Care Network of Wisconsin
414–784–0223
Employer Health Care Alliance Cooperative
608–276–6620

Caution: Leaving Your Employer

All this talk about working for yourself assumes that you can legally do so. If you currently have a job, you may not be allowed to leave your old company one day and start your new venture the next.

The reason: You may have signed a contract or agreement that prohibits you from competing with your employer, typically for a specific period of time after you stop working for that employer. Agreements may also bar you from using for your own purposes any confidential information you learned while working for the company.

What these agreements mean in practical terms depends on the precise wording of the contracts and how attorneys interpret it. Exactly what constitutes "competition" can be open to interpretation; so can the definition of "confidential information." The length of time these agreements are in force, as well as the geographic regions to which they may apply and the types of business start-ups that fall under any restrictions will vary from one contract to another and may also be subject to interpretation.

"I've never had to butter up the boss. I've always been the boss."

Farris, Cartoonists & Writers Syndicate

You'll want to talk with an attorney about any restrictions that will inhibit your ability to work for yourself. To avoid any perception of conflict of interest by your employer, plan to use your own time, supplies and resources—not the employer's—to plan your new endeavor.

For a helpful overview of the legal ramifications of

leaving your employer, write to the Michael D. Dingman Center for Entrepreneurship at the University of Maryland's College of Business and Management (Bldg. 39, Room 4361, University of Maryland, College Park, MD 20742) and order a copy of *How to Leave Your Employer (to set up your own business)* DC-90-01, by Russell B. Stevenson Jr. ($10).

Choosing a Business

"Genius is one percent inspiration and 99 percent perspiration."

Thomas Edison

One of the most common routes to working for yourself is to take the expertise you've developed while working for others and put it to use in your own enterprise. Why not take advantage of your own knowledge, experience and interests *and* satisfy your wants and needs? (If you don't know what those are, see Chapter 3.) It's possible that, in effect, your business has already chosen you.

If you've spent many years in manufacturing, you may want to take your skills and knowledge of assembly-line processes and put them to work creating your own products. If, like Patricia and John Trotta in Chapter 2, you've handled one specialized manufacturing job for a company, you may be a short jump away from doing similar manufacturing on your own.

Similarly, if you've spent a decade moving from one line of sales to another, you could open a retail store that puts your selling ability to good use—a gift shop or a real estate franchise, for example. Or, you could become an independent representative of one or more companies or a consultant helping other salespeople improve their sales techniques.

If you've managed restaurants, you could open one of your own. If you've analyzed companies as a bank loan officer, you could identify a good existing company that you could purchase for yourself. If you've sold cars, you could start a leasing company. If you've been a construction worker, you could open your own general contracting firm. If your hobby is crafting leather goods, you could start a leather crafts shop.

Of course, it's possible that you want to work for yourself precisely because you *don't* want to do what you've done before. You also may have some idea about a venture but need help in verifying that your hunch can actually work. This chapter will give you tools with which to research opportunities and help you confirm whether the type of business you're thinking about is really a good fit.

All that said, I have to concede that Edison was essentially right. Regardless of your inspiration or choice of business, your ultimate success will depend on you and the energy and determination you bring to your venture. Get ready to work—hard.

Need an Idea?

Generating business ideas starts with you. Think now and think *long* about the products or services you'd like to see. Every time you find yourself saying, "There ought to be a..." or "I wish there was a place where you could get...," write down the missing ingredient, be it service or product. Also keep track of the "missing ingredients" your friends and associates mention. Every "Why isn't there a..." or "I can't find a..." is more than just an idle complaint—it's a need waiting to be met, and recognizing and filling a need for a product that currently doesn't exist is a pretty good recipe for success. Chances are you'll soon have a long list of things this country needs. You'll still have to go through the process of deciding whether *you* should be the person to provide this product or service, but you will have taken the important first step of identifying a *potential* business for you. For sources of brainstorming help when thinking of ideas for your business, see the accompanying list.

Which Type Is Right for You?

Whichever business you choose, it's probably one of a handful of general types. We discuss all aspects of these businesses throughout the book, but these brief descriptions may help jog your thinking at this point.

Providing Personal Services or Consulting

Consultants have an intangible product: knowledge. They take their expertise and package it into some sort of written form (booklets, brochures, manuals) and/or spoken form (lectures and presentations) and use these vehicles to sell their knowledge to their clients.

As with any business, successful consultants must have

Sources of Ideas

Business professionals

Your bank is as good a place as any to start—bankers deal with businesspeople every day and often know owners who are considering selling their businesses. Business lawyers also can be sources of information, as can marketing consultants and other entrepreneurs. And, of course, business brokers always have a list of businesses for sale. (Helpful professionals are discussed fully in Chapter 14.)

Directories

Library reference sections are full of books of lists, including books listing businesses and business opportunities. For example, the *Thomas Register of American Manufacturers* is a 29 volume directory of products and services—every one of which could give you an idea of something you can make or sell.

Your public library may also have catalogs listing companies that sell franchises to entrepreneurs. Such catalogs provide a brief description of the franchise, including the initial investment required and how to contact the franchisor. You can also get the

Franchise Opportunities Guide, a directory of franchisors, sources of financial and legal help, and other information (International Franchise Association; 800–543–1038; $15, plus $6 shipping). See Chapter 18 for more sources.

Newspapers and magazines

When you finish reading the funnies, turn to the classified section under "Business Opportunities," where businesses and franchises for sale are usually listed. You'll also find businesses for sale in the classified display ads or business section of the newspaper. Many magazines, including *Independent Business, Inc.,* and *Kiplinger's Personal Finance Magazine* are also sources of business ideas and specific business ventures. You'll find these and others at your public library. Take some time to browse.

Professional associations

The same trade associations noted in Chapter 3 that can help you decide whether to start a business can also give you information about the earnings prospects for newcomers to the industries they represent.

something to sell and must identify a market. Some consultants and their markets are easily defined: Many government bureaucrats have become consultants to organizations needing expertise in dealing with government agencies; ex-military officers regularly become consultants to defense contractors; and, of course, business managers often become consultants to other businesses. In other cases, the consultant is a bit more creative: At least one actress and drama teacher has developed a business advising lawyers on how to "act" in court.

Consulting may involve the smallest start-up costs of

Computer networks

Such on-line computer services as America Online, GEnie, Delphi Internet, Prodigy and CompuServe have become increasingly easy-to-use sources of information. You can find computer bulletin boards, and professional organizations, that are geared to the interests of small businesses, consultants and people working at home.

National newspaper and national magazine indexes

These are great ways of expanding on your initial newspaper and magazine search. The old days of searching through issue after issue of recent *Reader's Guide to Periodical Literature* are gone; today, if you're at a well-funded library and want to know what's been written about a particular industry or business in national publications in the past three years, you can find out by using an index that has been stored on compact disk (CD-ROM) and can be read on computer screens. One magazine index includes articles from dozens of nationally circulated magazines; a service called the National Newspaper Index includes *The Christian Science Monitor, The Los Angeles Times, The New York Times, The Wall Street Journal* and *The Washington Post*. It's also possible to search indexes at your home if you have a personal computer with a modem and subscribe to an on-line service such as CompuServe or Dialog. The full text of newspaper and magazine stories can be transferred (or "downloaded") from a data service to your computer using these on-line services, and some companies even offer less-expensive "off-peak" rates for these services when used during nonbusiness hours.

The Yellow Pages

This may sound too simple, but don't overlook this resource. The good old telephone book Yellow Pages (whether issued by your regional phone company or one of the many competitors that have sprung up in the past few years) are a great resource, simply because they include categories for just about every product and service a small business can offer (or need). Just by leafing through a major-city phone book, you can find business ideas you may not have considered. In short, the Yellow Pages can be a source of inspiration.

Consultants have to be prepared for the "out-front" work. Clients want to hire the consultant, not an underling.

any business. You don't need expensive downtown office space, manufacturing equipment, a showroom or a lot of employees. Even established consultants may run their businesses from their homes. For the price of a business card, stationery, a well-designed brochure listing your services and credentials, some postage and a telephone, you can be in the consulting business.

On the other hand, a consultant starting on that thin a shoestring is a real one-woman or one-man band. You can find yourself spending all your time answering the phone, typing letters, handling routine paperwork, trying to organize your schedule—and spending very little time doing the consulting work that brings in your income.

Since consultants usually are selling knowledge or information, it's also often difficult for them to build a business in which someone else does the front-line work and they serve as a behind-the-scenes manager. Clients want to hire the consultant, not an underling.

All in all, it can be a delicate balance. "I have a lot of work and a good reputation, and people in the business know me," says Debbie Slutsky, a San Francisco food-and-wine consultant who has worked with restaurants and wineries to develop menus and recipes, wine lists, and wine-education programs for employees. "But there were times when I was starting out when I wouldn't pay attention to the client-generating end of the business and would find myself running out of work, just because I was so busy I hadn't taken time to line up contracts with people who wanted me to work for them."

Selling Retail Goods and Services

This is probably the type of business you're most familiar with. After all, most of us deal with a retailer—a grocer, an electronics store, an ice cream shop, a dry cleaner, any store in any mall in any town—every day. So you've had direct contact with hundreds or thousands of retailers already.

But looking at it from the other side of the counter requires a whole different perspective. For example, you may stop and patronize any shop along your daily route without any advance planning. But with any retail operation, you'll have to carefully consider your location, how much space you need, how much revenue you can generate, and how you'll attract and relate to customers, before deciding whether to open your doors.

The right location
for the right customers

You'll need to put a lot of thought into deciding where your establishment will be. Choosing a place with a lot of traffic won't be enough. You'll also need the right *kind* of traffic—people who because of their age, interests, income levels and other factors are likely to be interested in what you have to sell. A third-floor mall location, no matter how popular the mall, is not going to prove too helpful for a convenience store selling coffee, doughnuts and newspapers to commuters.

"Successful retail-store owners are especially careful about where they locate their businesses," says Max Fallek, a consultant to small businesses, author of How to Set Up Your Own Small Business and creator and president of the American Institute of Small Business in Minneapolis. Fallek notes that your location will affect, among other things, your business's sales volume, overhead, hours of operation, access to good workers and amount of potential customer traffic.

What's happening in retail

Small, specialized retail service businesses—operations like dry cleaners, copy centers, gift stores, specialty clothing stores, repair shops (that means repairs of just about anything; as more and more products are understood by fewer and fewer people), and so on—have been a

> ## *More Retail Information*
> ●
>
> **The National Retail Federation** (325 7th Street, N.W. Suite 1000, Washington, DC 20004; 202–783–7971), which represents more than 55,000 department and specialty stores worldwide, offers information on the average costs and profit margins of different types of retail establishments. Its monthly magazine, *Stores*, discusses industry events, consumer research, information systems and other aspects of the retail industry. (Free with membership to the NRF, $49 for nonmembers; single copy $5.)

growing section of the economy, and are likely to remain so throughout the '90s in spite of a couple of factors:

Many such shops may find themselves competing sooner or later with such large discount chain operations as Walmart. The key to success will be to offer something *different* along with plenty of *convenience*.

Some marketing seers have suggested that as the babyboomers mature, they will spend less and save more, boding ill for retail business. But as babyboomers leave the child-rearing stage of their lives by the end of the decade, their need for all sorts of goods and services will intensify and their high incomes will let them both save and consume at strong levels.

(You'll find choosing a business location discussed in Chapter 9; researching your potential markets is covered in Chapter 8.)

Help for the Independent
● ●

The National Federation of Independent Business (NFIB) (600 Maryland Ave., S.W., Suite 700, Washington, DC 20024; legislative and public affairs, 202–554–9000; membership services, 615–872–5312) is the largest small-business advocacy group in the U.S. It represents the interests of more than 600,000 members—small businesses and self-employed people—to state and federal governments. Membership dues are a suggested minimum of $100 per year.

- Members receive the NFIB's magazine, *Independent Business* (published six times a year), a source of straightforward, nuts-and-bolts information about starting and running a business, as well as legislative updates.

- The magazine's "Resource Center" sells back issues for $5 and a wide variety of reprinted articles for $3.95 or $4.95 each. For an index, call 805–496–6156.

More retail realities

Retailers need to be as enthusiastic about people (who they're selling to) as they are about product (what they're selling). Success in retailing often depends as much on the art of small talk as on the science of selling. As one operator of a small business said, "If you can't smile, don't go into business."

The cost of getting into retail will depend on the type of business, size of your retail space and location. In all probability, though, the journey from initial idea to grand opening will cost more than $10,000, maybe more than $100,000 (see the description of franchising below).

Similarly, the hours you work will depend on the business. One thing you can count on, though: They'll probably be *long* hours. A frozen yogurt shop in a college town may sound like a pleasant, profitable and low-stress venture until you consider that you—or someone else—probably will have to work until 11 P.M. or later on weekends.

Buying a Franchise

Franchises are an attractive way to get into retail because they give you at least *some* existing structure—you have your own business, but you're operating it under the guidelines of a larger organization that includes similar operations. The franchisor (that's the larger company) gives the franchisee (that's you) the right to sell a product or service, typically under the franchisor's name. In exchange, you give the franchisor something—often an up-front fee and a percentage of sales or profits. Initial cash investments can range from less than $10,000 for lesser-known franchises to more than $500,000 for a McDonald's franchise.

The pluses

The main benefit of buying a franchise may also be the main drawback for someone who just wants to work for himself: You aren't going into business alone. You'll get some help in operating your business, and as part of a larger organization you may also get a break on buying goods that can be purchased in large quantities through the organization. Depending on the franchise, you may also have instant name recognition and proven products that sell.

The minuses

You won't have total independence. You'll have rules to follow, the franchisor's rules, which may cover everything from operating hours to the type of broom used for sweeping up at night. And, you could wind up having to pay too much for your franchise or products and getting too little support and expertise. Riches are not guaranteed; many franchise owners put in long hours and take home

The main benefit of buying a franchise may also be the main drawback: You aren't going into business alone.

With an existing business, you buy a track record— whether good or bad.

less than $25,000 in personal income annually.

In buying franchises, as with any other type of business, you'll have to take a hard look at the entire deal before signing up. (Franchises are discussed in depth in Chapter 18.)

Buying an Existing Business

There is one clear advantage to buying a business instead of starting from scratch: Your start-up venture will already have a track record—a history of profits (or losses), a regular supplier or suppliers, a customer base, a stable location, even trained employees who may want to stay with you. And, the business's start-up costs will have been handled by the previous owner. However, if it's a successful business, you could pay more to buy it than if you started from scratch.

That's all in the best of circumstances. In the worst of circumstances, buying an existing business can mean buying a heap of headaches—a bad or deteriorating location, a weak client base, even a bunch of debts. That's right— you may pay to assume someone else's debts. (The pros and cons of buying an existing business are discussed in greater detail in Chapter 20.)

Manufacturing or Wholesaling

Manufacturing runs the gamut from making something by hand and in small quantities to producing goods by the thousands or the ton. It can be a craft that turns into a money-producer with minimal expense for supplies and no value assigned to your time. Or it can be one of the most difficult and expensive of all start-ups, depending on the equipment, manufacturing space and other facilities you need. Don't think of manufacturing only in terms of industrial products or durable goods. If you have a great recipe for a gourmet cake and want to produce it in mass quantities and get it to market, you're a potential manufacturer.

You not only have to have a product (and preferably a

unique product) and a way to sell it (whether to whole-salers, retailers or consumers), but you also have to develop a way of *making* the product and achieving quality compa-rable to what you achieved with your prototype or small batch. Recipes, for instance, may need to go through nu-merous alterations to be successful in mass quantities.

Alternative approaches

A couple of options can ease the pressures and cost of starting a manufacturing business:

It's possible to develop a product and pay someone else to produce it. In essence, you're subcontracting the manufacture of your product to an established company. You'll have slightly higher pro-duction costs (because the cost will now include a profit for the company you've contract-ed with), but your start-up and overhead costs will be much lower because you won't be taking on direct responsibility for manufacturing and capital investments.

Another possibility is to manufacture the product but pay someone else to sell it. This representative—either a sales-man pitching your product to other businesses or a retailer selling to consumers—will, again, take a slice of your profit from every sale. But by letting go of this part of the business and trading greater sales for smaller profits per sale, you may actually increase your overall profits.

Bond, Cartoonists & Writers Syndicate

Then again, if you combine both alternatives, you can wholesale a product that another company has manufac-tured and pocket the difference between the cost of manu-

A part-time business is a business—not a hobby. As such, it requires the same treatment and attention to details that a full-time business demands.

facturing and the wholesale price.

Or, you could sell your idea for a product to another company. Product ideas can be sold for a lump sum, for an amount based on revenues from the product, or for some combination of these and other formulas. The beauty is that you're getting paid for just your idea—others are taking the responsibility and risk of manufacturing and distribution. The downside is that you give up some control over how, or whether, the product is made and sold, as well as much of the profit that will be realized by the manufacturer and distributor. We'll talk about protecting rights to your ideas and other related issues in Chapter 7.

About Part-Time Businesses

Many new businesses begin as part-time ventures or grow out of hobbies. People starting a business in this way usually keep their start-up costs—and their risks—low and manageable. They also have the advantage of doing something that they already enjoy and in which they have some experience. Often the business begins as an enterprise run out of the entrepreneur's house or garage. Apple Computer is probably the best-known example of a company that started as a part-time, at-home venture, but countless companies can trace their lineage to a founder's spare room, attic, basement or garage. (See Chapter 21 for more on the particulars of having an office in your home.)

The thing to remember, though, is that a part-time business is a *business*—not a hobby. As such, it requires the same treatment and attention to details such as market research, record keeping, insurance and tax payments that a full-time business demands.

Business or Hobby?

Indeed, the Internal Revenue Service has two distinct sets of rules for the tax treatment of businesses and hobbies. In the eyes of the IRS (which are eyes every businessperson should keep an eye on), your activity can qualify as a business if you realize a profit from it in at least three years out of five. As a business, your part-time venture is then entitled to the same kinds of deductions that a multimillion-dollar corporation takes: deductions for advertising, business-related education, mailings, stationery, equipment, supplies, rent, and so on. You can deduct them in full on Schedule C.

If, on the other hand, your venture shows a profit in fewer than three of five years, the IRS may rule that you have a hobby, not a business. In that case, the government can tax any profits, but you can't deduct any losses. You can still deduct expenses, but they're limited to the amount of income your hobby generates and are considered miscellaneous expenses. That means you get the deductions only if you itemize on Schedule A and only to the extent that all your miscellaneous deductions exceed 2% of your adjusted gross income.

Make Money From What You Love

Tax status is just one factor in the hobby-business equation. When a hobby is successfully converted into a business, the results can be a delight. One example: Ralph Miller was always a horse nut. He went to prep school in New England, dropped out of college, hung around race tracks and rodeos, learned how to break colts and shoe horses. Eventually, he drifted toward Montana, where in 1975 he began putting his hobby to work, hiring himself out as a guide for horseback trail-riding groups in the backcountry areas of Yellowstone National Park. Soon thereafter, he bought enough horses to start his own outfitting operation—which he ran while earning a degree in veterinary medicine. Still mostly a summertime business for the year-round vet, R.K. Miller's Wilderness Pack Trips grosses about $70,000 per season from its Livingston, Mont., base. Not bad for a part-time business that never "graduated" to full-time costs and responsibilities.

When a hobby is successfully converted into a business, the results can be a delight.

Get-rich-quick opportunities are soon likely to be overrun with would-be entrepreneurs.

Avoiding the Fads

It would be par for the course for us to end this chapter by listing a bunch of rapid-growth industries and sectors that the potential entrepreneur should consider. For example, among the hottest franchise lines in the early '90s were house-cleaning services, printing and copying outlets, and diet centers.

There are two problems with lists of "hot" business opportunities. The first is that most business trends are cyclical, so this year's great opportunity could be next year's glutted market. Remember how popular video arcades were in the late 1970s? People saw children and adults pouring a seemingly endless stream of quarters into all manner of microchip-stuffed wonders, and the future revenue projections looked infinitely rosy. Then the market became glutted with video arcades, the novelty of many games wore off, and video games expanded from arcades to other retailers and finally to the home, where companies like Nintendo saw their sales boom. Video arcades still exist and still make a profit—but they're no longer looked at as licenses to print money.

Among the businesses I've seen touted as "hot" over the years: wedding videography, computer repair, lawn-mower repair, home day-care centers, medical-claims processing, baby-shoe bronzing, chimney-sweeping, carpet-cleaning, restaurant-grease collecting, pet-sitting, pet cemeteries, computer-generated portraits, computer-generated mail lists, computer-generated calligraphy (heck, computer-generated *anything*), frozen-yogurt shops, instant T-shirt shops, and lingerie sales through home parties (think the Tupperware concept).

Now these may have been, or even now may be, great money-making ideas. But anything that is commonly thought to be a get-rich-quick opportunity (or even a get-comfortable-quick opportunity) is soon likely to be overrun with would-be entrepreneurs, competing with each other and driving down prices and profits. As with video arcades, today's hot opportunity can be tomorrow's saturated market, as everyone jumps on the bandwagon.

That leads to a couple of "opportunities" listed. Do you really want to collect restaurant grease or open a pet cemetery? Do these interest you? There's nothing wrong with the businesses, *if that's your heart's desire.*

Which leads us to the second problem with lists of business opportunities: The "opportunity" is nothing of the kind if it's not something that you would enjoy taking on.

So when you come across them, take those idealized, generalized lists and treat them as a way to stimulate your thinking about businesses you can get into. The list that counts is the one you make—be it ever so humble, ever so simple, or ever so short—of the businesses you *want* to run. It's from that list that you'll find success. Trust yourself, and then confirm and verify that trust by developing a plan of action that will lead to your working for yourself.

Your Plan of Action

Once you have decided that you want to work for yourself, you have to figure out *how* you're going to do that. That means discovering the gaps in your knowledge about starting a business. This book answers many of the questions you will have about working for yourself, but in answering them, it will raise others. Take heart, though, because this book will equip you to find the answers.

Many of the questions you'll ask yourself when you read one section of the book will be answered in other chapters, and we'll refer you to them as you read.

Throughout, we'll also recommend other sources of information and expertise.

Remember, working for yourself will be one of the biggest and lengthiest information-gathering projects you will ever conduct. But this time, you'll be doing it for *yourself*—not for some corporation or agency.

Doing It by the Book

The chapters that follow are broadly grouped into two sections. The larger by far, beginning with the following chapter, discusses the big-picture questions that you'll have to come to grips with before you ever open your doors for business. The final section, beginning with Chapter 21, "Getting Organized," is more operationally oriented—a sort of to-do list of the nitty-gritty details and management issues you'll have to deal with when starting and running your business.

The chapters are ordered so that the information you gather and the decisions you make while reading one chapter will logically lead you to the issues addressed in the next chapter. You could simply follow the book chapter by chapter, developing your plan of action as you go.

Or, the cross-referencing from one chapter to another may lead you to weave from one chapter to another in no particular order. And that approach might more accurately reflect the nature of planning a business; it's not necessarily a linear or chronological process, but an organic one that demands that issues in several different areas seemingly come to a head at once.

Of course, depending on your interests, the type of self-employment you're pursuing, and how far along you are in your thinking and planning, not every chapter will be perti-

---

An Outline for Any Business Plan

• •

The essential elements of a formal business plan should describe and explain:

- Your business concept, that is, your business in a nutshell.

- Your product or service, in detail.

- Your market.

- Your marketing strategy.

- How you will produce what you sell.

- Your personnel.

- Your financial plans.

---

nent to your needs. (Even so, it would be wise to review those chapters that you think don't apply, just to challenge your own assumptions.)

Similarly, every plan of action or business plan will differ in its scope and focus. If you want to work alone and not in a partnership with someone else, you won't have a section on partners in your plan of action and you probably won't spend much time on Chapter 13, "Going Partners." A reader who feels he or she immediately needs information on leasing property and buying insurance may turn first to Chapter 21, "Getting Organized." Someone interested in purchasing a business may make a beeline for Chapter 20, "Buying a Business." Your own plan of action or business plan will reflect these types of decisions and concerns.

Your plan of action, in short, is not formulaic. Not only is there more than one way to come up with your plan, but there's also no such thing as a fixed plan: The way you're going to get your venture started will probably change over time as you learn more about your business and what it means to work for yourself. In fact, with each aspect of working for yourself that you explore, you'll develop new questions that need to be answered. One of the co-founders of Class VI River Runners, a white-water rafting company in West Virginia, recalls the one thing that stayed the same about his business plan over the years: "Our goal is to work hard and have fun."

Organizing Your Thoughts

A plan of action can take many forms. Some people keep their entire plan of action in their heads, never committing anything to paper. This technique isn't recommended for most of us mortals, but some folks make it work. Others keep folders in which they file notes, books, documents, articles and other information that applies to every aspect their project. Still others take everything they know about their new venture and put all that information into a coherent, well-organized and written form—especially if they expect to have to prove to potential lenders or investors that they've done their homework. People who do that call their plan of action a business plan.

Writing the Plan

Even if you have no intention of seeking outside financing, it will still pay off to create this outline of your research, your thinking, your decision-making, your goals, hopes and ideals—every aspect of how you're going to start working for yourself. It will be a plan you can refer to over time, and it will help remind you why you ever wanted to work for yourself in the first place.

Keys to Successful Planning

• •

- Planning is problem solving.

- A plan must be flexible as situations change.

- A plan must reflect reality.

- A plan should reflect the skills and knowledge of those who carry it out.

- A plan should state specific ways to achieve goals and objectives.

- A plan must be communicated to those who are affected by it.

A written plan can take many forms. At the minimum, it could be a few notes on index cards organized into categories. It could also be a typeset plan a half inch thick, with charts, graphs, photos, color-coded pie charts and an impressive cover for presentation to a banker or venture capitalist.

In any case, a properly developed business plan serves three important purposes:

- **It communicates** your ideas, research and plans to yourself—and to others.

- **It's a framework** on which to construct your business and manage it over time.

- **It's a yardstick** by which you can measure progress and evaluate changes in yourself and your business.

If your plan of action is something you wish to present to prospective sources of financing, as well as prospective partners, advisers and staff members, you'll want it to be well-written and neatly typed. You may want to hire someone, perhaps a free-lance editor, to help you make sure that your written plan is well-organized, easy to read, sound, logical and factual.

The specifics of what to include in a business plan and how to gather, calculate or quantify information are covered in the later chapters of this book. The accompanying checklist provides a more detailed overview of what each section could include and refers you to the corresponding chapters throughout this book.

Remember that, in order to be effective, your plan of action can't be cast in stone. You will probably discover it needs fine-tuning pretty frequently at first—particularly as you show it to your support network or prospective sources of financing and solicit their input. Ultimately, the idea is to make this plan serve *your* needs.

A Planning Primer

Planning is simply a way to organize your thinking, and good planning is the ability to translate your intuition

(continued on page 70)

Your plan of action can't be cast in stone. You will probably discover it needs fine-tuning pretty frequently at first.

A Plan in More Detail

Here's an overview of the essential components of any business plan. The information in parentheses is optional in a written business plan that will be read by outside sources of financing and advice, but it's important for your overall plan of action.

Your business concept

- The first and most important page of a business plan.

- This page presents a summary of your business idea: why you think it will work, how it fits into the marketplace, what the future should hold.

- It sets the tone for what follows, and it can be the "make it or break it" page in the eyes of a lender or investor.

- (Describes your personal goals; what you hope to accomplish.)

For more help, see Chapters 1, 2 and 3.

Description of your business

- Describes what, exactly, your new venture is.

- Gives a complete description of what you plan to sell—product or service, tangible or intangible.

- Emphasizes whichever aspect of your business will provide the bulk of your income.

- Explains advantages and benefits that will help "sell" your business concept to a complete stranger.

- If your product is still on the drawing board, projects when it will be available and includes any test data you have.

- Includes illustrations or photographs if appropriate.

For more help, see Chapters 5, 7, 18, 19 and 20.

Your market

- Explains the big picture first.

- Looks at the total universe of your market.

- Tells whether the industry is growing or declining, as well as:

- What is happening now or is expected to happen that will impact your business.

- Where you will locate your business.

- Who your competitors are.

- How successful they are, and why.

- What their weaknesses are.

- How your business will fill a need created by their weakness.

- Who your customers will be.

- Why they will buy your product or service.

For more help, see Chapters 8 and 9.

Your marketing strategy

- Discusses what you will name your business, as well as:

- How you'll legally protect your product, service, or business or product name.

- How your product or service will be sold.

- Pricing strategy, estimated sales and projected market share for each of the first three years.

- What you're going to do to get word about your venture to potential customers or clients.

For more help, see Chapters 7, 8, 10 and 12.

Operating (or production) plans

- Discusses how you're going to make your product or service "happen," as well as:
- All the specifics, such as how, where and by whom your product or service will be produced.
- What supplies you will require; availability and sources of supplies.
- The production process; your anticipated rate of production.
- (How you will run your venture on a day-to-day basis, including hours of operation, billing procedures, bookkeeping systems and quality-control safeguards.)
- (How you'll handle practical start-up details—setting up an office, hiring employees if needed, acquiring licenses, managing parking, arranging insurance and meeting other regulations and requirements.)

For more help, see Chapters 5, 16, 21, 22, 23, 24, 25 and 26.

Structure and key personnel

- Discusses whether your venture will be a sole proprietorship, a partnership or a corporation, as well as:
- Who else will be involved in the decision-making process of your organization.
- Who your supporting advisers will be (these may be other professionals on whose expertise you can rely).

- How many people are involved, and their skills and qualifications.
- When you will add personnel.
- How, if you're running a one-person show, your skills and talents are sufficient to achieve your goals.
- Includes an organizational chart, if appropriate.

For more help, see Chapters 3, 11, 13, 14, 15, 18 and 26.

Your financial plans

- Includes how much money you have, how much you might need, sources of start-up funds, anticipated revenues, as well as:
- A personal financial statement, if your business is a new one.
- A financial statement for the business as well, if it is already established.
- A discussion of how you plan to increase reserves and profits over time.
- (Be prepared to explain—line-by-line—how you arrived at each of your figures.)

For more help, see Chapters 4, 14, 17, 23 and 24.

into action and results. Chances are you already know the consequences of poor, incomplete or nonexistent planning or the inability to follow up on planning. It may be one of the reasons that you are leaving the workaday world to be your own boss. Good intentions, after all, don't get the job done. Use this opportunity to practice breaking "project planning" down into its most simple elements.

A Project Is Just the Sum of Its Parts

Planning is a matter of setting objectives and determining the specific time and resources needed to reach those objectives. An objective is a specific expression of what you want *to do;* a series of objectives is usually necessary to reach a larger goal. The time element sets a limit on how long you are giving yourself to do the job. The resources you will need to do the job should be spelled out, too: Who is going to do it? Who will follow up? How will you know when the job is completed?

For More Information on Business Plans

If you're concerned about the physical design or form of a business plan, there are several sources to which you can turn for examples and sample forms.

Books

- *How To Write A Business Plan,* by Mike McKeever (Nolo Press).

- *How To Start A Business And Succeed,* by Ripley Hotch (Stackpole Books).

- *Up-Front Financing: The Entrepreneur's Guide,* by A. David Silver (John Wiley & Sons), and

- *The Entrepreneur's Guide to Raising Venture Capital,* by Greenberg Consulting and Craig T. Norback (Liberty Hall Press).

Lenders

Loan application forms from banks and other lenders can function as plans of action for many people, since the forms ask for information on just about everything you have to consider in order to get a loan—and to start your business.

The Service Corps of Retired Executives

SCORE is supported by the U.S. Small Business Administration. Retired businesspeople are available to help entrepreneurs with their questions, including questions about business plans or plans of action. They may be able to help you design a plan or have an example of the kind of plan outline that is right for you (for more on SCORE's services, see Chapter 14).

A complete plan will also include:

- **Action statements.** Those are written descriptions of what you're going to do.

- **A ranking of each action according to your priorities.** Ask yourself, how important is each of these actions toward accomplishing my objective? What has to happen before something else can happen?

- **A schedule.** The closer you can get to a specific, believable date for each thing that needs doing, the better.

- **Assignments.** Who is going to check that something is being done and done right? You may be "it" in every case.

- **The results you achieved.**

- **Pertinent comments.** These could include reasons for delays, how actions or results will affect other people, how results will be measured, and so on.

You Won't Get There in a Day

In your planning, take into account short-, medium- and long-term needs:

- **the operational, day-to-day stuff** that you'll review daily or weekly;

- **the "big" objectives** that you'll probably review on a monthly basis;

- **and an outline of how you want your business to develop and grow,** covering three to five years and requiring review every six months or so.

Challenging Your Plan

And, finally, no plan is complete unless you:

Consider your constraints.

What limitations do you have to take into account?

Chances are you already know the consequences of poor, incomplete or nonexistent planning or the inability to follow up on planning.

Because most of your business will be running itself instead of running you, you'll have time to pay proper attention to the things that matter most.

What resources do you have, including money, people, time and equipment? What potential problems are you likely to encounter?

Establish control points.

You have to be able to tell how your plan is progressing, and you need to be sensitive to changes in direction. Your control points can be people, written reports, a sales ledger, a bank account or charts.

Chart your plan.

Devise a way to *show* the progress of your plan—for instance, on a timeline, a calendar or software designed for project planning.

Develop a backup plan.

If the worst happens and your plan falls apart, what will you do? In a critical situation, you may want to have two backup plans.

Planning will help you work things out on paper first and let you set up systems to handle routine needs. Then, because most of your business will be running itself instead of running you, you'll have time to pay proper attention to the things that matter most, as well as the inevitable roadblocks and unexpected occurrences. (For more on managing yourself and others, see Chapter 26.)

Protecting Your Idea

CHAPTER

7

Let's say that your new business is based on a new idea—a concept for a product or a process that nobody else is offering, or that you can provide better or cheaper or faster or more reliably than anyone else. Before you take your idea into the public arena, you have to *protect* that idea from those who would rip you off, taking your product and creating ersatz (and cheaper) versions that can be sold in competition with yours.

Copyrights, patents and trademarks are legal safeguards for your creative work, whatever its form. Businesspeople who are also inventors know this, or they learn it very quickly.

One example: Lyman Coddington had an idea for a set of toy blocks that could be used to teach small children about the metric system. The Washington, D.C., resident first designed the blocks—a group of cubes weighing a total of one kilogram (2.2 pounds). Then, before figuring out who might buy his "Merrie Metrics" blocks, before producing the blocks for sale, before raising the capital to get his fledging educational toy company off the ground, he got a patent for his invention. It took him a year and a half to get it, but U.S. Patent No. 4,838,794, granted for a system of ten blocks that in combination express metric weight, volume and length relationships, belongs to Lyman Coddington. "I knew it was a good idea, and I wanted to make sure that I could legally protect it," Coddington said.

Smart thinking. Here's a rundown on how copyrights, patents and trademarks can protect the fruits of your creative labors.

Copyrights

A copyright is the cheapest kind of federal protection available. It's also the simplest. How simple? Well, a copyright takes *effect at the moment you begin to create a work.* That's right: When you sit down to write something that can be copyrighted, that work is copyrighted—automatically, and whether or not it is published.

Copyrights are good for the life of the author plus 50 years with some exceptions on "works for hire" (commissioned for certain uses or prepared by an employee as part of his job). With a copyright, you and you alone have the right to reproduce, distribute, perform, display or make a "derivative work" from the work in question.

Work You Can Copyright

• •

Among the things that can be copyrighted are literary, dramatic, musical and artistic works, including:

- Books, magazine articles and plays.
- Computer programs.
- Videos.
- Sculptures, prints and other graphics.
- Maps.
- Songs and other musical works.
- Motion pictures.
- Training manuals.
- Management consulting plans.

What's Covered

Copyrights are mostly used to cover what can loosely be defined as creative works and "writings" (the legal language is "works of authorship"; see the accompanying box). That somewhat limits the effective use of copyrights for many small businesses. If you're writing computer software programs or developing topographic maps, the copyright laws will come in very handy. On the other hand, if you've invented a piece of computer *hardware,* or have created a tool to aid in land surveying, the copyright laws do you no good. For these and other creations, you'll need a more complicated form of protection (a trademark or patent) to keep someone else from taking unfair advantage of your bright idea.

It's also worth noting that an *idea* cannot be copyrighted. A copyright is created when you take an idea and express it in a particular or tangible way. For example, the idea that money and power do not necessarily lead to life-long happiness cannot be copyrighted. However, the transformation of that idea into the script for a movie or play could be copyrighted.

Marking Your Turf—Here and Elsewhere

To make people aware that you will protect the work from being unfairly copied, you can simply type the word "copyright" at the top of the work's first page. Your copyright will be more defensible if you pay $20 and register your work with the U.S. Copyright Office—and you should do so before there's a chance that your copyright will be infringed upon. You can use the copyright symbol—©—before or after registering a work. You should also use the copyright notice when you publish the work, although that's not required by law.

Copyright protection even extends to other countries. If your work is published in a country that subscribes to the Berne Convention, an international copyright agreement among some 65 countries in Europe and Asia, the work will automatically have copyright protection under the laws of that country. The U.S. also has agreements with other countries in the Western Hemisphere via the Buenos Aires Convention and with some countries via the Universal Copyright Convention (or bilateral treaty).

Copyright Violation

Now, if somebody copies your copyrighted work without your permission, that person is guilty of stealing—plain and simple. Large firms can be vociferous in defending their copyrights. For example, the Walt Disney Co. made news when it notified a daycare center in Florida that its hand-painted murals of Mickey Mouse and other Disney characters on the exterior school walls were unauthorized and violated the company's copyright. As you can imagine,

If somebody copies your copyrighted work without your permission, that person is guilty of stealing—plain and simple.

The Xerox Corp. does its best to remind people that not every photocopy is a Xerox.

such action doesn't always make for good publicity: People think of Mickey Mouse as belonging to the American public and don't necessarily see "theft" where Disney does. But for Disney, the issue is a simple matter of copyright violation, and the company is determined to protect its interests in and exclusive rights to the popular characters it has created. The company believes it has to be aggressive so that when it brings suit for unauthorized use, people can't defend themselves by asserting that Disney had abandoned its copyright or trademark rights.

Such vigorous protection can translate into high legal fees, of course—fees that many small businesses cannot afford. But if you're victimized by an unintentional copyright violation, you may be able to simply negotiate with the other party without hiring a lawyer.

For example, the author of a copyrighted article learned that a retail coat shop had reprinted her article in its promotional literature without her permission. The shop had disregarded the copyright law regarding "fair use," which allows limited reproduction of copyrighted material for news and educational purposes. She notified the shop that it had violated her copyright and demanded proper compensation. The shop negotiated with her, and the two sides eventually agreed on a fair reimbursement for the use of the article: a certificate for $1,000 that the writer could use to purchase goods from the shop.

Trademarks

A trademark is typically a name or logo that identifies the source of a product or service. The trademark helps identify the name of your product as being distinctly your own. For example, DuPont makes a point of reminding journalists that its brand of spandex fiber is called LYCRA, which is a DuPont registered trademark. While every LYCRA product can be called spandex, not every spandex product can be called LYCRA. Similarly, the Xerox Corp. does its best to remind people that not every photocopy is a Xerox and that the correct verb is "to copy" a document, not "to xerox" it.

Registered trademark status is usually indicated with the symbol ® following the registered mark. This symbol also represents registered *service* marks, which are used to protect the names or logos of services rather than products. The emblems of Blue Cross and Blue Shield, for example, are protected by service marks.

Keys to Identity

But a trademark can protect more than an emblem or a name. Any symbol or device—even part of a product itself—that serves to identify the source of the goods or services in the marketplace can also be protected. Kodak has succeeded in protecting its right to the yellow carton in which its film is packaged. The Coca-Cola Co. has trademarked its narrow-waisted bottle, the name of the soft drink that goes with the company name, the special script that spells out the words "Coca-Cola" and even the abbreviated name "Coke." The company is determined to make sure that when somebody talks about drinking a Coca-Cola, they're not talking about some other company's cola, soda or pop.

Even phrases can be trademarked. For example, Hallmark Cards has trademarked the phrase "when you care enough to send the very best." The phrase is part of the image and reputation the company has sought to build, and other corporations cannot use it.

Getting One

The application fee for federal registration of a trademark or service mark is $245. Federal registrations remain in force for ten years after registration and may be renewed indefinitely as long as the trademark or service mark remains in use in commerce. Getting a trademark registered doesn't happen instantly, however; the average application takes more than a year to wend its way through the governmental maze. In the meantime, you can use the symbol TM (or SM for a service mark) to indicate that you intend to defend your symbol against infringement.

Even phrases can be trademarked. For example, Hallmark Cards has trademarked "when you care enough to send the very best."

A state trademark

You can also choose to skip the federal level and get a state trademark in just those states where you expect to market your product. State trademarks are weaker than federal ones, simply because their jurisdiction is much more limited. Yet they can be inexpensive (for example, $50 for one in the state of Maryland) and useful alternatives to federal trademarks for those start-ups that intend to do business only in one state or small geographic region.

A trademark search

Although you're not required to search for conflicting trademarks before applying to register yours, the

Copyright, Trademark and Patent Resources

Associations

The American Intellectual Property Law Association (AIPLA) (2001 Jefferson Davis Hwy., Suite 203, Arlington, VA 22202) publishes a booklet, *How to Protect and Benefit from Your Ideas,* that serves as an introductory guide to cashing in on and safeguarding your creative works. By purchasing the booklet, you'll also be entitled to a free 30-minute phone or personal consultation with a member of the AIPLA. To get the booklet, send a check for $9.95 to the AIPLA.

Books

There are several good books available on protecting your idea and making money from it. Two in particular:

- For protecting your idea, *How to Protect Your Business, Professional, & Brand Names,* by David A. Weinstein (John Wiley & Sons);

- And for turning your idea into cash, *Millions From the Mind,* by Alan R. Tripp (Amacom Press).

From the government

The Register of Copyrights (Information Section, Copyright Office, Library of Congress, Washington, DC 20559) can provide more information on how to register your copyrighted work.

The U.S. Patent and Trademark Office (Department of Commerce, Commissioner of Patents and Trademarks, U.S. Patent and Trademark Office, Washington, DC 20231; 703–308–4357) can provide information and applications for patents and trademarks. Ask for a copy of the free booklet *Basic Facts About Trademarks.* You can also get a copy by calling the U.S. Patent and Trademark Office at 703–308–9000.

You can order another government booklet, *General Information Concerning Patents,* for $2.25 (Superintendent of Documents, Government Printing Office, P.O. Box 371954, Pittsburgh, PA 15250; 202–512–1800).

Patent and Trademark Office will do its own search. If it turns up a conflict, it won't refund your $245 application fee and it won't register your mark. If you want to do your own search, see the discussion below and "A Patent or Trademark Search," on page 80.

Patents

Patents are the U.S. government's way of protecting an inventor's property rights to his or her invention. A patent doesn't give you the right to make, use or sell something; it just blocks anyone else from doing that without your permission.

There are two general types of patents:

A utility patent

A utility patent can cover a new, useful and unobvious process, machine, manufactured article or composition of matter (such as a new drug). Utility patents can also protect improvements to any of those processes, machines and products. Utility patents now are typically granted for 20 years from filing.

A design patent

Design patents are more specific than utility patents. With a design patent, you can protect a design for the appearance of a manufactured item. Design patents are good for 14 years.

The Long and Winding Road

Getting any type of patent can be difficult and time-consuming. If someone else anywhere in the world published information on an idea clearly similar to yours before you created your invention, you can't get patent protection. Design patents are nice to have, but a design patent won't do you any good if a competitor makes even a slight modification to a design you've created. Before you apply for a patent, you can send the Patent and Trademark Office documentation showing the birth and development

If someone else anywhere in the world published information on an idea clearly similar to yours before you created your invention, you can't get patent protection.

of your idea. The PTO will save this material for up to two years. If you find yourself in dispute with another inventor, these records can help prove who had the idea first but they won't guarantee that you get the patent.

The wait for a patent can stretch for several years, and you can easily spend $5,000 or more on forms, drawings, legal help and filing fees. Once you've applied, you can use the phrase "patent pending" on every copy of your item. Though you can try to do it yourself, you'll probably have to hire a patent attorney or patent agent to search the files of the Patent and Trademark Office and make sure your invention is indeed unique (or at least an improvement on something that already exists) and to prepare the application and respond to PTO notices.

A Patent or Trademark Search

If you need help in conducting a patent or trademark search, consult the Patent and Trademark Office's register of patent agents and attorneys, who may also be listed under those headings in your local Yellow Pages.

Or request: *Attorneys and Agents Registered to Practice before the U.S. Patent and Trademark Office,* published by the U.S. Superintendent of Documents (Government Printing Office, P.O. Box 371954, Pittsburgh, PA 15250; $31). Write to this agency for current prices as well as a list of other potentially useful publications.

For the names of attorneys specializing in trademarks, look in the Yellow Pages under categories like "Trademark Agents and Counselors," or ask your family attorney or other business professionals for referrals.

If you're interested in conducting your own search of patents and trademarks, check out these sources of information:

- **The Patent and Trademark Office's Search Room/Libraries** operates from two locations. For patents only: 2021 Jefferson Davis Highway, Crystal Plaza, Building 3–4, Lobby Level, Arlington, VA, 22202; 703–308–0595. For trademarks only: 2900 Crystal Drive, Arlington, VA 22202; 703–308–9800.

- **The PTO's Patent Depository Libraries,** located around the country, provide free access to patent and trademark records on CD-ROM discs that are continually updated. Call 800–435–7735 for the address of the depository library nearest you.

- **The CompuServe and Dialog on-line computer services** allow you to do on-line trademark searches. Dialog features "Trademark Scan," a service that is updated three times weekly.

- **CompuServe and Mead Data Central** (its LEXPAT service) allow you to do patent searches.

If You Do Your Own Search

If you want to do a patent or trademark search yourself, you may need to go to the Patent and Trademark Office in Arlington, Va., or to one of the patent depository libraries around the country (see the accompanying box). It's not impossible to do your own search: Lyman Coddington, inventor of the metric cubes described earlier, hired a patent attorney to advise him but put his own time and legwork into the search, which consumed about 160 hours of his time.

Patent, copyright and trademark laws are complicated and subject to change. The sources discussed in the accompanying boxes can provide you with basic information. However, you'll also want to talk with a lawyer specializing in patent, trademark or copyright law if you need to protect the rights to your product. Patent law is tricky, and every word in a patent application counts: Faulty phrasing could cause you to lose some or even all of the rights to your invention.

The Importance of Documenting Your Work

Filing a patent can be just the beginning of your fight for the sole right to your invention. If someone applies for a patent on a similar idea around the same time, the patent office will step in to decide who is the first inventor. (This is not a new development, by the way; many people have charged that Thomas Edison was not the inventor of the light bulb but was simply quicker off the mark than others in patenting the process for sending electricity through a piece of metal.)

To really protect yourself, you'll need a written record of your work, starting at the moment of inception, lasting until you've received your patent, and dated and witnessed by someone else. "No scrap paper, no pads," said Calvin MacCracken, a lifelong inventor with 80 patents to his credit. Among MacCracken's inventions are a heating and

To really protect yourself, you'll need a written record of your work, starting at the moment of inception.

cooling system used in the space suits of astronauts and an "off-peak cooling storage" system that makes ice at night using off-peak-rate (and thus cheaper) electricity, then releases the stored-up coolness into air-conditioning systems the next day. MacCracken said his own organized records and notes saved him on the two occasions in his career when there was a conflict over who was the first inventor of something for which he'd applied for a patent.

Check, Check and Doublecheck

Perhaps the best way to document your work is by keeping track of it in a notebook—one bound with glue or

Analyzing Your Idea

A university department or other private organization specializing in start-up enterprises can analyze your idea and determine whether it is even worth legally protecting.

Colleges and universities

Check to see whether any nearby schools offer product evaluation services, which can be a real bargain. For example:

- **The Wisconsin Innovation Service Center** (University of Wisconsin at Whitewater, 402 McCutchan Hall, Whitewater, WI 53190), a nonprofit entity, can analyze your idea's legality, safety, functional feasibility, production feasibility and investment cost. You'll pay $175 for the service, which has evaluated nearly 3,500 ideas since 1980.

- **The Center for Entrepreneurship at Baylor University** (P.O. Box 98011, Waco, TX 76798) also offers evaluations, for $150.

Private and for-profit invention brokers and consultants

These folks can also help develop or sell your idea. Most of them will work on a contingent fee basis: They don't get paid unless your invention sells. Be wary of organizations that make promises in exchange for a hefty *advance* fee. There are legitimate companies that operate this way, but some companies have had action taken against them in various states for fraud after giving inventions glowing praise, collecting sizable fees, then doing little to turn the invention into a money-making product.

Consumer protection agencies

The Better Business Bureau, state and local consumer protection offices, and state attorney general's offices are good places to learn whether any complaints have been lodged against a company you're considering. Of course, you should ask your attorney to work with you throughout this process and especially before signing any contract with an invention development firm.

sewn together, not one of those three-ring deals in which pages can be added or removed. (No sense, after all, in leaving yourself open to an accusation that you pieced together a record of your work after the fact.) You can also number your notebook pages to further eliminate the possibility of being charged with modifying your records, and you can date and sign the bottom of each page, with your signature witnessed by someone who verifies with his signature that he has reviewed and understands the work represented on the page. As a backup and cross-check, keep a record of calls, meetings and correspondence related to your work, along with receipts for anything purchased relating to your invention. These conversations and documents can all be noted in a log or daily calendar.

Sound like a lot of extra paperwork? You bet. But this is part of what you have to do to ward off competitors before they get too far.

Choosing Your Protection

It's not always clear whether a product should be protected with a patent, a trademark or a copyright. Indeed, sometimes a trademark can be used in place of a patent. One example: In the mid 1980s, when Mark Achler and Charles Duff founded Whitewater Group (now Symantec Whitewater), a software development company in Evanston, Ill., they didn't patent their principal product. This was software called *Actor*, which was designed to support *Microsoft Windows*. But they did copyright the software, and they got a service mark for the company name as well as trademarks for the *Actor* name and logo. (The right to market the software was later sold to Genesis Development Systems.)

"Back then, patenting software was a gray area," said Ben Crown, who was the company's chief financial officer. "The guidelines were less clear. Also, a minor consideration was that the patenting process was much more expensive than the trademark approach."

Often, a company will safeguard a product with all three forms of protection. The inventors of Trivial Pursuit,

It's not always clear how a product should be protected. Often a company will safeguard a product with all three forms.

the board game that was all the rage in the early 1980s, copyrighted all the questions used in the game, applied for a registered trademark for the name, Trivial Pursuit, and got a design patent for the cardboard design used in the game. Their efforts came in handy when the company had to sue imitators of the popular game.

When Legal Protection Isn't Enough

Now that we've told you the importance of protecting your idea, we'll let you in on a little secret: Sometimes you can stand on legality, but it may not be enough—especially if you become a very well-known entity subject to an extraordinary amount of negative publicity in the course of protecting your rights to a very popular product.

In such circumstances, you could just throw up your hands in defeat. Example: In 1991, the slogans "Rip City" and "Red Hot 'N' Rollin" were all over the city of Portland, Ore., home of the National Basketball Association's Portland Trail Blazers. The Trail Blazers, a tremendously popular and successful franchise (it has been years since a home game did not sell out) decided to try to control use of the slogans, on which the team said it believed it had trademark rights. The slogans had appeared on many T-shirts, posters and other products that were not licensed by the Trail Blazers.

Reaction was swift—or, to put it another way, the public was red, hot and rolling in its anger at the Blazers. Fans held protests and wrote letters to the editor of the *Portland Oregonian*. Local newscasts reported on the controversy over what the fans clearly felt were *their* slogans. The shock waves rolled all the way to Los Angeles, where a *Los Angeles Times* sportswriter devoted one of his columns to the controversy.

Finally, faced with a continuing torrent of bad publicity, the team gave up. "Our fans, and virtually everyone in the media, have made it clear to us that they want the terms 'Rip City' and 'Red Hot 'N' Rollin' to be in the public domain," said team executive Marshall Glickman in announcing the change.

Call it a slam-dunk for public opinion.

Licensing Your Invention

Let's say you have a great idea but you don't want to have to personally produce or sell it—or you do, but you want to let others make use of your ideas in other ways. How do you protect yourself? The kind of proper legal protection we're discussing in this chapter can help you make money from your idea while giving somebody else the opportunity of, and responsibility for, bringing the potential product to market. Once you have a copyright, trademark or patent for your product or idea, you can do more with it than make money by selling the thing itself: You can also make money by selling the rights to it for use in other forms.

Giving somebody else the right to use your copyright, trademark or patent is known as *licensing*. Licensing an idea or product is sort of like renting it out: The licensor (that's you) gets a fee or royalty from the licensee, who gets the right to use or sell your product.

If you license the rights to your idea or product instead of marketing it yourself, you won't have to worry about product production, start-up costs, distribution, advertising, sales or anything else. This has appeal for people who get excited coming up with new

Harris, Cartoonists & Writers Syndicate

ideas but don't want the hassle and worry of trying to translate those ideas into concrete products. On the other hand, licensing means almost certainly giving up some potential future profit: The companies buying the rights to

You and your attorney will have to consider the many ways that your product could be licensed and give the rights only for those uses that you want to relinquish.

your creation will be looking to make more money from it than they're paying you for the rights to it. That's only fair, of course, given the investment they'll be making in your product. However, you'll want to be sure that you receive fair compensation for any rights you assign.

The Value of Your Idea

There's no way we can tell you here how much an idea or invention of yours is worth: Every potential product has, obviously, its own special value to a potential licensee. What's important is that with any licensing agreement you receive a fair contract and a fair amount of money for your efforts (you'll probably need an attorney or agent to figure out exactly what's "fair.") Licensing agreements can provide for royalties based on a percentage of sale revenues, profits, number of units sold and other variables. You could get an up-front payment plus royalties as part of an agreement, or you could simply sell the rights to your idea for a fixed lump sum.

Be Specific

Any licensing agreement should describe exactly what rights you're giving to the licensee: how long the license will last, what type of rights (local, national, worldwide) you're granting; what fees will be paid, and so on. It should also cover the forms or ways in which the product can be sold. For example, a written work could be sold on paper or in computer-disk form; a series of drawings could be sold as posters, silk-screened T-shirts, or even coffee-mug emblems. You (and, in all likelihood, your attorney specializing in intellectual property issues) will have to consider the many ways that your product could be licensed and give the rights only for those uses that you want to relinquish.

Money for Nothing

You'll also want to be sure you'll receive something even if the company does *nothing* with your idea. It's not unheard of for a corporation to purchase the rights to a product simply so it won't have to worry about something that could become a competitor to its own products.

How Licensees Protect Themselves

Finding someone to license your idea can be difficult. Corporations are often reluctant to look at ideas that come in unsolicited, in part because they worry about being hit with lawsuits for misappropriating or stealing an idea. For this reason, your first contact with any potential licensee may be through its legal department, which will want you to agree that your legal rights will be restricted to whatever patent protection you have or will eventually receive. That keeps the company from worrying about its own research and development being limited by anything other than your patent rights, which the company would have to honor whether you'd made contact with it or not.

Some companies won't even give you that option, though. To prevent any lawsuits alleging misappropriation of an idea or breach of a confidential relationship, some companies simply won't look at *any* ideas submitted to them by outsiders.

Their loss

That seemed to be the case for Keith Scripps, who got virtually no show of interest when he first tried to commercialize his idea for a new kind of smoke-detector—one that would plug into a standard light socket. "I put together a list of all the smoke detector manufacturers and sent each of them a letter, but the companies simply weren't interested," said Scripps, who calls himself a "gadgeteer."

A year after those rejections, he got a call from a hardware company in Kansas City. Someone within the organization had had an idea for a smoke detector that

Corporations are often reluctant to look at ideas that come in unsolicited.

would plug into a light socket. When they did their patent search, they found—surprise!—Scripps's patents on his invention. The company agreed to license Scripps's patents and produce his invention, paying him a royalty on every sale.

Scripps's baby came to be called the Generation 2 Smoke Detector and was voted best new product at a national hardware show. That's where the CEO of one of the companies Scripps had originally contacted saw it and asked why Scripps hadn't called his firm. Scripps had the pleasure of telling the CEO that his company had turned him away.

Market Research: Who Is *Your* Customer?

8

This chapter is all about knowing who your customer is. If you don't find that out, you won't know how to properly reach your customers, meet their needs, set a price they'll gladly pay or identify competitors for their business. Market research is the means to this end. It can be done by anyone who can ask questions, record the information and take the time to learn what it means. Investing time and money (not necessarily a lot) on market research before you start your business can reduce some of your risk and may save you from expensive mistakes later on. It could tell you what to do, or it could tell you what *not* to do. And, with any luck, you might discover an unmet need that will give you the ultimate competitive edge.

Identifying your customer is intertwined with locating your business, which is an important enough topic to warrant a separate discussion (Chapter 9), in which some market research techniques that apply specifically to location are outlined.

What Experience Teaches

Consider these three marketing situations:

Talk is cheap, and it pays

I know a woman who always made a point of talking to customers at the flower shop where she worked, asking them what kinds of flowers or arrangements they would like that the shop didn't currently have. After talking to hundreds of customers, she realized there was a market for a shop that would specialize in unique flowers and designs. Her conversations led to her eventually opening a shop of her own.

Suiting yourself doesn't always suit others

I also know a man of great taste and refinement who owns a jewelry store. He didn't get very many customers when he started his store—lots of lookers, but not many buyers. Those people who did make purchases tended to keep coming back, but they were simply too few to support the business. After observing and thinking about the situation, he realized his problem: He thought everyone in the market for jewelry would like what he liked, and he bought almost exclusively pieces that he liked. "Being a retailer and buying merchandise only for yourself isn't very smart," he said. "You have to realize that you're buying for everyone else, not for yourself, and you have to respond to what they want." He still brings many things he would be pleased to own into his store, but he also offers many styles that he doesn't care for but that potential customers will find to their liking.

Make no assumptions

And I know a man who was hunting for a house in Portland. A real estate agent asked him where he was moving from, and he said, "Southern California." Immediately,

---

Key Questions

· ·

- Who are the people or businesses who will want to buy my product?

- What do they want or need? What don't they want or need?

- How does my product or service meet my prospective customers' wants?

- Will they buy my product or service?

- Who are my competitors? How much business are they doing?

- What can I do to make my service or product more attractive to prospective customers?

- What type of advertising can I use to attract them? (See Chapter 10.)

- Where should I locate my business? How much business can I expect there? (See Chapter 9.)

- What are the long-term trends that could affect my business?

the agent began pitching him on the advantages of living outside the city, in one of the suburbs south of downtown. "It's just like Orange County 20 years ago," the agent said.

Unfortunately for the agent, that was exactly what this customer did *not* want. He was looking to live close to downtown, to be able to use public transit, to be close to restaurants and shops—in short, to live in a vibrant and compact urban environment. He found exactly what he wanted five minutes from downtown Portland. The agent who based her pitch on his answer to one question and assumed that he wanted to re-create the home of his youth assumed wrong. And she did not get the sale.

These examples highlight why you'll want to learn about your customers and test your assumptions about them. Knowledge indeed is power, and the more you know about your market, the more you'll know about how to sell your product and run your business.

Research on the Grand Scale

Market research can be as simple as chewing the fat with the people with whom you think you'll be doing business. It can also be remarkably sophisticated, and major corporations—successful operations that you would think already know their markets—devote huge sums to it.

For example, I belong to several airline frequent-flier clubs. Periodically, an airline will send a letter offering me some free miles on my account—1,000, for instance—if I'll just take a couple of moments to fill out a short form with a few questions about my flying habits. I normally toss surveys into the trash, but, well, for 1,000 miles...why not? I take a minute and check the appropriate boxes. For the airline, the reward is information on how much I (and my fellow box-checkers) fly, how much we pay, where we travel, how and why we choose one airline over another, what we value in traveling, and so on. That's all market research.

Another example: At some grocery stores, customers can get a free plastic card with a magnetic strip on the back—much like a credit card—entitling them to discounts on certain items each week. The store isn't just giv-

Knowledge indeed is power, and the more you know about your market, the more you'll know about how to sell your product and run your business.

Here are some other factors that can affect your business and your market:

- Preferences.
- Opinions.
- Habits.
- Trends.
- Plans.
- Geography.
- Demographics.
- The psychology of the market.

ing customers a small discount, though. It also can be collecting a tremendous amount of information about customers and their shopping habits. By "swiping" the magnetic strip through a machine that can read the information encoded on it, the store can build a detailed profile of *everything* purchased by a household. And, it can combine information for several households to create a picture of consumer preferences from neighborhood to neighborhood, from one age bracket to another, even from one side of a street to the other. That information may influence a store's choice of inventory and pricing.

Starting on your own, you're probably not going to be handing out cards with magnetic strips to thousands of people. Nor are you going to take the path of a multinational consumer products company like RJR Nabisco and "test market" your product or service to tens of thousands of people across the country.

But that's all okay. You don't have to do that kind of market research to develop information that will make a difference in how you start your business. What you want is research on your market.

Who Are You Really Selling To?

This is a key question. Having a great product won't do you much good if you're not marketing it effectively. For example, consider a businessman I know who ventured into selling smoked salmon. This was a top-quality product—the best salmon, smoked using new equipment and the most efficient techniques. The only problem was that this businessman didn't really think about how potential customers were going to look at his product. He would have succeeded if he could have sold his salmon to retailers, but those he approached already had reliable sources of smoked salmon. And even though his salmon was of a high grade, that made little difference to the retailers who were his potential market. His salmon was no cheaper than that produced by other companies, and retailers who already had a good source of salmon had no financial incentive to switch suppliers. Nor did they have the space or money to expand their display areas; the new product could be introduced only at the expense of current sellers.

In this case, quality was in many ways irrelevant. There's no "brand name" for the smoked salmon being sold behind a deli counter; a retailer's customers ask for a particular type of salmon, not salmon provided by a specific smokehouse. So long as those customers are satisfied, the deli has no reason to switch suppliers. In short, even though this businessman had a good product, he had no way of differentiating himself in the marketplace. He wound up selling his equipment at a loss, and he, his family and his friends had a ready supply of tasty—but ultimately very expensive—smoked salmon for several months.

Market research in this businessman's case would have included not only the people who would end up eating the salmon, but also the people in the sales chain—the retailers or food brokers on whom he would have had to rely. Getting direct feedback from the sales chain as well as from ultimate users can be important. As happened with the salmon smoker, conflicts with other product lines, financing problems or plain old self-interest can keep a product from succeeding even if someone wants that product.

Market research in this businessman's case would have included not only the people who would end up eating the salmon, but also the people in the sales chain.

The Real Product

You may also discover that your product is not quite what meets the eye. For example, Class VI River Runners offers white-water rafting trips down the New and Gauley rivers in West Virginia. But, said co-founder Dave Arnold, it turns out that the company is selling more than just a ride in an inflatable boat. "We're really selling a first-class look at and an educational introduction to what is an incredible natural area," he said. "You get the great ride, sure, but I think it also makes a difference to our customers that our guides have been doing this for a long time and really know the river, that we provide a buffet-style lunch on land we own rather than just some quick sandwiches handed out wherever we can stop…there are a lot of ways of differentiating our product from other companies that also do a good job of taking people down the river."

*The simplest way of
doing market research
on your own is to
engage in the
common-sense
method.*

At the highest level, a product can be far more than just a functional item for sale. Certainly, sometimes a shirt is just a shirt. But when the shirt is sold by Ralph Lauren (born Ralph Lifshitz), it becomes much more. For many customers it can be a symbol of a certain way of life, a talisman for the way people with Old Money would dress and act when being casual but still proper at a WASPish country-club event. Careful marketing and advertising are as important to creating this image of Ralph Lauren as the product itself.

Learning the views of potential users of your product is best accomplished, of course, by talking with those users. It's through market research—old-fashioned asking people what they think—that you can learn whether the big selling point you think your product possesses really is crucial, as well as discovering what other features of the product will turn potential customers on—or off.

Doing It Yourself

There are a couple of ways of compiling information about your market. The first is to do it on your own—a viable option for most small start-ups. Or, you can hire someone to do it (see below).

The simplest way of doing it on your own is to engage is some common-sense market research—variations on the steps discussed in the opening chapters and recommended when trying to figure out whether you should work for yourself: Ask your friends and family for anything they know about your potential customers. Go to trade shows or engage in networking with other professionals. Talk to pedestrians who shop in the area where you think you would like to set up shop. Subscribe to publications that cover the business or trade you're interested in.

A more complicated way of doing it on your own—and probably a more accurate way—is to conduct a full-fledged market research survey. There are three steps in a standard market research survey:

- **Create your "typical" customer profile,** that is, figure out who you think your customer is.

- **Conduct a survey** or surveys of people fitting that profile.

- **Analyze your results** to determine whether you can put information you've learned about your market to profitable use, then follow up on your findings.

Once you have your tentative customer profile, you'll want to find and survey people who fit it.

Imagine Your Customer

The first step in this process is to think about and (hey, why not?) *write down* everything you *think* you know about the folks who are going to buy from you. This list could include such variables as those listed on the accompanying customer profile worksheet.

If you're planning to sell to businesses rather than to individuals, a similar list can be developed that is oriented to prospective corporate customers.

This information about your potential customer adds up to a profile of your typical customer—the person you're going to be depending on for business. The profile could be very specific: For example, if you're going to become an independent cabinetmaker specializing in custom-made jobs, your customer could be the owner of an older home, living within a short drive of you, with enough discretionary income to pay for custom work, and without a background as a do-it-yourselfer. Or, you could be targeting two-earner households with no children for a cleaning service. On the other hand, the profile could be very general: For example, just about anyone who takes pictures and lives within a couple of miles of the business could be a potential patron of a camera shop.

Choose Your "Sample Population"

Once you have your tentative customer profile, you'll want to find and survey people who fit it. Correctly identifying people who fit your profile and interviewing enough of them is crucial to the success of any survey. The wrong people or too few people could result in false information.

A quick and early word of warning and encouragement about this: *Don't despair.* For many retail businesses,

Your Customer's Profile

Use this worksheet to help you imagine the person you think you're most likely to do business with.

Age _____

Sex _____

Income level _____

Education level _____

Geographic location _____

Marital status _____

Number of children _____

Race _____

Religion _____

Employers, position, and jobs performed _____

Special interests or hobbies _____

Health _____

Age and type of car _____

Age of home _____

Home owners or renters _____

Buying habits _____

Eating habits _____

Vacation habits _____

Other _____

a good sample population is just a random collection of the people who walk or drive by the potential site of your business.

Why you want to meet the right people

Having said that, here's why it's important to have people who really are potential customers in your survey: If the people in your sample population are indeed the people who are your most likely customers, any results from the survey (assuming it is properly constructed) will be meaningful; you'll be able to confidently make decisions based on the information you glean. However, if the people in your sample population are *not* probable customers, it doesn't matter *what* they say or what you find out—their answers will be irrelevant to you and your business. Why ask vegetarians what their favorite cut of steak is?

Here's the flip side of this challenge: If you've done a good job of identifying your customer profile and sample population, you won't need to interview huge numbers of people to come up with a statistically valid survey. Even national pollsters rarely include much more than 1,000 people in any poll they conduct. The reason? The pollsters know that a scientifically designed and conducted poll of a little more than 1,000 people will yield results that are, 19 times out of 20, accurate to within three or four percentage points. (That is, if 70% of the people polled give a particular answer to a particular question, chances are that 70% of the entire population, give or take three to four percentage points, would give the same answer.)

Get a Handle on Your Market

• •

There are many books on surveying and analyzing markets and using public and private research sources. One of the best guides to what you can get and where you can get it is the second edition of *The Insider's Guide to Demographic Know-How* (American Demographics Press, a division of American Demographics Inc.; $49.95 plus $5 for shipping and handling). The book provides a useful overview of demographic trends in the U.S. and is full of primary and secondary sources of demographic information. Check your local library or call the publisher at 800–828–1133.

Also look for *American Demographics* magazine (monthly; $69 per year if they bill you; $59 if you prepay), an interesting source of consumer information and discussion of related issues.

Even a well-designed poll of as few as 100 people can be accurate to within about ten percentage points. Far from perfect, but it may be as good as you need—so long as you recognize the limitations. If 70% of the 100 people you survey say they would buy your product, the actual figure among the entire population could be as low as 60% or as high as 80%. You'll have to judge for yourself how accurate your numbers must be.

Where to find them

So much for the miracle of statistical research and random sampling. For you, the important point is that the people you survey be people who could actually become customers. Next, you'll have to find a way to reach them (if

Sources of Mailing Lists

The Direct Marketing Association

This organization (1120 Avenue of the Americas, New York, NY 10036–6700; 212–768–7277) represents the interests of its 3,000 member direct-mail companies.

- *Direct Marketing Marketplace,* available from the association, lists information about direct-mail firms and firms that rent lists. It can be found in the reference section of many libraries.

State licensing offices

This is where certain types of businesses and professionals—for example, contractors, veterinarians and medical professionals—must register to perform their services. You can usually select their names using such sorting options as zip code or county. For example, in Arkansas you can purchase for $10 a mailing list of all licensed contractors in the state. This could be a good way to determine how many competitors or potential clients or customers are in a geographic area.

State divisions of motor vehicles

DMV data bases typically compile information including name, address, age, sex, zip code and make of car; sort the information according to one or more of these variables; and provide the mailing lists on computer printouts or magnetic tape. You can expect to pay a set-up fee plus a charge for every 1,000 names.

Free lists

Don't overlook these possibilities if you think they'll accurately represent your prospective market. Free lists can come from:

- church, social, fraternal, political or professional organizations.

- schools and alumni organizations.

- athletic and recreation organizations.

- groups of hobbyists or collectors.

standing on a street corner isn't going to make it).

If you want to survey members of your local community, you could pick, say, every tenth name from the local telephone directory. It will probably be a little tedious, but at least it's free.

Mailing lists are "rented" for a certain amount per 1,000 names (many lists are available for $40 to more than $100 per 1,000, although the cost can be much greater). You can find names of companies specializing in this service under "Mailing Lists" in the Yellow Pages. Such companies could, for example, rent you a list of all the addresses in a particular zip code (usually about 5,000). See the accompanying box for other ideas.

If your customer profile is particularly tough to pinpoint, you may have to conduct a general survey to start with and then try to extract a smaller group that matches your profile.

Four Kinds of Surveying

Depending on your needs and resources, you can use one of these approaches to get at your prospective customers' needs, desires and opinions.

Personal interview

Survey professionals regard this as the most accurate, complete and valuable kind of interview. You (or whomever you hire) conducts a one-on-one interview with the subject. Someone planning to work for himself in a venture serving other businesses (for example, a commercial architect) could conduct personal interviews simply by contacting potential business clients and making appointments to discuss what their needs are and how they would use the services of a new venture.

Personal interviews give you the chance to ask detailed questions, to follow up on those questions, to show pictures and diagrams, and to get a variety of answers and unsolicited comments that could be surprisingly enlightening. You get all the benefits of a "regular" conversation with this technique—you can see how the individual reacts, you are not separated from the subject by a technological or physical barrier, and you can get highly nuanced variations in the answers you receive.

On the downside, personal interviews can be very expensive in terms of time, especially if you're trying to interview people in a number of different locations. But balancing that is the likelihood of a 90% response rate—that is, 90% of everyone you want to speak with will complete the interview with you.

Telephone interview

Telephone interviews can be conducted from any home or office and can be less time-consuming than personal interviews, though they may cost you a tidy sum if

Creating Survey Questions

Well-designed survey questions and methods are essential for the success of whichever market research method you choose. These rules will help you.

- **Have a standard set of questions for every participant.** Ask everyone the same questions in the same order. Whether they're part of a written survey or a list of interview questions, it's a good idea to try them out on your friends and family first. If they don't understand them, your respondents probably won't either.

- **Keep your questions as brief, clear and unambiguous as possible.** A store manager who wanted to know why people chose his establishment once asked in a written questionnaire, "What brought you here?" Among the responses: "My car." "The bus." Factually correct, but not very helpful.

- **Keep the overall questionnaire as short as possible.** Whether over the phone, in

person or via mail, people have a limited amount of time and energy to devote to these things.

- **Ask questions that can be answered with a yes or no** when you're trying to get clear-cut responses.

- **Follow up yes/no questions with** "why" if you want to develop more information.

- **Ask some open-ended questions** (those that cannot be answered yes or no) as well.

- **Introduce only one issue per question,** unless you're actually trying to group topics together. If you ask, "Where do you buy books and computer software?" you may get inaccurate responses as people who buy those products from two different locations try to decide on one place that would carry both. Instead ask, "Where do you buy books?" and "Where do you buy computer software?"

you're dialing long distance. You can anticipate about a 60% response rate from all the people you call. Shorter telephone surveys are more likely to succeed than long ones, simply because most people don't have the time or patience for a long "cold call" survey. C'mon now, be honest—when's the last time you were willing to take the time to talk to a pollster who called you out of the blue?

These interviews don't have to be complicated. Here's an example of one: I was recently called by someone working for himself who wanted to know if I use a lawn-mowing or gardening service. I don't, nor do I want to. End of interview—but he has some information about his market.

- **Try to avoid bias in your questions.** Instead of asking, "Would you like a shop that's not surrounded by other businesses and lots of traffic?", ask, "Would you like a shop that is a stand-alone—that is, a shop that is by itself instead of being in a mall?" While we're on the subject, try to avoid the word "not" in questions—it's an easy word to miss, and people also find themselves forming double- and triple-negatives when they answer. ("Well, no, I wouldn't not like a shop surrounded by lots of traffic.")

- **Put the questions about each topic together** if you have questions about several products or issues.

- **Make a written survey as attractive as possible.** Double- or triple-space the sentences, so people won't get confused or skip over lines. Simpler is better—no fancy typefaces or colored inks. Stick with black ink on white paper.

- **Be honest about your intentions.** Make your questions understandable to a wide range of people, and make sure your questions won't grossly offend anyone.

- **Give your respondents time to answer your questions.** Don't cut them off arbitrarily. Make sure you understand their answers. And don't answer the questions for your interviewees; putting words in their mouths won't help you find out what they think. Live with their silences.

- **Be polite.** Don't get upset with people who brush you off—they have lives, too, you know. Let people know you would appreciate their taking the time for the survey. Always thank them afterward. This all seems so obvious and commonsense...but in the heat of the battle (or the data gathering) it's the commonsense that can get left out.

If the group is composed of people who know you already, you could wind up with an overly generous judgment of your product—flattering, but not very useful.

Mail interview

You can use the mails to reach a large number of people over a wide or narrow geographic range who might not be available by phone, such as businesspeople. However, mail surveys are not as inexpensive as they may first appear. For openers, you'll have to send out more surveys—a *lot* more—than you actually need to get back. A response rate of 5% (that is, five completed surveys returned for every 100 that you send out) is considered excellent for this kind of direct mail. And don't forget about the cost of return postage, plus return envelopes, plus printing up the surveys, plus tabulating the results that do come in.

The kind of mail survey more likely to be useful and successful is one that you can target to potential customers you already know you want to reach. A businessman interested in opening a warehouse, for example, could mail a survey to every business within a three-mile radius of his planned location to see how strong demand is for warehouse space.

Group interview

With a group interview, or "focus group," you can get reactions and opinions from several potential consumers at once. Members of the group can see, taste or otherwise test a product and give you immediate and detailed feedback. By interacting with each other, participants may also spark some creative and helpful suggestions that wouldn't develop out of other survey methods.

There are a couple of risks to group interview setups: If the group is composed of people who know you already, you could wind up with an overly generous judgment of your product. That will make you feel good, but it won't help you accurately gauge the market for what you're selling. It's also possible that a couple of stronger personalities will dominate a group, quashing less-assertive but equally important participants who have differing views. It's up to you or whoever oversees the session to keep the group on track, give everyone an equal chance to speak honestly and let the group act without influence from you.

It's a wise idea to conduct two or three focus groups

to verify your findings. Focus group participants are frequently paid a nominal sum, say $40 to $50 per session, and offered a free meal for their trouble.

Test Marketing

Another step you can take is to invest in some test marketing of your product or service. When you test market something, you put a small number on the market and see how they do—the business equivalent of "running it up the flagpole to see who salutes." Test marketing is more advanced than surveying in that it usually means getting someone to actually *spend money* on your product, rather than just say that they would buy it if they could. It's a big distinction: There's nothing like having someone open her wallet to affirm your feeling that people will indeed pay for what you have to offer.

Whether they realize it or not, many people who start small businesses test market their product before wading into the selling sea. Anyone who starts a business on a part-time basis while still holding a full-time job is, in essence, test marketing.

As a consultant or independent contractor, you could try to pick up just one or two clients to see how they like your work—and how you like working with someone on a contract, rather than a full-time, basis.

Or, you can test market by selling a product out of a little kiosk, or by producing a few copies of something and getting one store in your area to carry the item—perhaps on consignment—for a couple of weeks. That will give you the opportunity to ask customers how they like the item, whether they think it's worth the price, and how you could improve it.

Competitor Intelligence

Another way businesses can research their potential market is by studying what their potential competitors are doing—or not doing—for their customers. The whole area of scoping out your competitors—also known as competitor

Anyone who starts a business on a part-time basis while still holding a full-time job is, in essence, test marketing.

intelligence—is a growing part of many business operations.

Major corporations hire consultants who specialize in competitor intelligence to research what other companies are up to in terms of product lines, pricing strategies, customer service and profits. But you don't have to pay an outside firm to gather such information. You can have an in-house "department" of one person: yourself.

Here are some ways of getting and using competitor intelligence:

Look at local want ads.

Competitors looking for new employees may be planning to expand their present operations or enter new fields. On the other hand, a company that is constantly advertising for the same job opening may be having problems finding or keeping good help—either because it's not a well-run company (which can mean a

---

Getting Help With Market Research

Magazines and reports

Go to your local library and look in the *Encyclopedia of Associations* for trade associations that represent the kind of business you're considering. From that directory you can get addresses and phone numbers of associations that can provide you with information about all aspects of the business you're considering. Also check out the U.S. Department of Commerce's *U.S. Industrial Outlook*, which provides an overview, by industry, of predicted future economic conditions.

Local colleges and universities

The marketing department of a local college's business or management school can be very helpful. The school's library may have several specialized texts or papers on marketing and market research; the school may also have an intern or counseling pro-

gram that can line you up with a graduate student who could help design your market research program.

Chamber of commerce and other local business groups

Chambers and other groups are not just boosters of the community; they are also great collectors of information about local business trends and developments.

U.S. Small Business Administration

The SBA's Service Corps of Retired Executives (SCORE) can provide one-on-one counseling on how to properly research and develop your market potential. Contact your local or regional SBA office, listed in the blue (or government) pages of your phone book, for more information on SCORE programs. (For more on SCORE, see Chapter 14.)

---

potential opening for you) or because there just isn't much quality help available in that field (which can mean potential problems for you.)

Read your local newspapers as well as larger papers.

Business sections are full of information on trends in many industries, probably including the field you're entering. Local papers feature news on the local economy and on businesses that may be your direct competition. Nationally circulated papers—particularly *The Wall Street Journal* and *The New York Times* —contain a wealth of information on national business and economic developments that could affect your start-up.

Talk with potential customers.

Find out what they're paying for the goods or services

Small Business Development Centers

There are 56 SBDCs nationwide, most located on college and university campuses. SBDCs, underwritten by the SBA, provide counseling, training and technical assistance to business start-ups and existing businesses. Funding is always uncertain, but as of this book's publication the SBA was funding more than 900 service centers around the country that offered general guidance to small enterprises. Call your nearest SBA office or the Office of SBDCs (202–205–6766) for more information.

Wholesalers and manufacturers

You may be able to get a lot of information from these businesses—especially if you'll be buying goods from them.

Media advertising representatives

Perhaps nobody knows local markets, economic conditions and demands like the folks who sell advertising space for newspapers, magazines, and radio and television stations. Many media companies have research departments that compile extensive information on the composition of local markets, and they make that information available to potential advertisers. Guess what? You're a potential advertiser. Go get 'em!

they now receive. Ask if they feel like they're treated well as customers by the businesses they now patronize. A field of unhappy consumers is fertile territory for a start-up looking for customers or clients.

Visit competitors.

If you're considering a manufacturing operation, go to a competitor's plant and hang around outside the main entrance. You can eyeball how many employees the company has—one more little piece of information on what you're up against—and maybe take the time to talk with them. Or just call the company and ask what you want to know—many companies will be happy to tell you, and if it's a publicly traded company, they'll also probably send you an annual report.

Check local government records.

City Hall or the county courthouse can be a mother lode of competitor intelligence (see also the box on page 104). You can check the property-tax rolls to determine what land or buildings a business or individual owns. You can look at planning department records and find out whether any permits have been filed to expand an existing business. In some areas, you may even be able to find out how much a business pays in local sales, license or revenue tax, which can be a good clue to how successful the business is. (The offices and departments where you'll find all this information vary from state to state and municipality to municipality, but local government officials should be able to point you in the right direction.)

As you can tell, competitor intelligence isn't some dark, nefarious cloak-and-dagger operation. It can be accomplished with basic initiative and shoe leather, with trips to libraries and businesses, with time spent thumbing through public files. So slip on some comfortable loafers and get out there.

In the Final Analysis

Once you've completed your research, you can put the information you've gathered to good use. You can modify your products, services or location, do more research to make yourself more distinctive in the marketplace, or otherwise act on the material you've gathered to improve your start-up prospects.

What happens if the results are negative? Do you give up on your idea? Not necessarily. You'll have to use your own judgment and consider the survey a guide, not a final answer. You'll have to analyze why you think people answered the way they did, maybe test your hypothesis, and revise your strategy accordingly. How you act on those results is up to you. And, of course, you can get help and direction from some of the same sources that can help you determine whether your overall idea is a viable one. Check the listings at the ends of Chapters 3 and 7 for more information on this.

Another Option: Paying a Pro

You don't *have* to do all this research work yourself. You can pay someone else—a professional market researcher—to do it for you. Figure on paying $2,500 and up, depending on just how much work is required. But remember: Most small-business start-ups can do at least some, and often most or all, of their initial market research.

"We need a bit more science in our market surveys."

Toos, Cartoonists & Writers Syndicate

If you opt for help from a market research firm, try to check its qualifications. Ask for examples of reports the firm has done for other clients. Look for objective analyses that sound specifically geared to the clients; beware of analyses that sound like generalized boilerplate demographic statistics that could apply to any (or no) business. Research

Setting a price on your products presents one of those times in life when the twin instincts of greed and fear wrestle for rights to your thought processes.

methodology should be clearly explained in detail. And, of course, always contact the firm's recent clients for recommendations and comments.

Pricing Your Product, or, What Will the Market Bear?

Financial forecasting—predicting how many sales you can make of your products or services, and at what price—is an art, not a science. Part of your market research involves developing some idea of how much you'll be able to charge for your product.

Setting a price on your products presents one of those times in life when the twin instincts of greed and fear wrestle for rights to your thought processes. The struggle is a simple one.

The greed instinct in us wants to charge as much as we can, because the more money we receive for each sale, the more money we make and the less time we have to spend producing our goods or services.

The only match for greed is fear—the simple, sweaty-palmed fear that nobody will ever want to pay for what we're trying to sell. Fear compels us to price our products competitively to lure customers, in the hope that we'll at least be able to make a little money on a lot of sales. Fear finds its purest expression in the impulse to cut your prices so much that you actually lose money on every sale after your operating costs are properly accounted for. Not a good idea.

A More Reasoned Approach

Determining how much of your goods or services you'll be able to sell at a particular price is part of market research. Before you start the business, you'll have to decide on a general price range for your goods. Usually, the price of any item has to cover the cost of the item, a prorated share of the costs of running your business (that is, your overhead), plus a profit on the sale. The difference between your cost to buy or create an item and the price you charge for it is known as the markup .

You can ask potential customers what they would pay for your products, of course. You can also see what your potential competitors are charging. And, trade or business associations may have information on typical pricing strategies or average profit margins in your industry.

(Financial ratios for businesses and ways of determining the break-even point for your venture are discussed more fully in Chapter 17.)

And, Then There's Strategy

There's no one rule on how to price something. You can try to operate on a razor-thin profit margin which, if your prices are low enough, could result in a larger market share and even eliminate some competition as other businesses are unable to compete with your aggressive pricing. Alternatively, it is sometimes possible to price your goods or services higher than the norm and still maintain a healthy sales volume, either because your higher prices are combined with better service or because of the appearance of exclusivity, which is sometimes known as snob appeal. We all know of products that are sold in name-brand as well as generic form, manufactured in exactly the same way and containing exactly the same ingredients. The only apparent difference is the lower price for the generic item. Yet both the name-brand and the no-name survive. Apparently, consumers are buying something more than just the product in question when they buy the name brand.

Selling to Your Customer

Don't forget, in the midst of all this research, to figure out how you'll best get to your customer. Determining that is a final area of market research. You'll choose from among these methods of selling:

The personal sale
You personally get out in the field, develop contacts

Manufacturer's reps can be effective and may be the only way to get through some retailers' doors.

and make your sales. Most common in consulting businesses and with specialized products that rely on delivery of personal service.

The hired guns

If you have something you'd like to market to retailers, you pay someone else to go out and make the contacts while you stay behind, presumably working on the business. This is a good alternative if you can afford it and if the prospect of "showing your portfolio" makes your palms sweat. You can either go with *an in-house sales force* or with an *independent* (or *manufacturer's representative*). Manufacturer's reps can be effective and may be the only way to get through some retailers' doors. For example, you may be able to go into the boutique on the corner, show the owner your handmade aprons and make a deal for her to sell them in her shop. But if you tried the same approach at Kmart, you'd probably be turned away and told it deals only with reps. Unlike an in-house crew, whose loyalty is presumably to you and you alone, independent reps will have many masters. They're going to represent many products in addition to your own—and may not always give your products the attention or "push" you think they deserve.

Catalogue and direct-mail sales

These are alternative ways of selling products that would traditionally be sold by retailers. Shopping by mail boomed in the 1980s; one effect of that boom was a reduced tolerance among some consumers for mail solicitations. That's not to say that direct mail won't work; we're just pointing out that it can be both expensive and unproductive.

The retail operation

This is the most common method of selling goods to a general consumer market. Your market research, as well as your research into where to locate your business (see Chapter 9) should help you determine where to open your retail operation.

Every business has its preferred method of selling, and there's no one right way to sell anything. You'll have to determine what's right for you. Sometimes, the methods can be startling in their simplicity. For example, Randall Grahm runs Bonny Doon Vineyard, a small producer of wines in the style of France's Rhone Valley. It's not unusual for the owners of small wineries to go personally to retail outlets and restaurants and ask the owners of those businesses to taste (and hopefully purchase) their products.

The feeling is that the winemaker can be his own best sales force. Randall Grahm, however, takes that principal one step further: his head salesperson is his mother. "My God, it's difficult enough to say no to a winemaker who comes around trying to sell you his products," says one restaurateur. "But what on earth can you say when the *mother* walks in selling her son's products?"

CHAPTER

9

Where Will You Find Your Customers; Where Will They Find You?

Location, location, location. Most people give long and hard thought to location when deciding which home to buy. You should give at least as much thought to where you're going to locate your business—whatever it is. What qualifies as an ideal location depends on the individual business, your needs and desires, and those of your customer (discussed also in Chapter 8).

Valerie Greenbaum chose a storefront within a string of retail shops as the location of Eiger Ice Cream in West Los Angeles. The store is in an affluent section of town populated by people who can pay $2.25 for a cone of her ultrarich, superpremium confections, but it gets nowhere near the casual foot traffic from office workers that national ice-cream chains seek when looking for high-density business-district locations. There are no high-rise buildings in Eiger's neighborhood.

But that's okay. The lack of office workers is offset by the presence of the many locals who live in the area or patronize the other small stores and restaurants nearby, as well as by a huge plus for an ice-cream store: the nearby Brentwood School, which funnels a daily stream of children and parents to Eiger. Eiger Ice Cream is so popular that families who no longer live nearby will get in their cars and drive several miles specifically for an Eiger outing.

What may seem to be an obvious spot for a business isn't always the best choice.

A More Complex Issue Than Meets the Eye

What may seem to be an obvious spot for a business isn't always the best choice. It's possible that a business you'd usually think of as retail (and thus needing easy access to potential customers) can survive, and even thrive in a location that renders it out of sight to most clients. Travel agencies, for example, usually need ground-floor locations, or at least locations where they're visible from the street to individuals who are potential clients. But many travel agencies have chosen to specialize in corporate travel. Their clients usually just use the telephone when making travel plans for employees. Agencies catering to corporate clients don't need high-profile, street-level—and expensive—locations.

As we've pointed out previously, with advances in both high-tech communications systems and low-tech delivery services, many people working for themselves now have a wide range of options about where to set up shop—and it may be nowhere near Main Street. Documents—even many types of artwork—can be electronically transmitted. When an original has to go, it can travel via express mail services that have transformed a coast-to-coast delivery from a week-long odyssey into an overnight journey.

As a result, the self-employed—especially those in information-related industries—often don't have to be located within minutes of their clients. Illustrators who depend on New York publishers or Chicago advertising agencies for work can leave those cities, setting up shop instead in upstate New York or a midwestern lakeside community and driving into town only on those occasions when face-to-face contact is essential. I know someone living in Portland who coordinated development of a Caribbean resort from the Pacific Northwest. Many accountants, architects, attorneys, photographers and other self-employed individuals have clients who live in different time zones and whom they see only rarely. All benefit from these changes in technology.

> ## *The Importance of Location*
>
> •
>
> Where you set up your business affects:
>
> - Your sales.
> - Operating hours.
> - Overhead costs.
> - Advertising.
> - Access to good employees and supplies.
> - Ease of delivery and pick-up.
> - Access to storage.
> - Many other factors that are directly related to your profitability.

People with such a wide range of options are, however, still in the minority. And whether you can work from anywhere or will depend on customers from a relatively small geographic area (as with most small retailers and service providers), the location of your business is a key start-up decision that will affect your customers' access to you and your access to suppliers, storage and other resources.

But even the meaning of "access" will vary by business. If you're starting a company that provides a service to other companies—computer software consulting, for example, or a plant-care company for all those businesses that want indoor plants but don't know how to keep them from dying—it may be important that you be centrally located or at least able to get to your clients quickly and easily.

Unlike the customers of a downtown sandwich or ice-cream store who are on foot and can pop in on a whim, customers of a retail furniture store are likely to plan a store visit when they're purchasing something as substantial as a couch or a kitchen table. That means making it as easy as possible for them to get there—and to park. Add to that a furniture store's need for easy access by delivery trucks and for adequate and inexpensive storage space. Hence, you're more likely to find such a store in the suburbs, maybe close to a major highway, and in either a detached building or a strip mall.

The whole question of location is predetermined if you're buying an existing business. However, even in this case you'll want to look at the current performance of the business and consider whether a move would be beneficial. (The ins and outs of buying an existing business are covered fully in Chapter 20.)

There's another huge component to consider when weighing different locations: how much you'll have to pay for business space. Locations that generate lots of foot traffic (and lots of potential customers for retailers), like shopping malls and lively downtown areas, will cost you a lot more than a spot that is more "destination-specific"—that is, a place where people are likely to go only when they *specifically* want to visit your business.

Any business that can start as a one-person operation is a candidate to begin life as a home-based business.

Stretching Your Dollar— Starting From Home

Your search for the ideal workplace may start, and end, at home. That can be the ideal option for many people working for themselves, especially those who:

- **are starting a part-time venture** while keeping their regular, full-time jobs.

- **are turning a hobby or craft into a business.**

- **want or need to be in the home** to provide or supervise care for their family members.

- **require an environment custom-designed** to best accommodate their disability.

In fact, any business that can start as a one-person operation—tax preparer, lawyer, editorial consultant, fashion designer, architect, independent sales representative, computer technician, housing contractor, importer, furniture maker and on and on—is a candidate to begin life as a home-based business. It's an option that's easier financially than even the best bargain-basement lease and you can't beat the commute.

*Check with your
town clerk or zoning
board and your
local homeowners
association to
see if there are any
restrictions.*

The Issues

You'll get the most out of your home office only if
you're physically and emotionally able to work at home—
and if you're careful to follow any zoning laws and tax regulations that can affect your business.

Is it legal?

Local zoning ordinances could prevent you from
working from home. Typical restrictions prohibit the use of
toxic or combustible materials, unsightly outside operations, displays of products and supplies that would turn residential properties into de facto retail stores, and activities
that would cause traffic congestion. Check with your town
clerk or zoning board to see if there are any restrictions on
home-based businesses and whether they'd affect you. You
might also need a license, a fire inspection, even a permit
from the health department if, for example, you're catering or preparing baked goods.

Check in, too, with the local neighborhood association. One graphic designer nearly made a down payment
on a new home but thought first to speak with a neighborhood association officer. She answered his question and
more. No, the association wouldn't allow him to post a dis-
creet brass plaque at his front door for delivery people,
and furthermore, the rules prohibited running a business
from home, period. No problem. He bought elsewhere.

Is it practical?

Take a personal inventory of whether you're able,
from an emotional and practical standpoint, to work out of
your home.

- **Can you work without the hubbub and distraction** of co-
  workers? Might you even thrive?

- **Do you have the discipline** to get up every morning and
  plant yourself in "the office" if your commute is measured in footsteps instead of miles?

- **If you have children at home,** will you be able to focus on work instead of on them? Will they let you work at home, even if you hire in-home day care?

Can you set aside a work space?

It will help you focus if you can designate a portion of your home for work, only work, and nothing but work.

A clearly defined space for "the business" serves a second purpose: It allows you to take a deduction on your tax return for costs related to devoting one section of your home solely to running a business.

The Tax Facts

Take another look at the wording in that last sentence. It's important that you devote one section of your home *solely* to your business. Convert a single room, two rooms, even an entire floor to business use and you can deduct a prorated share of many home expenses from your taxable income, so long as the home office is your principal place of business.

Deductions

You can deduct as a business expense part of your mortgage interest, property taxes, insurance, utilities, general repairs and pest-control costs as business expenses, which can reduce your self-employment taxes as well as your income taxes. The percentage you can deduct is equal to the percentage of your home that is used for business. For example, if two rooms totaling 300 square feet in a 2,000-square-foot house are used for business, you can deduct 15% of the above expenses.

Depreciation

You also can take a deduction for depreciation on the portion of your home that's used for business. Depreciation deductions are calculated as a percentage of the tax—or adjusted—basis of your house, which is essentially what you paid for the house, plus the cost of any improvements (not routine repairs), minus the value of the land on which your house sits.

The percentage of your home-related expenses that you can deduct is equal to the percentage of your home that is used solely for business.

Limits to a good thing

Unfortunately, depreciating the business portion of your house could later (and depending on what Congress and the IRS do in the meantime) cost you added taxes if you eventually sell your house at a profit. That's because business property does not enjoy some of the tax advantages of a personal home. The depreciation you've previously declared would reduce the adjusted basis of your home, meaning that a larger amount of the profit on your home will be subject to tax. One easy way around this is to convert the office back into personal space and don't claim it in the year you sell the house (three years before you plan to sell if you're planning to take the one-time $125,000 capital gains exclusion).

And be aware that, if you don't show a profit from your business in at least three out of five years, the IRS may label some dubious businesses as hobbies only. In that case, you deduct your expenses, but they'll be considered miscellaneous expenses; you will be able to deduct them only up to the amount of your hobby income, only if you itemize on Schedule A, and only if your miscellaneous deductions exceed 2% of your adjusted gross income (see page 60 for more on the tax rules for hobbies versus businesses).

The IRS frowns on deductions to people who claim they're starting an in-home business but have no proof that they can sell a product or serve customers. So keep track of meetings, letters and contracts that will show you are in business even if you don't have immediate revenues. You should also know that the deductions for an office in your home cannot be used to

"This town isn't big enough for both of us—
let's merge."

Harris, Cartoonists & Writers Syndicate

produce a net business loss for tax purposes.

You'll want to talk with your accountant about how to calculate all this. You can also find more information about home deductions on your own in *Kiplinger's Cut Your Taxes,* by Kevin McCormally.

Leasing Versus Buying

If you can't or don't want to work from home, then you'll have to lease or buy another place of business. It's great to imagine buying a cozy clapboard cottage in a mostly residential area and converting it to your private work space, or building a bright, spanking-new, all-steel structure to your specifications. But most often, leasing will be less expensive and a better choice, especially during the first several years of your business.

Buying a building or a site on which you'll erect a building can add a tremendous amount to your start-up costs. There's no good reason to spend money on a down payment and closing costs when you could put it into developing your product or service or use it for a few months of living expenses. Nor is it wise to burden yourself and the liabilities side of your balance sheet with a mortgage or a commercial construction loan (if you can get one).

Presumably, your goal is to find a place where you can work, not to invest in real estate. If investment is a motive, then you'll be interested in the potential advantages of price appreciation and leverage (using borrowed money to amplify any gains). But the tax advantages of buying and leasing will probably be a wash. If you lease, you can deduct your monthly rent and any related business expenses and depreciation won't be a concern. If you buy the property as both an investment and as space for your business, you can deduct the mortgage interest, property taxes and depreciation—but you don't get double the advantage.

Leasing gives you flexibility. With a lease, you're not locked into one fixed space of one fixed size. If your business expands, you can move into larger quarters. If it turns out you need less space than you thought, you can switch

Presumably, your goal is to find a place where you can work, not to invest in real estate.

to a cozier location—depending on whether or when you can get out of the lease. If your business doesn't pan out, you won't face a forced sale of property.

How Much Will You Have to Pay?

In real estate all values are local, and that's as true with business sites as with anything else. People in different parts of the country don't even use the same units of measure when discussing costs of business sites. In much of the country, leasing costs are expressed in annual cost per square foot. So, when someone in Philadelphia says their 400-square-foot office costs "$20 a foot" you know they mean they're paying $20 per square foot per year, or $8,000 in all. But in California, costs are often expressed in *monthly* rates. This can cause initial confusion when someone from the East Coast hears about space in fashionable Los Angeles office buildings going for "$1.50 a foot." That translates to $18 per square foot per year.

Customer Location Profile

Here's an exercise to help you when considering a business location: For whatever business you're starting, make a list of your prospective customers' desires. Then think about what you could do in site selection that will help you accommodate those desires and attract the customers you want. In effect, you're adding to the client/customer profile that you developed in Chapter 8.

The focus here is on determining why people will want to buy from you. Among the questions you can ask yourself:

- **Will they buy because I'm convenient** to their jobs? their homes? or, where they go for relaxation and recreation?

- **Will they buy because it's easy to park** near my business?

- **Will they buy because they can walk in** on their lunch break?

- **Will they buy because I'm close to public transportation?**

- **Will they buy because I can quickly reach** their home, office, or another location?

- **Will they buy because I can deliver** my product to them quickly or for a low price?

- **Will they buy because of the quality (or rarity)** of my goods or services, even though I'm not conveniently located?

- **Will they buy because a low rent allows** me to pass lower prices on to them?

The amount you pay for your location depends not just on its desirability but also on local market conditions and real estate values, availability of competing business space, and what the space will be used for. A 1,000-square-foot space that leases for $2,500 a month in a major urban center could cost one-fifth that amount in an outlying area or a small town. A warehouse in an industrial park will lease for a fraction of the price of a comparably sized space in an area dominated by retail stores.

It's possible to sign long-term leases with fixed annual payments or with rate increases that are spelled out and can be prepared for. It's even possible to pay *less* for a lease down the road than you pay initially. In many regions of the country, overbuilding and a glut of office space have led landlords to offer space at far less than they would have charged several years ago. Businesses have been offered months or even a year or more of free rent, reduced maintenance charges, cleaning services and other inducements to sign lease agreements. Competition for tenants in several markets has become so fierce that landlords have negoti-

- **Will they buy because I have enough storage area** to maintain a large and varied supply of products?

- **Will they buy because of the other stores located in my area,** or because I'm in an area with a reputation for quality merchants?

- **Will they buy because they feel safer** coming to my location than that of a competitor?

- **Will they buy because I'm convenient to many other places** where they also do business?

- **Will they buy because I'm enclosed with many other merchants** under one roof and they can avoid the elements?

- **Will they buy because I'm in a storefront on a main street** that makes them feel part of the "street scene"?

- **Will they buy because of the atmosphere of my neighborhood or building** (artsy, hip, historic, upscale, downscale, small-town, sophisticated)?

Before committing yourself to a potential business site, you'll need to test your assumptions about it.

ated rate reductions with their existing tenants rather than risk seeing them go to a newer—and cheaper—competitor. (The ins and outs of negotiating and signing a lease are discussed more fully in Chapter 21.)

What Do Your Customers Want?

Whatever you do, don't fall in love with a location because it's near *your* favorite shopping center or jump at a trendy office complex whose address will impress *your* friends—at least, not unless those factors are going to bring you customers or help your business! Instead, think about those customers and what is important to them in terms of your location (see the checklist on page 120).

Learning About Your Location

Before committing yourself to a potential business site, you'll need to test your assumptions about it. This is especially important if you're entering a retail business and will be depending on the surrounding community for support. With the proper research, you can determine the composition of the neighborhood and surrounding area and decide whether it fits in with your customer profile.

Among the factors you'll want to explore:

How big a population of potential clients/customers will be available?

A small neighborhood retailer or restaurant could draw from an area of only a square mile or so for most of its business; a shop in a mall could pull in customers from 20 or 30 miles away. A real estate agent might be willing and able to list or show houses on the other side of town, but home sellers or buyers may want to work with someone who is located in their area and knows it well.

How much money do people in this area make?

A trendy and expensive clothes boutique should be easily accessible to people who can and will pay for such purchases. A convenience store, on the other hand, could go in almost any area where people need an alternative to driving a few miles to a shopping center.

What are their educational, professional and lifestyle differences?

Someone wanting to open a specialty bookstore could look for a neighborhood whose residents' appetite isn't being met—say, for mysteries; romance novels; nonfiction in the social, political and economic vein; military or local history; works related to the curriculum at a local school or university; or books directed at alternative lifestyles. A women's clothing boutique would want to know whether an area was populated mostly by stay-at-home moms who need casual clothing or women who work outside the home and need appropriate work attire.

Do they own their homes?

If you're opening a home- and lawn-care center, you'll want to be accessible to families who own houses or townhouses and are likely to need yard equipment, home supplies and tools. Renters of apartments—no matter what their incomes or interests—are not likely to spend money on gear used in maintaining the great residential outdoors.

How many singles are there? How many couples or families?

A store specializing in children's toys or clothing is likely to do better in an area with lots of young families than in one dominated by retirees, even if they are grandparents.

Your Friend, the Census

One way to learn about the demographic characteristics of an area is to delve into U.S. census information. The U.S. Bureau of the Census conducted its most recent survey in 1990, and the result is the most complete demographic picture of the country yet. The census brought with it an explosion of data that can be useful to small businesses. "Someone interested in starting a business has the capability to find data that we have collected through every one of our surveys," said Joe Wade, one of the customer service representatives in the Census Bureau's Data User Services Division.

The breadth of information available is stunning. The Census Bureau has divided the entire nation into what it calls blocks—that is, areas roughly equal, conveniently enough, to a city block. These census blocks can be formed by such physical features as streets, railroad tracks and rivers. Four streets that form a square can constitute a block, of course, but so can two streets that end at a stream. A block comprises only a few hundred people; the census combines blocks into "tracts" that have an average of 4,000 people living in them.

In fact, the array of information available can be overwhelming. There's more than one way of narrowing that information down, however. Census information is used by local chambers of commerce, real estate firms, banks and other business organizations in assessing their markets. It can pay to take the time to contact those sources and ask what information they have on the areas you're considering. They may already have taken census data and analyzed its meaning or combined that data with their own research to develop new findings that could be helpful to your start-up.

If you're going to go it alone, you can get census information in the form of printed reports, microfiche or CD-ROM disks. CD-ROM disks can hold two or three times the data that can be stored on most computer hard drives. They generally cost between $20 and $250, depending on

What the Census Knows

• •

Here's just some of the information you can get from the Census Bureau, down to the block or tract level:

- Total population in an area.

- Average age of residents.

- Income of households.

- Education levels.

- Average number of people per household.

- Average number of rooms per house.

- Percentage of people who own or rent their own homes.

- Average rents paid.

- Value of owner-occupied homes.

- Number of vehicles owned.

the amount and complexity of the information provided. (Of course, you'll also need a CD-ROM drive on your PC.) You can get on-line data reports through the CENDATA feature offered by Dialog and CompuServe.

Checking Out the Traffic Flow

If you'll be dependent on existing traffic for business, you'll want to know a few things about it. How much traffic is generated by existing businesses and travel patterns? Is there convenient public transit? How about parking—off-street or on-street? Free or paid?

There are two ways of doing a traffic count that can help determine how many potential customers your business could be exposed to. One is to write to your local or state highway and roads department and ask for a copy of its traffic count material for the street and intersection you're considering. The other is to simply take a day of your time and spend it counting the number of people who pass by your potential location.

How to Locate Census Information

Your local public library (or at least a nearby college library) should have copies of census data and reports that can help you. They may be able to retrieve data and reports for you from an on-line service for a fee.

The best starting point for Census Bureau data is the *Census Catalog and Guide,* which includes information on everything the bureau collects and has available, including all prices for reports. There are order forms in the back of the guide. If your public library doesn't have it, you can order it from the Government Printing Office (Superintendent of Documents, P.O. Box 371954, Pittsburgh, PA 15250; 202–512–1800). The guide costs $22 and

can be charged to a major credit card; when ordering, you must specify stock number 003–024–08752–9.

Two particularly helpful publications:

- *The Census Bureau's State and Metropolitan Area Data Book 1991* ($26; number 003–024–07259–9), which offers more than 300 pages of local demographic and economic facts and figures by region, and

- *The County and City Data Book 1994* ($40; number 003-024-08753-7), with 1,000 pages of similar, though even more current, information. You can order either book from the Superintendent of Documents (see above).

Hands-on location research

You can use the time spent on a traffic count for a lot more than just adding up pairs of feet. You can conduct your very own in-depth, targeted research survey and, in the process, learn as much or more about a location as you could find by reading scores of reports and studies. (This is an aspect of the kind of market and survey research discussed in Chapter 8, particularly personal interviewing.)

Here's how you can do this:

- **Get yourself a clipboard, a legal pad and some business cards.** The cards don't have to identify your non-existent business; just something with your name, address and phone number will do fine. Dress nicely, and go out to the location.

- **Count the number of cars driving by and note their condition**—new, old, expensive European imports, practical econoboxes, and so forth. That will give you some idea of

Getting Help With the Census

The Census Bureau has hundreds of specialists who can help you find and understand the material you need—information on everything from construction statistics to livestock data to fertility rates.

Census specialists

These people are dedicated to studying and understanding demographic data on a particular subject, such as housing, education or aging.

- For a free list of specialists, call the bureau's public information office at 301–457–2794 or Customer Service at 301–457–4100 (see below).

- For help in locating the department that can help you with your specific question or problem, call 301–457–4608. A recorded message will lead you through a series of options for locating the division you need.

- You can also get information on bureau publications and services by calling the Customer Service Division at 301–457–4100. Several phone calls to this number have convinced me that this is one of the friendliest and most helpful departments in the entire government. Be prepared to wait on the line for a few minutes, though—others have also discovered how helpful these folks can be.

the demographics of potential customers already passing by the area.

- **Approach people walking by.** Explain that you are considering opening a business at this location and are surveying people to see if it would appeal to them. Always start by saying, "Excuse me, I'm considering starting a business here..." at the same time you hand out your card. That will immediately let people know you're not asking for money, you're not selling anything (yet) and you're not going to mug them. Handing them a business card establishes that you're "for real," with a real card. It also forces them to stop and focus for a second on the card, giving you a chance to continue with the conversation.

- **Continue:** "...and I was wondering if I could ask you whether you would visit a (insert your type of business here) if it were to be opened here."

Private services

Several companies now specialize in massaging census data and other information into more digestible (good for you), saleable and profitable (good for them) forms. For around $250 to $500, most of them will prepare a report that lists basic demographic information on your metropolitan region. Among the biggest companies:

- Claritas (703–812–2700),
- Conquest Market Data Line (800–866–2255),
- CACI (800–292–2224),
- National Decision Systems (800–866–6510),
- Urban Decision Systems (800–633–9568).

Your state's economic security department, economic development office or state data center

Contacting these sources can be a particularly cost-effective way to get data in digestible form. These departments receive data from the census bureau as well as from state sources, and they provide it free or at cost to the public in the form of off-the-shelf and customized reports. They typically give first priority to preparing customized reports in an effort to attract prospective businesses to their states. Most of these offices will also field brief questions by phone.

By shopping the competition, you can learn how their customers—your potential customers— are being served.

- **Once you get an answer to that question, you can move forward,** asking these potential customers what sort of goods they would be interested in buying and—just for the heck of it—what kind of business they would like to see at this spot or think there's a need for that's not being met.

These questions will take only a couple of minutes of their time, and will give you unique information and a few ideas that can help in assessing a location.

Checking Out Your Competitors

While you're scoping out the location, you should check out your competitors, too. Here's the easy way: Pretend you're a customer. Pay a visit or make a telephone call. By *shopping the competition,* you can learn how their customers—your *potential* customers—are being served. You'll also learn more about how much of a market exists for your potential business in any location, including your home.

Here's how to do it:

- **Walk into the business, noting the overall appearance.** Is it clean? well-organized? If it's a retail outlet, is it an easy place to shop? If it's a restaurant, are tables clean and inviting? How about the bathrooms? If it's an office, is it professional-looking and inviting? Does it look like the abode of someone you'd like to do business with?

- **Pretend you're a serious customer.** Note how long it takes for someone to notice you and offer to help. Explain that you need some information about a product or service. Be ready with a relatively tough question about something you know they provide. Follow up with questions about prices and other options, and note whether the folks you speak with seem to know their business. If you're in a restaurant, simply order something and note what kind of service and quality of food you get.

- **Ask for a copy of any descriptive literature,** price lists or catalogs. These will help you with your own marketing program.

(continued on page 130)

Competitor Analysis Form

Name of competitor _____

Address _____

_____

_____

_____

	Yes	No	Comments

High traffic area _____

Adequate parking _____

Easy access by car _____

Business neat and well-lit _____

Prompt attention _____

Courteous staff _____

Knowledgeable staff _____

Complete array of services/
selection of products _____

Competitive fees/prices _____

Credit cards accepted _____

Will deliver to customers _____

Will place special orders _____

Repair service available _____

Open seven days a week _____

Looks busy and successful _____

Other notes on services/brands _____

How do prices compare with what I would charge? _____

What can I do to be better than this competitor? _____

_____

Nothing stays the same. Once you have an idea what an area is like now, consider what it will be like in the future.

• **Finally, fill out a "competitor analysis" form,** like the one shown on the preceding page, for each establishment you visit or speak with.

If you find another business that's offering top-quality goods and products at a low price, can quickly serve all its customers and can provide any special services that might be needed, you have a fierce competitor on your hands. You could be better off looking for a different location. On the other hand, any weakness—slow service, uninformed salespeople, poor selection, high prices, shoddy organization—represents a weakness in the competition and an opportunity for you at that location.

Other Factors to Consider

Here are a few other factors you should keep in mind as you explore different locations:

Market trends

Nothing stays the same. Once you have an idea what an area is like now, consider what it will be like in the future. An area experiencing population growth, for example, can mean an increasingly large market.

How can you assess market trends? Begin by reading local and neighborhood newspapers, looking for news of any new developments or business projects that are being planned. Also talk with business owners already in the area—they have a vested interest in knowing what's going on around them. The local planning department, zoning commission and permits or licensing office can give you information on zoning regulations in the area and on any new commercial, industrial or residential projects that have been filed for consideration.

Local legislation

Find out now whether there are any legal impediments, such as zoning or licensing, to the location you have in mind. You don't want to try opening a business that isn't appropriate for the zoning in an area. "High-impact" businesses like restaurants, bars, liquor stores and anything involving a manufacturing process may have to meet special requirements.

Stay aware of any impending changes in the tax structure, building codes and zoning ordinances or any other regulatory changes that would decrease or increase the desirability of a location you have in mind.

Local sentiment

Aside from legal considerations, use your common sense. For example, you should be cautious about trying to open a business that's going to create a lot of traffic, noise or controversy near a residential neighborhood—even if it's legal to do so. Hell hath no fury (and rightly so) like homeowners who perceive a business as diminishing the quality of their neighborhood.

Get the Word Out: Advertising and Public Relations

Okay. Let's say you've defined what business you're in. You're ready to give your clients or customers their money's worth and plenty more. But what happens if nobody else knows that you and your business even exist?

The answer, of course, is not much. A great product or service doesn't translate into a successful business unless someone out there knows you exist, and understands what makes you different from your competitors or otherwise worth patronizing.

That's where advertising and public relations come in. With good advertising and public relations (or PR, as it's commonly referred to), you'll be able to get information about your business to customers who would never have heard of you otherwise, and people who *you* would never have realized could become good customers, despite your best efforts at market research.

Some start-ups do fine without advertising. If your only client will be your former employer, for example, you won't need to spend any time or money on advertising. If you already have a great reputation for your work and you will have as many contracts as you want through current clients and word of mouth, you also may not need to advertise.

While advertising specifically promotes the sale of a

product or service, public relations promotes good news about a business to clients and the general public—and helps create a positive image for the entire enterprise. You can succeed without good public relations, too, but it never hurts. Good PR will help make yours a name that people think of when looking for the kind of goods or services you offer. And it will provide the kind of positive reinforcement that keeps customers coming back.

Advertising and public relations are two related parts of a unified effort to create and promote your business image. Their uses and methods can be analyzed separately.

Advertising

Many people think of advertising as television and radio commercials, newspaper and magazine advertisements and other "paid media messages" such as billboards and airplane banners. A complete ad campaign can include all of those things, and more.

Advertising is, simply, any communication of a sales message. It attempts to persuade someone to do something—"Buy this today!" or "Call me tomorrow!"—and it's paid for by an identified sponsor, you.

Planning Your Campaign

There are six basic steps in developing an advertising budget and media plan:

Decide what it is you're selling.

This seems, initially, like the easy part. Once you know your product or products, you know what it is you want to promote. But your "product" can be more than just an item. It can be:

What Advertising Can Do

Good advertising can:

- Sell your products or service and promote your business.

- Increase the number of people who recognize the name of your business.

- Make your sales efforts more effective because people already know something about you and your product before they meet you.

- Create the "need" for what you have to offer.

- Stimulate steady demand and sales.

What is special or unique about your business? That's something that you can highlight in your advertising.

- **the lowest cost.**

- **a convenient location.**

- **extraordinary service**—quickest turnaround time, never-miss deadlines, delivery anywhere, emergency service and so on.

- **special expertise.**

- **helpful referrals** when you don't have what the customer or client needs.

- **consistent availability or longer hours.**

- **quality and reliability.**

What is *special* or *unique* about your business? That's something that you can highlight in your advertising. Chances are that what you "sell" in your advertising will combine several such features. Know your product and then you can begin taking steps to establish your market position through advertising.

Target your audience.

You'll have to know who your potential customers are before you can advertise to them. Are they people in certain businesses? neighborhoods or other regions? professions? age groups? (Go back to Chapter 8 for a refresher on market research.)

Choose the best means to reach them.

Each medium has its own advantages and disadvantages, discussed in the box on pages 138–140.

Consider the cost per thousand.

Divide the cost of your ad by the total number of people, in thousands, who listen, read or subscribe. That's the cost per thousand, and you can use it to compare costs of various media outlets.

Decide how much you can–and should–spend, and what means are most effective.

This can be especially tough for start-ups with no

track record. One of the best things you can do is ask other small-business owners (preferably not direct competitors) which types of advertising have worked for them and how much they spend on advertising annually.

Of course, as a start-up you can't say for sure what your sales will amount to. But you can estimate how much business you'll reap in the first year and use that projection to calculate what you can afford to spend in advertising.

You may choose not to spend much. If you're a hobbyist, posting notices at your office, your place of worship or the public library could be all the ad campaign you need. If you appear at local craft shows, you pay for advertising when you pay for your display space.

For people working independently (consultants, free-lancers and other professionals), the most cost-effective approach could be direct mail sent to everyone in their Rolodex. The mailing could include a specially printed note card, hand-signed and with a brochure enclosed. Or, if appropriate, you could spend time and energy walking door to door in your neighborhood, introducing yourself and handing out your business card and other materials.

Schwadron, Cartoonists & Writers Syndicate

An important point: Self-employed individuals may be tempted to send out résumés. Don't. That's a tool for job hunters seeking employment. Do send a brochure that describes the products and services you sell.

For small retailers, the best media buys are usually in the local newspaper, direct mail, and circulars or fliers. Plenty of carry-out restaurants get a lot of bang for the buck by distributing copies of their menus, with their phone number prominently printed, to offices and households in their neighborhood. But retailers focusing on mail-order, regional or nationwide business may find the expense of advertising in nationally circulated or specialty magazines worthwhile.

Help With an Ad Budget

● ●

Many trade groups compile information on the average amount member businesses spend on advertising as a *percentage of sales.* Dun and Bradstreet, Standard & Poor's, and Robert Morris Associates have all published guidelines for advertising expenditures in many industries; their publications are available in many public libraries.

When you open your doors for business, plan to hear from local advertising sales representatives. Ask about the service they can offer and the efficacy of their publication or other media outlet. But don't feel compelled to commit, even if they play on your secret fear, "What if I gave a party and nobody came?" If you know your audience, a modest but well-aimed rifle shot may be more powerful than an expensive shotgun blast.

Follow up.

Ultimately, you'll want to know whether your ads really work. Here are some ways to determine how effective they've been:

- **Ask customers how they heard about you.** This is the simplest and most direct follow-up.

- **Advertise a promotion or special sale through only one outlet.** Track your sales following the campaign. If your sales increase significantly, ads in that outlet are probably making a difference.

- **Include coupons in your printed ads.** If people bring or mail them in, you know that your ads are having an effect.

- **Assign key numbers in ads that require a response.** If your ad gives people a phone number or address to contact, include a "department," "box," or "suite" number that lets you know which ad they're responding to. For example, a January 23 newspaper ad could instruct people to call your business and ask for "Department

NP123" (your own code for a newspaper ad that will run on the date 1–23).

Getting Help

There's one big problem with conventional advertising for a start-up: It's expensive. Even so, many new businesses open with big advertising splashes to develop instant name recognition, spending much more initially on promotion than will be necessary later.

Conceivably, you could save money by doing all the work involved in putting together an advertising program—developing the concept, drawing or writing the print advertisements, hiring someone to photograph or film ads, buying print space and TV time. That's conceivable, but not probable unless you have experience as a graphic artist or advertising-agency account executive, for example. If you need only a little advertising in local publications, you can often get by with your own ideas and the help of the advertising departments selling you space. But if you have more complex needs and you aren't an advertising expert, hire an ad agency or a graphic design firm that does advertising work. You'll have to pay a fee for these services—either a flat sum or, more commonly, a percentage of the total amount you pay to newspapers, TV stations and other media for ad space—but it can be money well spent.

Fees and commissions can be negotiated, and you should shop around for the services you need, both by talking with agencies directly and by asking other

---

Ways to Advertise

• •

The means of advertising are limited only by your imagination. Besides the usual media outlets, you can reach your prospective customers with the following:

- Postcards, fliers, brochures and other literature that may be sent out in mass mailings or made available at your place of business.

- Products (pens, calendars, chocolates, T-shirts, free samples) imprinted with the name of your business.

- Signs outside your business.

- Wall or window banners.

- Business cards left wherever you go.

- Notices posted publicly on electronic bulletin boards.

- Free samples given out on the street corner or at any public event.

(continued on page 141)

Ways to Get Your Message Out

TELEPHONE DIRECTORIES

Pluses

- Cover a specific region appropriate to local businesses.

- Used by individuals actively looking for specific goods and services.

- Good for most kinds of businesses.

Minuses

- Businesses with potential clients or customers spread over a wide geographic area could have to advertise in several directories to cover their market.

- Directories attract only active shoppers who happen to look up the specific category under which you've advertised, so you have to choose your category carefully, and you may need to advertise in more than one category.

Costs

- Anywhere from less than a hundred dollars for a listing in a small directory to $5,000 or more for a full-page ad in a big-city directory. A two-inch advertisement in US West's Portland, Ore., Yellow Pages is $1,073 a year; buying a half page would set you back more than $20,160 a year.

NEWSPAPERS

Pluses

- A good way of reaching a large number of people within a specific geographic region.

- Frequent publication allows you to get your business in front of the public eye on a regular basis.

- Short lead time—your ad will usually appear the day after you order it.

- In-house help designing and developing ads is often available from the newspaper's own ad department.

- Discounts for frequent advertisers.

Minuses

- Short shelf life—your ad goes out with the next day's trash, or the next week's in the case of a weekly or a free "shopper" paper.

- Not usually effective for businesses seeking to advertise to other businesses.

- Difficult to target a particular group of people within most geographic markets.

There are some exceptions to this last rule. *The New York Times,* for example, is valued by advertisers who believe that the paper, which is read by only about one of every seven New Yorkers, reaches the highly educated, high-income section of the local population as well as a sophisticated audience that receives the national edition.

Costs

- Anywhere from less than $25 for a weekend classified in a big-city paper to more than $10,000 for a full-page ad in a big-city paper.

MAGAZINES

Pluses

- You can target your audience through specialty publications aimed at virtually every sort of subgroup in the population: young, middle-aged and older people, cyclists, craft enthusiasts, horse lovers, business owners, middle managers, homemakers, physicians, gardeners, skateboarders and film buffs—even skateboarding film buffs who tend gardens and have seen Elvis at the local fast-food franchise. You name 'em, there's probably a nationally circulated magazine for 'em, and maybe a regional or local version to boot.

- Magazines have a longer life than newspapers, staying on the family coffee table for a week or month and often being passed along from reader to reader.

- Discounts on rates for larger advertisers.

Minuses

- The more highly targeted audience typically comes with a higher price, which can put magazine ads outside the budget of many start-ups.

- Magazines also require a longer lead time—you'll want to plan ads at least a couple of months in advance.

Costs

- Depending on the publication, anywhere from around $100 for a small ad to way, way more. You can advertise your expensive hand-knitted sweaters with a one-inch, one-column ad in the New Yorker for about $1,080 for a direct-response mail-order ad; a full-page color ad in the same magazine will set you back more than $42,000.

DIRECT MAIL

Pluses

- You can make a personalized pitch to an audience you choose. Detailed demographic lists allow you to send your ads to specific groups: corporations that spend more than $1,000 annually on office paper supplies say, or single men earning $20,000 to $30,000 who rent apartments, subscribe to Sports Illustrated, buy three pairs of running shoes annually, eat out at least twice a week and belong to a health club.

Minuses

- You'll have to live with the knowledge that what you're sending out is called—and treated like—junk by most of your recipients.

- The quality of mailing lists can vary widely. Some lists may be revised monthly and have up-to-date addresses; others may be falling out of date and include many old and duplicate addresses or "nixies." You'll want to try and get some guarantee that no more than a certain percentage of the names sold to you will be those nasty nixies.

To find a mailing house that can label your fliers, insert letters into envelopes, sort your direct-mail pieces by zip code and deliver them to the right postal terminal, talk with advertising and PR people—they should have recommendations of houses that can give you price estimates. You can also find direct-mail specialists in your local Yellow Pages.

Ways to Get Your Message Out (cont'd.)

DIRECT MAIL (cont'd.)

Costs

- Can be pricey. You'll usually have to pay to create a brochure, buy the mailing list (for a flat fee or for a base rate with a fee attached for each name), and pay for stationery, envelopes and postage. A mailing to 100,000 people that yields the typical response rate of 1% to 3% (and responses are not necessarily purchases) can easily cost $30,000 or more.

RADIO

Pluses

- You can reach large audiences in specific regions.

- You can also target particular groups such as teens, commuters or older listeners by advertising on stations whose "format" is aimed at such groups or by buying a "spot" during a certain time of the day.

- You can start or change an ad campaign on short notice. You can produce your own spots; many stations have in-house help to assist you in developing or producing ads.

Minuses

- Radio advertising usually works only if it's repetitive. You'll have to run your ad a lot to get someone's attention.

- Radio listeners are also distracted listeners, typically doing something else (working, driving) when the radio is on.

Costs

- Vary widely depending on the size of the station, the time of day (rush hour, when more people are in cars and listening to radio, tends to be most expensive) and the number of times you want the ads to run.

TELEVISION

Pluses

- Huge audiences for national markets or simply large ones for local TV advertising; you can target a specific region with local ads.

- Works well for products with wide potential consumer appeal.

- Effective in its ability to appeal to consumer senses of sight and sound.

Minuses

- The reality is that few start-ups can afford the huge costs of paying for commercials to be produced and then paying again for them to appear on TV. Smaller TV outlets—local or specialized cable channels, late-night programs, low-rated shows—are more affordable, but they are also often less effective than the network shows most of us would like to see our products advertised on.

Costs

See "Minuses."

small-business owners about their experiences with various agencies. This is a good occasion to look for advertising and graphics professionals who are also working for themselves and can offer you fees that reflect their low overhead. In any case, it certainly makes sense to spend a little more on an advertising professional and get ads that work for you than to pour a lot of money into your own program and miss the mark.

Truth in Advertising: Your Best Weapon

One last thing about advertising: Just because you're paying the bills, don't think you can say anything you want. Your ads should always be accurate and truthful, in spirit as well as in law. If you're less than 100% above board, customers will eventually recognize that, and your ads will lose credibility. Just as bad (or worse), the people responsible for regulating advertising will eventually take notice. These may include your state consumer agency, the office of the state attorney general, the Federal Trade Commission or the federal Food and Drug Administration. The Council of Better Business Bureaus also makes an effort to scrutinize its members' advertising. Food companies that had advertised as "fresh" orange juice made from frozen concentrate got a lot of unwanted publicity in the early 1990s when the FDA persuaded them to remove that adjective from advertising and container labels.

Public Relations

What you really want as a start-up is exposure. You want people or businesses—your potential clients—to know you're out there with something that they can use. You want them to know you exist. And you can accomplish that *by generating publicity about yourself and your company.* We're talking public relations here: a way of letting people know about yourself, often for far less than what you would pay for advertising.

Public relations is, basically, anything that conveys information about or promotes your business. For starters,

If you're less than 100% above board, customers will eventually recognize that, and your ads will lose credibility.

Truth in Advertising

For information about deception and substantiation in advertising, contact the Federal Trade Commission (Document Division, 6th and Pennsylvania Ave., N.W., Washington, DC 20580; 202–326–2222).

it's networking through business, professional and community organizations. Call it "personal public relations." Every contact you make with a potential customer, or with anyone who might interact with anyone who might be a potential customer (in short, just about anybody), represents an opportunity to effectively promote your venture.

Public relations in the form of nonmedia contacts—sponsoring a Little League team, for example, or making a donation to a charity fundraiser—won't necessarily come with a direct "plug" for your business attached but it will increase your name recognition and the good feelings of potential customers toward your business.

Unlike advertising, public relations via the media isn't something you can control. Advertising is placed with advertising salespeople; you pay for the ad and know exactly what the message will be and when and where it will appear. Public relations that leads to media publicity is placed with journalists who, after getting information on you or your company, decide on their own whether—and what—to write about you.

That said, good PR also can be amazingly effective at enhancing your company's public image because the publicity you get is objective. The public knows that, at least in the case of any reputable publication or show, you did not pay for the nice things being written or said about you and your company. That kind of credibility is, in many ways, the best publicity of all.

Nothing Beats Good PR

The impact of good public relations can be tremendous for a small business. For instance, when *Reader's Digest* published an article about Tracers Co. of America Inc., an investigative firm that specializes in finding the missing—whether the "missing" be people, bank accounts or whatever—the company was flooded with more than 400,000 letters. That is, admittedly, an unusual example, especially when you consider that more than 27 million copies of *Reader's Digest* are sold every month. But the point made is valid: The kind of free publicity generated by mention in the right place can mean a lot of money for a small business.

When an East Hampton, Long Island company called MapEasy, which produces tourist maps of several U.S. and international cities, was featured in a small item in *Travel & Leisure* magazine, the owners thought they might get a few telephone calls for orders. "Our phone started ringing the first day the story came out," said MapEasy founder Chris Harris. "We got hundreds of orders from individuals, plus bulk orders from corporations that wanted our maps for their employees. Even six months later, we were getting a couple of calls every week."

The key for MapEasy was that mention of the company's product was made in a publication read by people interested in traveling who would probably be attracted to that product. Targeting your market is as much a part of good public relations as it is a part of good marketing: You should look for publicity from outlets that are attended, viewed, listened to or read by people who would have reason to be interested in what you have to offer.

> ## *Ways to Promote Your Venture*
>
> Public relations can include:
>
> - A press release.
> - An interview with a newspaper.
> - A feature in a magazine.
> - A radio interview.
> - A guest appearance on a television show.
> - A letter to the editor.
> - An open house for the community.
> - A press conference.
> - A company logo on your car.
> - Even the attitude and personality of you and your employees.

When working through media outlets, you have a silent ally: the editor, reporter, host or booking agent of the show or publication you're contacting. It's tempting to think of these people as "the enemy," the folks you have to get past to reach that pot of gold known as free publicity. But remember, they're in business, too, and they're doing everything they can to appeal to their customers. Yes, you have to "sell" them on yourself and your business, but if you do have something that appeals to their audiences, you will get the coverage you crave.

Targeting Your PR Efforts

The right target for your public relations efforts will not always be readily apparent. Take, for example, the happy case of Patrick Dunne.

Dunne owns an antique shop called Lucullus, which specializes in what are probably best categorized as culinary antiques. His store, located in the French Quarter of New Orleans, is filled with all sorts of items that one would have found in the finest kitchens and dining rooms of the 18th and 19th centuries—not just hand-crafted chairs and dining tables but also silverware, wine goblets, corkscrews, decanters and napkin holders. He's even purchased antique breast pumps. If it relates in any way to food, Dunne says, he's interested in it.

The best prospects for free public relations for Dunne and Lucullus might appear, at first glance, to be local: area television and radio talk shows; the arts and entertainment section of the *New Orleans Times-Picayune*, the city's daily newspaper; city magazines. National travel-oriented and collector-oriented magazines would be great prospects as well, although the bigger the outlet you're shooting for, the harder it is to compete for the coverage you desire.

But some of the best PR Dunne ever received came from none of these sources. One day, a reporter on assignment for *The Wine Spectator*, a twice-monthly magazine covering the wine industry for oenophiles, walked into Lucullus. She'd heard about the shop and wanted to see what it was all about. The result, after some months and several

---

Discovering the Media

• •

To locate media outlets, try these directories that you're likely to find at your local library.

- *The Editor & Publisher International Yearbook* lists key editorial personnel for nearly every daily and weekly newspaper in the U.S. and Canada, and to a lesser degree, for newspapers abroad.

- *Writer's Market* lists information on the kinds of stories more than 1,000 magazines are looking for.

- *Standard Rates and Data, Consumer Magazine* and *Agrimedia Rates & Data* gives names, descriptions, and advertising rate information for just about every consumer magazine.

- *Broadcasting and Cable Marketplace* is the industry source for radio, television and cable.

interviews, was a 1,500-word feature in the magazine that focused on the wine-related items collected by Dunne.

The reaction was phenomenal. "It was a very focused article for a very specialized readership, and it exposed me to a whole new clientele," Dunne said. "After the article came out, everyone who was serious about wine who came through New Orleans made a point of stopping in to see me and to find out what I had for sale."

For any start-up, of course, simply the fact that you're opening a business is newsworthy, and your local papers and other publications may be interested in that.

Even so, be creative. Use your imagination. Don't blindly try to get your business in every media outlet available, but do think of any outlet that would be interested in some aspect of your business.

Entrepreneur, Slant Thyself

Any publication or show geared toward people like you or written for your potential clients is a possible source of free PR. However, you'll have to slant your "pitch" toward the interests of the reporter or editor of each outlet, and its readers.

For example, let's say you're starting a hair salon in a section of town that hasn't had many new businesses open in recent years. Possible PR outlets would include:

- **local newspaper business sections** ("Local Woman Opens New Business").

- **local business magazines** ("New Shops May Signal Rebirth of Area").

- **local newspaper feature or fashion sections** ("The Kindest Cuts of All for Fall").

- **local radio talk shows** ("Today's Topic: The Long and Short of It: Hair-care Products That Make a Difference").

- **local and national women's business magazines** ("Going From Employee to Owner").

You'll have to slant your "pitch" toward the interests of the reporter or editor of each outlet, and its readers.

Getting In

Whether you're trying to get into a newspaper or magazine or on television, the process is the same.

Know your audience.

Be aware of exactly who you want to reach and who you will be reaching through a particular media outlet.

Know the outlet.

Read the newspaper or magazine; watch the television show you're interested in.

Know your objective.

Do you want to make people aware simply that you've started a new business? Or is there something you specialize in that you think will interest people? Think

---

Profiting With News Releases

The best way to contact a media outlet is almost always through the mail, at least initially. Editors and reporters don't usually have much time for out-of-the-blue phone calls, and unless you've got some great news story that must be reported on today, a good journalist will simply tell you to send him or her something in the mail. So do that to begin with.

The one thing you can use a telephone for initially is to call the organization and get the name of a specific person to whom you can write. It's easy to do. Just look up the name of the organization in the phone book, call, and ask whoever answers the phone who the managing editor, business editor, fashion reporter, guest booker or other contact is. Confirm the address of

the publication or station, and send off your news release.

Now, here's a quick list of do's and don't's for news releases.

- **Do make your news release read like a journalism story.** Put the most important information you're trying to transmit in the first paragraph (the "hook"). Follow that with the next most important piece of information, and so on. In short, make "finding the story" as easy for a reporter as possible. Don't know what's most important? Ask yourself why the reader or editor should care about what you're saying, that is, "so what?" The information your reader should care about should be up near the beginning of the release.

about what the most interesting or unusual things are about the business you're starting—they'll be good things to promote and will probably also rate as newsworthy with the editors and reporters who are the gatekeepers to the publicity you seek.

Contact the right person.

If you're reading a newspaper or magazine regularly, you can figure out who the best person is to write about your business. Simply note who writes stories that come closest to covering the business or field you're in, and contact him directly. If there aren't any bylines, write a letter to the editor of the publication or the section that you're interested in. You can usually get the editor's name by calling the publication or checking the masthead (usually printed in the first few pages of the magazine).

Don't just address a letter to "Editor" without a name attached. Depending on the size of the organization, your

- **Do put the name and telephone number of whomever can be contacted** for more information prominently at the top of the page.

- **Do be descriptive, but don't use lots of adjectives.** Again, let the journalists decide whether what you're pushing is "wonderful," "fantastic," "great," "special," "fabulous" or whatever.

- **Do follow up with a phone call, but only after a couple of weeks have passed.** Simply call and ask if your news release was received, and if there are any questions you can answer. Also ask what kinds of stories they are looking for— you might think of an angle you could use in a later press release.

- **Don't start out, "I have something I think you should write about."** Let the recipient decide what she wants to write about. Just describe your business, service or product and explain why it is newsworthy.

- **Don't "happen to mention" that you're interested in advertising** with the publication or station. Editors don't like feeling as if someone is trying to bribe them to run a story.

letter may get passed from in-box to in-box or thrown in the garbage without a second glance. Lack of a name means you haven't done your homework.

If you want to promote yourself on radio or a television show, contact the producer of the show, the "booker" (who is responsible for scheduling guests) or the reporter. To find out exactly who you should contact, simply call the station and ask who books interviews on the show that interests you.

Don't just have a company—have a story.

Tell the editor why your story is an interesting one. Make it relevant to his or her reader or listeners.

For TV and radio, consider a coach.

You'll have to pay, of course, anywhere from $200 to $4,000, depending on the degree of coaching you want. Dr. Margaret Cary, a Denver physician, went to an acting coach when she shifted career tracks and began developing a medical show for television.

Help With Giving

Want to contribute, but don't know who to give to? Don't worry after you've advertised or promoted yourself, organizations looking for help will have no trouble at all in finding you.

There are some charitable groups that are good sources of "one-stop" giving—they take contributions and distribute them to several worthwhile causes—and information about charities. Two especially worth mentioning:

- **Your local United Way.** The 800-pound gorilla of charitable groups, the United Way conducts annual fund-raising drives in virtually every community, collecting money and distributing it to a wide range of groups and causes. Check your phone book for the nearest office.

- **Local volunteer clearinghouses** list many organizations that depend on volunteers to survive.

- **The National Committee for Responsive Philanthropy**, a federation of smaller charities, most of which are not affiliated with the United Way. Contact the committee at 2001 S Street, N.W., Suite 620, Washington, DC 20009.

"I needed to learn a lot of structural things—how to look at the camera, how to deal with the sense of intrusion you can feel from having a camera watch you all the time," she said. "A good coach helps you get comfortable with the simple act of being in front of a camera."

Doing Well by Doing Good

Some of the best public relations can come out of your own good and charitable impulses.

Certainly, you're not going to be mistaken for the Ford or Rockefeller foundations anytime soon. After all, they give away millions of dollars annually. No matter, though: Even small contributions, made properly, can generate goodwill within the community, and that goodwill can only help you and your business.

Good works don't have to be confined to the writing of checks. Some of the best charitable assistance, from a public relations standpoint, is "in-kind" service: A small restaurant could donate sandwiches to a volunteer neighborhood cleanup effort or give leftovers to a homeless shelter; a print shop could design and print the invitations to a charitable fund-raising event. Donating goods, services or your own time to an auction or public-radio membership drive gets your name out to people and allows you to give something of value to a worthy cause.

This is a form of what I'll call incidental public relations: The purpose of your contributions is to "do good"; the secondary effect of doing good is to help create a positive image of you and your business within the local community. It's important to remember the order of those priorities and not make your contributions based only on the public-relations value to be gained from them. Give to those causes you support and feel are doing a good job; the recognition and appreciation will follow.

Some of the best charitable assistance, from a public relations standpoint, is "in-kind" service.

The Form
of Your Business

After getting a batch of business cards with your name and phone number printed on them, it's tempting to think, "Okay—now I'm a business." In a way, you are. But before you're really in business for yourself, you'll have to decide what *legal form* your business will take. The form of your business can affect your potential legal liabilities, the kinds of paperwork you have to complete to satisfy the government, the tax forms you fill out, even the amount of tax you pay and the amount of money you'll be able to set aside for retirement.

There are several choices for the self-employed to ponder: Your business could take the form of a *sole proprietorship*, a *general partnership* or a *corporation.* Each has intrinsic advantages and disadvantages. Here are some factors to consider when choosing the legal form of your business.

Sole Proprietorship

A sole proprietorship is subject to the least amount of red tape of any form of business. That's probably why it is the most common form a new business takes.

You call the shots.

It happens to be, logistically, just about the best a one-person shop could hope for: a legal form in which you and your new business venture are one and the same. You don't have to consider the desires of partners or other owners; you don't need to worry about the opinions of a board of directors. You get to keep all the profits, and you maintain personal control over your business.

You don't have to file any forms with the federal government.

When starting a sole proprietorship, you probably won't have to file anything more complicated than a fictitious business name or "DBA" (or "doing business as") form for the record with your state or local government. (Check Chapter 12 for more on naming your business.)

You don't even have to fill out a separate income-tax form for your business.

You simply report all revenues and expenses from your business on a form called Schedule C, which you file with your personal tax return. Profits from your business are reported as earned income; losses may be used to offset income you earn from other sources, such as interest or salary from another full-time or part-time job.

The Risk of Liability

Sole proprietorships are simple, but they also have a significant downside: a lot of financial risks. With full control of the business comes full liability for the debts of the business. "There is a simple hierarchy of legal protection for operators of businesses, and sole proprietors are at the bottom of that hierarchy," says Jonathan Kirsch, an attorney with the Los Angeles firm of Kirsch & Mitchell who represents many small-business owners. "A sole proprietorship offers no distinction between the assets of the business and those of the proprietor, so any assets of the individual can be at risk for the debts of the business. In a sole proprietorship, the individual is the business."

Since the individual is the business, the individual's bank account can be wiped out by the business's misfortunes. If you sign a two-year lease on office space but have to close your business after three months, you're still personally responsible for the remainder of the lease—business or no business.

Similarly, if a client is injured while on your business property, or if an employee is involved in an accident while using a business vehicle, you could be personally li-

"There is a simple hierarchy of legal protection for operators of businesses, and sole proprietors are at the bottom of that hierarchy."

able for injuries or damages. Your personal bank account as well as your business could be wiped out because, again, there is no legal or financial distinction between you and the proprietorship.

General Partnerships

Partnerships are sometimes thought of as being one level up from sole proprietorships in the financial security they give you. They are usually defined as agreements by two or more people to operate a business for profit.

Partners share and share alike

Partners may pool their resources—money, ideas, labor—and share in the liabilities and profits of the business.

Forms of Businesses

	Sole Proprietorship	Partnership	Corporation
Start-up	Easiest to form; usually no documents more complicated to file than a "doing business as" notice.	Need DBA and partnership agreement in most cases.	Formal application and registration can be costly.
Daily operation	Simple—you do the work, you get the money.	Need to spell out responsibilities of each partner.	Can be complex if several employees involved; must treat business as separate financial entity from self.
Liability	Unlimited personal liability for financial claims.	Unlimited personal liability for financial claims.	No personal liability if corporation operates in legal and independent manner.
Taxation	Same as owner's rate.	Same as partner's individual rate.	Corporate rates—may be lower than owner's individual tax rate.*

*A Subchapter S corporation's income is passed through to its stockholders and taxes at stockholders' rates.

The shared work load and responsibilities can make the business easier to manage, and the pooling of talents can make for a more successful venture. (Partnerships are discussed in detail in Chapter 13.)

Contain the risk with a contract

No formal contract is required between partners. Still, a written agreement is a good idea. A written agreement will make clear the rights and responsibilities of each partner and spell out what percentage of the profits each partner is entitled to receive. Partnerships, though, can be just as financially risky as, or even risker than, sole proprietorships.

Here's why: You are still liable for all the debts you incur while operating your partnership, just as you would be with a sole proprietorship. However, in a general partnership you are also responsible for debts that your partners incur on behalf of the partnership. Say, for example, one of your partners purchases some equipment or takes out a loan. If the partner is acting on behalf of the partnership, you could be fully liable for repayment—even if you weren't told about or didn't approve of the transaction. The potential for financial disaster is obvious.

"You have to figure you're at risk...unless you have a high level of confidence that your partner is going to check things out with you before making any business decisions," says Kirsch.

Limited partnerships

While most people who want to enter a partnership will be interested in general partnerships of the type just described, some may be interested in taking on *limited* partners. The liability of such partners is limited to the amount of money each has paid into the partnership as a capital

---

> ## *For More Information*
> •
>
> The U.S. Small Business Administration has two publications that can help you start the process of sorting out which form your business should take (to order by mail, call your local SBA office; see also page 22):
>
> - *Selecting the Legal Structure for Your Firm*, Management Aids Number 6.004.
>
> - *Incorporating A Small Business*, Management Aids Number 6.003.

"If you're going to have employees, you're crazy not to be incorporated."

contribution; however, they generally act only as investors and don't participate in the day-to-day management of your business. The structure of limited partnerships can vary greatly; you'll need the help of an attorney if you're interested in this form of partnership. (See also Chapter 17 on financing.)

Corporations— The Pinnacle of Protection

Unlike sole proprietorships and partnerships, corporations are legally considered separate entities from the people who operate or own them. This gives entrepreneurs who form corporations far more legal protection against personal liability than those who operate as sole proprietors or partnerships. All you can personally lose is the money and time you've put into the company. (Of course, this doesn't protect people who use their business to purposely trick or defraud creditors.) Your house, car and personal bank accounts are safe, even if your corporation is sued or goes bankrupt. That's a big difference from the unlimited liability that sole proprietorships and partnerships can face.

"If you're going to have employees, you're crazy not to be incorporated," says Jim McGrath, a financial planner and certified public accountant in Rockville, Md. "At least if you're incorporated, your personal assets are protected from problems with employees' either being injured or causing damage to someone else's property; things like that become the company's problem and not yours."

There are a couple of exceptions to the general rule that incorporation protects you against business debts and liabilities:

In case of a loan

First, even if you incorporate, banks are still likely to ask you to personally co-sign any loans, pledging your house, car or other personal assets as collateral.

You don't live up to the rules

Second, you can lose the legal protection of a corporation if your firm does not act like a corporation. Corporations have to adopt bylaws (rules for conducting the business of the organization), keep financial and business records, and conduct themselves as the independent entities they are.

For you, that means (among other things) not mixing the corporation's finances with your own. You have to have separate checking accounts, separate savings accounts and separate tax returns if you are going to be truly separate entities. Writing a company check to your personal account when you need a little extra money is strictly a no-no, unless the corporation formally makes a loan to you. If you don't conduct your personal financial affairs separately from the finances of the corporation, creditors and the IRS may try to have you declared personally liable for the corporation's debts. Of course, keeping your personal and business finances separate is a good idea from a tax and record-keeping standpoint even if you're *not* a corporation.

"Unless the corporation is maintained in good standing and as a genuine business entity, a creditor can ignore the corporate structure and 'pierce the corporate veil,' as lawyers say, to get at the assets of the owners," says Kirsch. "The greatest mistake I'd say that entrepreneurs make is to incorporate and then ignore the corporation and continue to do business as if they were a sole proprietorship. They don't hold annual meetings, they don't elect officers,

"Now I understand why it's a limited partnership."

Schwadron, Cartoonists & Writers Syndicate

If you have ownership in an S corporation, you can apply losses from the business against other income on your personal tax return.

they don't keep minutes of meetings, and so on."

States license corporations and specify the rules covering incorporation, including those covering election of directors, conduct of meetings and records of corporate decisions.

Incorporating isn't cheap: Depending on where you live and the complexity of the corporation you're starting, it can cost anywhere from several hundred to several thousand dollars to pay the state fees and have a lawyer draw up and file all the necessary paperwork.

The Advantages of Subchapter S Corporations

"S" corporations are similar to other corporations in most ways except that, as with partnerships, all their income and losses flow directly through the firm to its owners or "shareholders." (Unlike partnerships, you may be the only owner.) That allows the corporation to avoid being taxed on profits, which it then distributes as dividends. (See discussion of tax treatment of businesses below.) Many small businesses can opt to be treated as S corporations; you should consult with your accountant about IRS requirements for S corporation status.

There is another tax-related advantage to S corporations: If you have ownership in an S corporation, you can apply losses from the business against other income on your personal tax return. The savings can be significant if you're keeping your current job while starting a new business and expect the new business to lose money in its first couple of years.

You, Your Business and Your Taxes

Whether you operate as a sole proprietor, partnership or corporation, you'll have to pay taxes on profits. However, the way you pay those taxes will vary with the form of your business.

Sole proprietors

Taxes on sole proprietors are relatively straightforward. To oversimplify somewhat, you add up the money your business took in, subtract the money your business spent and report the difference as your income. The federal income-tax rate on your business profit is the same as if that profit were paid to you as salary.

Partnerships

Partnerships are taxed like sole proprietorships. You pay taxes on your share of the partnership's net profit at the same income-tax rate as on your other personal income. If the partnership had a profit of $60,000 and you own 50% of the partnership, you'll report $30,000 income.

Corporations

Much is made about corporate tax rates and the tax advantages or disadvantages of incorporation. This is one debate that may contain more heat than light. If you incorporate and draw a salary from the corporation, you'll pay personal income tax on that salary. Corporations also pay taxes on their profits, and if a corporation distributes some of its profits to shareholders and owners (yourself, for instance) in the form of dividends, taxes will also have to be paid on those dividends.

That "double taxation" on profits (salary and dividends) is often cited as a reason *not* to incorporate. But with help from your accountant, you can minimize the amounts distributed as dividends and subject to double taxation. Furthermore, although the tax code and tax rates are always subject to change, corporate income-tax rates for small businesses are often lower than rates for individuals. (For more information on tax rates, check *Kiplinger's Cut Your Taxes,* by Kevin McCormally.)

It's tempting to look at how the tax laws are structured and say, "Ah-ha! I'll just take all my compensation from the company in the form of salary and not have to worry about any dividend taxes." Don't try it. The IRS is wise to such tactics and will go after people who flout the rules.

Although the tax code and tax rates are always subject to change, corporate income-tax rates for small businesses are often lower than rates for individuals.

Talk with your accountant, attorney and other advisers about the potential benefits and pitfalls of each structure.

One other advantage of corporations: They can deduct much of what they contribute for employee benefits, including life insurance and health insurance, even if they have only one employee. Neither S corporations nor sole proprietorships can do that.

Beginning in 1995, sole proprietors will be allowed to deduct 30% of their health insurance premiums for themselves and their families from their taxable income. (The legislation covering this deduction also restored the 25% deduction for 1994. If you were denied the deduction, you are eligible for a refund by amending your return with Form 1040X.) As a sole proprietor, you can't deduct your premiums if doing so will result in a net loss or if you, or your spouse, are eligible for coverage through an employer.

Words to the Wise

Remember that much of the tax code is subject to annual review and potential modification by the government, so decisions about what form your business takes should not be based solely on tax considerations. Instead, talk with your accountant, attorney and other advisers about the potential benefits and pitfalls of each structure as it would apply specifically to your business and personal situation before choosing the one that's best for you.

One other thing to remember that may put your mind a bit more at ease: This decision doesn't have to be permanent. Many businesses start as sole proprietorships and evolve into partnerships or corporations. You can begin with the simplest form of business, then change to a partnership or corporation as your business grows in size and complexity.

What's in a Name?

Ti Martin, Dick Brennan Jr. and Bradford Bridgeman spent a lot of time thinking about what they wanted to call their New Orleans restaurant. The trio were opening what was certainly a "city" restaurant—a glittery new establishment into which they had put $2 million worth of construction and planning. But it would also be a restaurant with the atmosphere and attitude of the grand cafés of Paris, from which they had drawn much of their inspiration. And it was a venture being launched by three people who represented the next generation of New Orleans's best-known restaurant family and were cousins as well.

The first name they came up with, Cousins' City Café, was an inspired creation, linking key elements and feelings that the cousins had about their restaurant. It conveyed the idea of a sophisticated café, and it also offered a clue as to the forces behind the restaurant—in New Orleans, it wouldn't take long for people to learn and remember that the "Cousins" were all part of the famed Brennan clan.

There was just one problem. They couldn't use that name. There was another business in another part of the country that also called itself Cousins, and it wasn't about to give up the name. If these three cousins had opened their business with that name, they could have been sued. "It wasn't likely, but we talked with our lawyer and we knew it was possible," said Martin. "Having that name didn't seem worth the potential hassle."

So Martin, Brennan and Bridgeman went back to the drawing board, and came up with an alternative: Palace Café Seafood Roti. The name retained an oblique reference to the grand cafés of Paris and, even better, linked the

First impressions count, and one of the first things people are going to notice is the name of your business.

restaurant's name to its architecture, which features a dramatic, curving stairway rising to a wraparound mezzanine. Using the words "Palace Café" preserved, and probably strengthened, the family connection: the trio's parents were co-owners of Commander's Palace, one of the best-known restaurants in New Orleans. "It's kind of important to have a name that says what you are, and we think "Palace Café Seafood Roti does that for this restaurant," said Martin.

The process these three restaurateurs went through illustrates the issues involved in naming your business. You'll want:

• **an appealing name** that describes something—preferably something unique—about your business.

• **a name that customers will recognize,** especially if you're starting a retail business.

• **a name that won't cause you any legal problems.**

These concerns will apply equally, regardless of whether your business will be a one-person shop (you) or involve a corporate cast of thousands.

Your Name, Your Message

First impressions count, which is one reason people go to the trouble of paying attention to their appearance. First impressions count in business, too. And one of the first things people are going to notice is the *name* of your business. Ideally, your business's name is the one that will jump out from the jumble in the Yellow Pages, catch a buyer's eye on a newsstand, or simply linger in the mind of a potential client even after he has misplaced your business card.

Perhaps fortunately, business names are not judged by the same standards as one's personal appearance. A business name doesn't have to be attractive or handsome or even dignified; it just has to offer information about the business. If it conveys some essential attribute—reliability, aggressiveness, creativity, prudence, speed—it's doing its job. If it is something that people can easily remember—because it's such a common name or such an unusual one (or just because it has that *something* that sticks in people's minds)—then all the better. After all, if people can more easily remember the name of a business, they'll more easily find it in the phone book and will more likely think of it when they want to refer other potential customers.

Your Own Good Name

It's tempting to use your own name for your business (see the discussion of legal angles later in this chapter). It also may be a good idea, especially if you're starting a business that will draw customers from an area, either geographic or professional, in which your name is already known. And it may make for a great play on words, as in the case of Flowers & Flowers, the Reston, Va., floral-design business run by—and we are not making this up—Sandy Flowers.

Will it fit?

Using your name will be an even better idea if it just happens to be no longer than three syllables, or about ten characters, and if it's not hyphenated. Business names have to fit on signs, letterheads, advertisements, and so on, and shorter names have the advantage of fitting more easily into a relatively small space. Don't worry, though, if you're a Dornenbergerman or a Phongphouthai: Modern typefaces have rarely met a name they couldn't adapt to a space.

Hyphenated names

Hyphenated names pose a slightly more practical problem: They may be confusing as well as lengthy. For example, is Hughes-Waterman a partnership or one person's company? Having to explain such a thing to your customer takes time from what you should be doing—selling and serving. There's also the inevitable problem of which name customers will look under when they try to find your company in the telephone book.

Hyphenated names present the inevitable problem of which name customers will look under in the telephone book.

Choosing a name beginning with A is no guarantee of getting an "up-front" listing in the telephone book.

Descriptive Names

A descriptive name somehow highlights some essential, unique or laudable aspect of your business. Consider the following points when mentally thumbing through descriptive names:

Emphasize what you're selling or what makes your business unique.

For example, if you're the only bagelmaker in the area, say it: Dave's Bagel Bakery. If quality is key, say so: Stan's *Gourmet* Ice Cream. If service is king, highlight that in the name, or perhaps in a motto or tag line. For example, one national house-cleaning franchise calls itself ServiceMaster.

Avoid a name that begins with the letter *A*.

Lots of people have already thought of this, and it's no guarantee of getting an "up-front" listing in the telephone book. Because so many businesses start out with that letter, the front of the book is characterized by nothing so much as, well, Anarchy. The C&P Suburban Maryland White Pages, for example, lead off with five full pages of businesses whose names begin with one—or more—A's.

Don't use an initial followed by a name.

You're just asking for more confusion. Yes, a company, even a retail company, can succeed with such a name—for example, B. Dalton in books or H. Salt in fast-food fish. But it's still not usually your best option. Don't believe me? Then answer this: If you had to find out, right away, the address for the nearest B. Dalton Bookseller and had access only to the local White Pages, would you look under *B*...or under "Dalton?"

Watch out for a case of the cutes.

A decorative rock-garden business run by a woman named Agnes could be called "Rocks of Agnes." Cute, but if people come into the store looking for paving stones or diamonds, Agnes has a problem.

Besides, what you think is a witty double-entendre may not strike your potential customer the same way. Humor is truly a funny thing; If someone is not amused, the effort can actually backfire. I have a friend who won't get his hair cut at any salon that makes a pun about hair. Hair Today, Gone Tomorrow; Headlines; Mane Event— names like these stop him at the door.

Make it easy to pronounce and remember.

Foreign words and phrases can be wonderfully exotic or memorable and can even create an air of exclusivity. (A certain car company probably hasn't been hurt because not everyone is sure whether the car name is pronounced "Porsh" or "Por-Shaa.") But they can be difficult to say or remember. You probably have better things to do with your time and money than to spend it educating the public about how your company name is pronounced. Keep it simple.

If you choose to sell your goods or services internationally, you could encounter a related problem: The innocent name of a company or product can have a distinctly different meaning in another language or within the slang of another culture.

Choose a name that won't become dated.

That is, unless you're deliberately trying to create an "old-fashioned" image with something like "Ye Olde Chocolate Shoppe."

Be wary of high-tech names.

This is especially true if you're not a high-tech company. There's been a real love affair in recent years with giving companies "techie-sounding" names. Such names—Genentech, Centocor, Intel, Autodesk—are just fine if you're in the computer or high-tech industry. But they can also backfire. Remember "Allegis Corp."? If not, don't worry—you're not alone. Allegis was, for a blink of the eye in the mid 1980s, the name given to what was, and is more commonly known as, United Airlines, or UAL. It was reported that Allegis/UAL spent more than $7 million

Be wary of high-tech names. This is especially true if you're not a high-tech company.

Registering your business name protects you from others' infringing on your business identity, and vice versa—now and in the future.

creating and promoting the new name, only to eventually go back to the old, better-understood and more sensible, descriptive name.

Watch out for alphabet soup.

Similarly, think twice about names that are collections of initials. Sure, IBM has done just fine (though it began its life as the Computing, Tabulating and Recording Co., changed its name to International Business Machines in the '20s and evolved into calling itself IBM). But using only initials for your company name usually means missing out on an important chance to tell your potential customers something about yourself and your business.

A Legal Name

In general, anyone starting a business must register its name in the state or states where the start-up will be operating. This protects you from others' infringing on your business identity, and vice versa—now and in the future. The name of your new business can't be the same as, or often even close to, the name of an existing U.S. corporation or foreign corporation authorized to do business in a state in which you plan to operate.

Some states also will reject names that are identical or similar to existing limited partnerships, trade names (the name under which a company does business or that it assigns to its product or service) and trademarks already registered by the state. Existing corporations are usually protected against new names that—just because of the *name similarity*—could present a threat to the existing corporation's market. The idea, and fear, is that similar names could confuse the public, affect the reputation of the existing corporation and even cause that corporation to lose business.

There's actually a gray area around the issue of similar names. Simply put, some similar names will slip through the legal safety net, while others won't. A name may pass muster because state employees overlook an existing business whose name is in conflict or because the officials in charge of making these decisions determine that the name wasn't so similar to another as to be confusing to the public. But the other business in question doesn't have to accept that judgment without a fight. It can challenge the start-up in civil court, charging that its name has been infringed upon. Obviously, the safest route you can take is to avoid, to whatever extent possible, any appearance of similarity between the name of your business and the names of businesses who "got there first."

Because of the many legal entanglements that can ensnare you, it simply doesn't make sense to try to whimsically play off the name of a better-known company, no matter how tempting the urge. Your last name may indeed be Westing, but if you name your appliance shop "Westing House," a certain corporation is sure to be on top of you like a moth on a light bulb. Same goes for such circumlocutions as "Windy's Hamburgers" and "McDouglas's." Corporations are very determined and very successful in protecting their good names from unauthorized incursions, no matter how witty.

Harris, Cartoonists & Writers Syndicate

A Name Search

David A. Weinstein, a lawyer specializing in trademark and copyright law and the author of *How to Protect Your Business, Professional, & Brand Name* (John Wiley & Sons), says that anyone starting a business should do as thorough a name search as possible. "They should do everything they can— check corporate records with the secretary of state, check directories, check data bases," he says. "Everything helps, although no one source is ever absolute."

Remember, you have to avoid conflicts with existing businesses in every state in which you'll be doing business, not just in the state where you incorporate. Even if you don't plan to do business regionally or nationally, it's possible that you'll do business in more than one state. Consider such metropolitan areas as New York City (New York, Connecticut, New Jersey), Washington, D.C. (the District of Columbia, Maryland, Virginia), Minneapolis–St. Paul (a stone's throw from Wisconsin), and Kansas City (Missouri and Kansas).

The search takes time. Fortunately, most states let you reserve a potential corporate name for about three

Researching Your Name

The phone company

Before you commit to a name, look for duplicates among your competition. A check of your area Yellow Pages and a call to the telephone information operator will tell you whether someone is operating a business with a name close to yours.

The state

You can continue your own limited search by contacting the state agency with responsibility for corporate names (usually the secretary of state or the state revenue department) and asking if a name can be registered—or by simply going to your statehouse and checking the records yourself.

Directories

Publications like *Brands and Their Companies,* the *Business Organizations and Agencies Directory* and *Thomas Register of American Manufacturers* are all sources of information about consumer product and trade names.

Private search companies

Your attorney may, in fact, use such a company if you ask him or her to research a name.

Experts say that you'll almost certainly need help if you have to do a national name search and that the only way to be even reasonably sure a name isn't already being used is to hire a professional research firm. The burden of trying to verify the acceptability of a name in 50 states—which you'd have to do if you're planning to market your product nationwide—can make these firms virtually essential. For fees that can range from a few hundred to about a thousand dollars, they'll check federal and state registrations, industrial directories and other data bases.

An attorney or accountant specializing in business formations and incorporations should be able to help you with your search, or with your search for a search company.

Actual filing procedures for business names vary from state to state. The state office in charge of filings, or your attorney, can give you more specific information.

months, during which time you can conduct your own search or get help with it. If, like many people, you have the name of your business before you have the business itself, that should give you enough time to confirm or discard a name.

Don't overlook this important process. It may not seem vital now—because you're local, small, unique or not likely to attract attention (or be discovered). But it may not always be that way. If you succeed beyond your wildest dreams, you could find yourself doing business in unexpected markets, with unexpected competitors and an unexpectedly high profile.

Other Legal Angles

Some other information that can help you:

Filing your business name

You usually don't have to deal with any special filing requirements if you don't incorporate your business and you use your full legal name to identify your business. Thomas C. Yorkshire Fisheries won't have to bother with any filings if Mr. Yorkshire is an unincorporated sole proprietor and the owner of the business. (The legal form of your business is discussed in detail in Chapter 11.)

However, people who don't incorporate but who use something other than their full legal name to identify their business will have to file fictitious name statements. "Tom's Fishy Business" would have to be registered, as would "Yorkshire Fisheries." That's because these last two names don't give customers (and potential creditors) as much information about who actually *owns* the business as does the first example. The basic rule to keep in mind: if you use only part of your legal personal name as your business name, you have to file that "adapted" name with the state.

If you're incorporated

If you incorporate your business, most states will want that reflected in the official name of the business. Thus, "Sam's Security Systems," if it isn't a partnership, would ac-

People who don't incorporate but who use something other than their full legal name to identify their business will have to file "fictitious name statements."

tually have to be called, "Sam's Security Systems Corporation," "Sam's Security Systems, Limited," or "Sam's Security Systems Incorporated." Abbreviations—Inc. for Incorporated, for example—are generally allowed.

If you're "doing business as"

If Sam (or Samantha) doesn't want that corporate moniker at the end of the business name for everyday use, he or she can also file an assumed name. In fact, every year thousands of business start-ups file "fictitious name statements" or "DBA" (doing business as) notices. You'll have to pay a filing fee, often less than $75, and may also have to pay to publish a notice about the new name in a "general circulation" newspaper—often a publication that exists to

---

Filing a Name Wires You In

A funny thing happens when you file for and publish a notice of your business name: All sorts of people and companies start writing to you, offering their services to help you and your business.

Here's why: When you announce the presence of your business to the state, you also announce the presence of a potential client to a whole bunch of other businesses. Businesspeople read those legal notices or use the services of companies that compile the notices into market lists and mailing lists.

Let me tell you about just some of the mail that I received after filing a "doing business as" form. Among the things people and companies were eager to sell me:

- Accounting services.
- Business credit cards.
- Printing services.
- Advertising services.
- Direct-mail services.
- Mailing lists.
- Business stationery and cards.
- Financial management services.
- Legal services.
- Office-equipment installation.
- Office supplies.
- Computers.
- Computer software.
- Books.
- Magazine subscriptions.
- Filing systems.
- Insurance.
- Delivery services.

The moral: Don't worry about finding experts when you start your business. They—or at least some of them—are sure to find you.

do little other than print such legal notices. You can often get the names of these publications from the office of the local clerk of court, from the state office where you file the name change, or by looking in your local yellow pages under "Newspapers" and calling around to find out which paper offers the lowest prices on legal notices. Figure on spending another $15-$85 for the legal notice.

DBAs are also commonly used for businesses that have an unwieldy or unknown corporate name and a better-known public name. For example, Time Inc. Ventures is better-known for the names it does business as, which include *Parenting* magazine.

What's off limits?

While some phrases are mandatory, others are prohibited or restricted. Don't plan on using such words as "insurance," "trust," "medical," or "bank" in your application unless your business literally can be described by one of these words.

Put it to the test

A good quickie test for the viability of a business name: If it's easy to recognize and pronounce, if it describes some aspect of the business, and if it is unlikely in any way to cause a consumer to confuse the business with an already existing entity, it's probably a good name. (Protecting your rights to that great name is covered back in Chapter 7.)

Going Partners

Chapter 11 dealt with the legal, organizational and tax aspects of different forms of business, including partnerships. Chapter 17 will deal with financial partners who invest money in your start-up in exchange for controlling a share of the business. There is, however, another kind of "partnership": the human partnership of two or more people working together toward the same goal, in this case the goal of running a successful business. This chapter is mostly about the personal, as opposed to legal, considerations of partnerships.

Most of the reasons people give for going into business with a partner instead of going it alone are based on the simple idea that two heads are better than one. Starting a business can be daunting, and a partner can share the burden and contribute ideas that help get things off the ground. One partner can pick up the slack when the other's exhausted, or handle some aspect of the business that the other doesn't enjoy. Two people interested in the same business, but with different skills or specialties, can complement each other, efficiently filling in each other's gaps. Someone who likes to travel to make sales presentations could be a blessing for someone who prefers to keep the office running efficiently. A person who likes the glad-handing aspect of customer relations may be a nice fit for someone who prefers the hands-on work of providing the product or service.

Ken Cosgrove and Zane Carter made just such a partnership. Co-founders of Carter/Cosgrove & Company, an Alexandria, Va., corporate communications and multimedia design and production firm, the pair work off each other's strengths. "In a small firm, you cannot make something solely one person's responsibility, but you can have areas of focus," says Cosgrove. He takes main responsibility for day-to-day management, while Carter focuses on longer-term goals and business objectives. "Together," says Cosgrove, "we're one hell of a businessman."

Picking a Partner

Most often, your potential partner will be someone you already know—a friend, a relative, someone you've worked with, a business contact. It's logical that you'll already know your potential partner: Most people talk about their business with lots of associates before actually starting it, and anyone who's interested in being part of a venture is likely to make the desire known. In many cases, partners are people who have developed the idea for a business together.

On the other hand, if you want a partner but don't have anyone in mind, don't worry—your attorney, accountant or other associates and friends can probably suggest a good one.

Personal Considerations

Your partner could be anyone—depending, of course, on the skills you have and what kind of expertise or background you're looking for in a partner. There's no one clear method, set of questions or "process" to invoke in picking a partner, beyond knowing that the partner is going to be able to make a material contribution to the business in terms of know-how, time or money. However, it is best if he or she is someone you feel confident you will:

- like,
- respect,
- trust,
- understand,
- enjoy talking to, and
- be comfortable spending lots of time with.

These basic emotional or personal issues (as opposed

Most of the reasons people give for going into business with a partner are based on the simple idea that two heads are better than one.

to financial or professional considerations) are a key part of the partnership decision. Chances are that if you and your potential partner can deal with many of the basic issues involved in starting your business with a minimum of conflict and a maximum of understanding, honesty and goodwill, you'll have a good shot at building an effective partnership. And the only way to tell whether you can do those things is to discuss your goals and dreams for the business, and how you wish to work at it, before actually forming a partnership. (Reading Chapter 3 and discussing the issues raised in it is a good exercise for people considering becoming partners.)

Where to Find One

● ●

People make connections with prospective partners through:

- Professional and fraternal organizations.
- In school.
- At professional seminars.
- Other career networking events.
- During trade shows.
- Advertising in the local or trade press.
- Approaching people already in business who could be a good fit.
- Just talking over the fence with neighbors.

The Business Side of the Relationship

Considering some of the nitty-gritty aspects of a partnership should reinforce why it's so important that you find the right person. Issues to consider include:

How you'll split the work

Who's going to take responsibility for what? Few businesses will work efficiently with two people splitting all duties right down the middle. Besides that, one of the goals of a good partnership is to have each person do what he or she's good at—not to split all the responsibilities 50–50.

So, if you're skilled at writing and editing corporate videos, you might want a partner with a strong background in sales or one who has plenty of experience hiring the actors, camera people and other specialists you'll be needing in your business.

A pair of retail partners could divide their duties into

"front-room" and "back-room": One could handle the aspects of the business that customers can see (hiring salespeople, managing displays); the other could take responsibility for areas that may be out of sight but that can never be out of mind—inventories, cash flow, monthly bills.

Who will pay into the company checking account?

Quite simply, who is going to pay how much of the company's expenses? What happens if your estimates of the amount needed for the start-up are wrong and the business needs a first-year cash infusion? Often, two or more people who start a business as "equal" partners will be putting the same amount of money into the business, but it's also possible that one partner will contribute more than the other or that one partner will make an "in-kind" investment of something other than cash—office equipment, for example, or the patent rights to a product. In any case, the amount that each participant is putting into the business, and will put into the business in the future, needs to be spelled out early on. Any noncash contributions will have to be assigned an agreed-upon value. Your accountant or attorney can help you develop a proper agreement, including clauses covering the value of contributions, as part of your business plan. (Accountants and attorneys and their roles are discussed fully in Chapter 14.)

How much money will be taken out of the business and when?

Put another way, how much will you and your partner(s) be paid for your efforts? Partners often simply divide the profits of the business. However, some partners might need something resembling a regular paycheck to cover a mortgage. It is possible for a partner to also receive

Resources

• •

Partnerships are tricky. One book that does a good job of anticipating the legal or professional complications that can result from taking on a partner, whether business acquaintance or close friend or relative, is *The Partnership Book: How to Write Your Own Small Business Partnership Agreement,* by Dennis Clifford and Ralph Warner (Nolo Press). The book takes readers through everything involved in writing their own partnership agreement.

What happens if one partner dies, becomes disabled or just wants to get out of the business?

a salary for work performed. However, you need to be clear on methods of compensation before you're caught up in the middle of running a business.

Who will have access to the company checking account?

If you have a partner, you'll have to decide who can write checks on the business account, and for how much. If you're both comfortable with just one of you having total responsibility for check writing, fine. But it's more likely that each of you will want to know where the money is going. In that case, it will make sense to agree to go over the bills that need to be paid and the checks that need to be written on a regular basis—say, every week or even every few days. Another, probably more manageable, option is to give each of you the power to write checks for small amounts but to require two signatures for payments of more than, say, $250 or $500.

How will you handle decision making?

Even if you've already agreed to divide the day-to-day responsibilities, larger issues will inevitably loom that require joint decision making. If you both agree, no problem—although you could take turns playing devil's advocate and challenging each other's assumptions. But if you disagree, you'll have to find a way to work it out for the good of the company. You'll have to compromise or let the person to whom it means the most make the decision.

Handling the Worst Case

What happens if one partner dies, becomes disabled or just wants to get out of the business? It's only natural to give little consideration in the start-up stages of your business to what will happen if one of your partners will not or cannot continue to participate in the business. But the formative stages are the best time to plan for this theoretical question.

For example, without a written agreement stating your right to buy out the ownership interest of a partner, someone who decides a few years down the road to sell his or her interest in the business could sell it to anyone.

Buying Out a Partner

Your partnership agreement should include a clause giving you first crack at buying out a partner who wants to sell or who can no longer work in the business. This is usually called the right of first refusal. If there are more than two partners, all partners should have the right to buy equal shares of another partner's interest. The agreement should also specify how the buyout price will be paid (for example, 25% up front with the remainder to be paid over several years). Again, the attorney helping you decide the form of your business can draft the proper language for these cases.

In the Event of Death

If a partner dies, things get a little trickier: Your partner's share of the business usually will be passed (through the partner's will or under state law) to his or her heirs—usually a spouse or children. Everything you've heard about the problems of going into business with relatives goes double for being unwittingly thrown into business with a partner's relatives. That's why it's important to have an advance agreement that requires the estate of a deceased partner to sell the partner's interest to the remaining partners or to give the remaining partners the right of first refusal.

The agreement will also, of course, require the remaining partners to buy the shares that the deceased owned, and it may specify how the value of the deceased partner's interest will be determined.

A buy-sell agreement

Here's how such an arrangement, known as a buy-sell agreement, usually works: When drawing up the agreement, you and your partners, working with your accountant, establish a method for setting a price on the business.

If your partner dies, his or her share of the business usually will be passed to heirs—usually a spouse or children.

Most businesses rely on formulas using book value or some multiple of the business's earnings or sales. It's also possible to pick a fixed dollar amount, but if you go with a fixed price you should review it regularly to take into account changes in the direction and value of the business.

One of two basic buy-sell agreements is typically activated if a partner dies. In both agreements, the money for the purchase comes from insurance policies on the lives of the co-owners. This makes funds available to the surviving partner(s) without their having to borrow. One advantage of insurance policies is that the face value of an insurance policy can easily be adjusted upward as the business grows to reflect the increased value of the business.

"I told you: you marry me, you marry the company!"

Bart, Cartoonists & Writers Syndicate

A cross-purchase agreement

In a cross-purchase agreement, each partner takes out an insurance policy on the other's life. If a business is valued at $500,000, for example, each partner will purchase a $250,000 policy. The partner buying the policy is named as the beneficiary and can use the proceeds from the policy to buy the deceased partner's share of the business from the estate.

If you only have one partner, a cross-purchase plan is an easy way to go. With lots of partners, though, cross-purchasing can be tough: If you start a partnership with ten other people, for example, you would have to buy ten policies—and each partner would also have to buy ten policies!

A stock redemption agreement

In a stock redemption agreement, the corporation, rather than a partner, is listed as the beneficiary of the insurance policies on the lives of the partners. The corporation then pays the proceeds from the life insurance policy to the deceased partner's estate in exchange for his or her share of the business.

My Partner, My Spouse

One of the most common partnerships is between two people who are already partners in another respect—couples who start businesses together.

Even though spouses who are also partners already share affection, respect, trust and understanding—all traits of good partnerships—the second merger can still be as emotionally and logistically tricky as the original one.

J. Michael Martin and Mary E. Martin had spent 23 years building a life together but working separately—financial firms for him, a double-duty shift of raising four children and teaching for her. Then they switched gears and together started Financial Advantage, a financial-planning and publishing firm that has produced products including "Billpayer" and "The Financial Planning Organizer." The change in roles and routines took some getting used to. "I'd always been very fortunate that all I had to do was handle my job and Mary had taken all the pressures and responsibilities of raising a family," remembers Michael Martin. "Then all of a sudden we had new corporate roles, and we had to have a lot more clarity about tasks and divisions of responsibilities, figuring out who had to handle different aspects of the business. There were even things we didn't recognize about each other at first. It started when we went to buy furniture and found that, at least in terms of business decor, our tastes were different."

Address the Issues

The Martins successfully negotiated their new business relationship, and their marriage and business thrived.

When spouses go into business together, the second merger can be as emotionally and logistically tricky as the original one.

Do each of you see the other as equally important to the success of the business?

Such happy endings, while not universal, are also not unusual. Despite all the talk about how hard it is to work with the one you love, business partnerships between husbands and wives can and often do succeed. Even so, any couple contemplating this second great leap of faith needs to enter the venture with eyes wide open—just like the first time around. Among the things to consider:

- **Sharing your bed is one thing.** How do you feel about sharing decision-making responsibilities for ventures outside the home?

- **Can you separate your business discussions and battles from your home life?**

- **Do you have trouble just deciding where to go to dinner?** Or, have you worked well in the past in making decisions on such things as how and when to buy a house, or in taking on a project like planting a garden?

- **Have either of you had experience making business decisions before?** Prior experience never hurts.

- **Do you have complementary skills, talents and temperaments** that are going to be useful in your joint venture?

- **Do you each recognize areas in which one of you is more skilled than the other,** and are you willing to give each party the responsibility—that is, the power—for that area?

- **Is your business venture a fervent and shared dream,** or is one of you pulling the other one along? It's not necessary that you be equally possessed by the vision, but you should each want the venture to succeed and should understand the other's hopes, fears and desires.

- **Do each of you see the other as equally important** to the success of the business? People who are partners in a business don't want to be taken for granted any more than people who are partners in a marriage.

The Martins decided to divide responsibilities and power within their business: Mary became president of the publishing side; Michael became president of the financial-planning side. The Martins discuss possible projects for their publishing arm, but all final decisions in that area rest with Mary.

Again, you don't have to have the exact same attitudes, skills or even authority within the business. What is important, though, is that both of you are clear about what you want from each other and from the business. "There's so much you learn about yourself and each other," says Michael Martin. "It really forces you to grow."

One way to clarify the issues is to read Chapter 3 together, focusing on why each of you wants to start a business,

> ## *A Great Idea for Anyone*
> •
>
> Long before J. Michael and Mary Martin created their financial-planning and publishing business, they began keeping an idea file. The Martins had a folder they informally called "the business" that grew fat with clippings—business ideas, tips on running a business, publishing industry news and anything else related to their goal of running a business together—which they each contributed over several years. By the time they made their shift, there was no doubt the new venture was something that they both wanted.

why you want to do it together and what your goals are.

Cousin—Cuisine

Going into a partnership with a relative other than a spouse can be tempting, but it may be even less of a sure thing. In the best cases, of course, a family-staffed business can be an entrepreneur's dream, with motivated, dedicated and loyal people working together to make a vision become reality, or even to extend it beyond the business founder's wildest imaginings.

This dream really can happen. The Brennan family of New Orleans (introduced in Chapter 12) has garnered national fame for its restaurants, led by Commander's Palace. Four Brennan brothers and sisters, operators of Commander's Palace, gradually introduced the next generation to the restaurant business through part-time and summer jobs. (Dick and Bradford, co-founders of the Palace Café (mentioned in Chapter 12) eventually crossed over to management positions at Commander's Palace.)

*"Don't hire relatives
...that's like civil
service. You can't fire
them."*

Many of those children, now adults, have started their own restaurants, in partnership with either siblings or cousins. In New Orleans' French Quarter, several restaurants are now run by the next generation of Brennans, all operating on their own but benefiting from the experience of their elders.

Just as often, though, personal family conflicts can spill over into a business, and business problems can sour previously strong blood relationships. It's hard enough for someone working for himself for the first time to run a business and manage any staff members; trying to simultaneously manage personal relationships can qualify as an unfair burden, especially if relatives are not on golden terms to begin with. Emotional baggage from family relationships can get carried into the business relationship, making it tough to decide any issue involving a relative.

It's easy to suffer misunderstandings with relatives, as most of us know. When that happens in our personal lives, there's an emotional price to pay. But when it happens in our professional lives, the costs can be emotional and financial. As the owner of a printing company said: "Don't hire relatives...that's like civil service. You can't fire them."

Even the successful Brennans have had their disagreements: In the early 1970s, conflicts about the direction of the business and the best way to manage it split the family. Family members are polite and circumspect about the dispute; suffice it to say that by the time the dust had cleared from that long-ago but still seldom-discussed feud, one group was no longer involved with Commander's and instead had full control of Brennan's, the family's original restaurant, which also continues to prosper.

Of course, you needn't have a legal partner to get the support and expertise you lack. You can, in effect, hire a partner by the hour. That's what the next chapter discusses.

The
Good Guys

You may be able to single-handedly do everything associated with running a small business. You may be able to keep your own financial records, do your own taxes, negotiate and review your own contracts. Somewhere in there, you may even find time to serve your own customers and make your own coffee.

But chances are that at some point (and probably early on) you're going to need some help—financial assistance, tax counseling or legal advice. Turning to other people for assistance may seem like the last thing you want to do if one of the reasons you're starting your own business is to gain a greater degree of independence in your professional life. But you'll find that advisers like bankers, accountants, and attorneys —some of the people we refer to as "The Good Guys"—can do far more to liberate you than to pin you down.

Since all these professionals are dedicated full time to keeping on top of their respective fields, they can actually give you more freedom, namely the freedom to focus on other aspects of the business you're starting. Other people familiar with the business field you're entering, or with start-up concerns in general, can also help you at the beginning and become part of *your personal brain trust.* These are all people you may turn to when you're trying to get off on the right foot by setting up your business properly and avoiding long-term problems, and as you grow and encounter new opportunities and challenges.

What follows is a discussion of some people you can ask for help, and explanations of what they can do for you and your venture.

Bankers

When we talk about bankers, what we really mean are loan officers—the folks you'll probably be seeing if you decide you need to borrow from the bank. But getting a banker on your side should start, ideally, before you ever apply for a loan.

This is important because initially bankers probably won't know much about you or your business. Unless a local banker is your friend or social or business acquaintance, he or she isn't going to know anything about your background, how your business works, how you make your money or what you do on a day-to-day basis. Often, he won't know if he can give you a loan even if he wants to; that's because your loan may have to go through his boss or a loan committee for approval before he can give you any good news.

"Your accountant won't be able to bail you out this time, Mr. Potter."

From the Wall Street Journal, Permission—Cartoon Features Syndicate

Because of everything they don't know, bankers will ask you to fill out pages of what may seem like meaningless (or incredibly personal) forms before even considering a loan. Those forms yield a wealth of financial information about you. Bankers like them precisely because bankers *know* how much they *don't* know.

What a banker knows, however, includes plenty that could help your business—little things like:

• **whether your business plan makes sense;**

• **whether your cash-flow projections are realistic;**

• **which experts**—accountants, lawyers and others—could help you;

- **what the outlook is for development in your locale** and for the business climate in general;

- **where you might look for potential clients;**

- **what you can do to make your business most attractive** if you ever need to apply for a loan.

Some banks actively recruit small business accounts; others can't be bothered.

Where to Find a "Good Banker"

Finding the right banker isn't easy. There are no set rules on where "good" bankers (that is, bankers who will understand the needs and concerns of entrepreneurs like yourself) are located. Some banks actively recruit small business accounts; others can't be bothered. Some banks periodically offer or sponsor small-business educational workshops, but such sponsorship doesn't necessarily indicate greater willingness to lend to small businesses. Small local or regional banks often are perceived as being more interested than big banks in smaller loans and accounts, but that isn't always the case: One employee in the local office of a major, multibillion-dollar West Coast bank where I keep an account has gone out of her way to tell me about borrowing opportunities if I want to expand my present business or start a new one. If I ever want a loan, you can bet I'll be checking with that bank first.

One thing's for sure: If a prospective banker expresses a strongly negative opinion of your type of business—perhaps because he or she has been burned on loans to businesses like yours—keep looking.

Maximizing the Benefit

To get the most you can from your banker:

- **Think of him or her as a team member.**

- **Talk to the banker about your endeavor** and see whether he or she has any ideas or recommendations.

- **Have your banker review your business plan** and visit your business to see what you do and how you do it.

- **Stay in touch and let the banker know what's happening** with your business. That's true even if the news is bad—better for the banker to hear it from you than through the local grapevine. (And bankers, remember, are people who generally hate surprises—hence, those forms.)

- **You could even take your banker to lunch.** I know one woman who owns her own business and who takes her banker to lunch once a month, whether or not she's doing any business with him at the time. Does it make a difference when she needs a loan? "I'm sure it doesn't hurt," she says. "I have his undivided attention for an hour and can use that time to tell him everything good that's happening with my business and to learn anything about the bank or business in general that he can share with me."

Other related factors to consider are covered later in this chapter.

Accountants

Many people who work for themselves need at least basic assistance in keeping track of the financial side of their business. That can mean professional help in preparing their tax returns or in setting up a bookkeeping system.

Working With Your Advisers

Here are tips for making the most of your team of outside experts:

- **Batch your questions,** rather than calling your adviser each time a question arises.

- **Teach your adviser about your endeavor.** Send her copies of your brochures, newsletters, price sheets, ads, and so on.

- **Include her on your list of people to "copy"** with pertinent memos. Invite her over for a visit or a tour.

- **Ask for your adviser's point of view** on any important decision, and if you're going to ignore her advice, tell her why.

- **If you don't understand what you're being told, say so.** Ask for whatever interpretation or explanation that you need.

- **If you don't like the service you're getting,** say so or find someone new.

- **Avoid giving your adviser "garbage-bag" projects.** Disorganized messes cost her time and you money.

Others want more sophisticated financial analysis, with someone to prepare and interpret spreadsheets and pie charts showing profit centers, cash flows or various financial ratios. Either way, enter the accountant.

Far More Than Bookkeeping

Yes, your accountant can do your annual tax return. But a good accountant can also:

- advise you on how to put together a record-keeping system that you can live with for a long time.

- help select or train bookkeepers.

- keep track of your income, payroll, accounts receivable and payable, and other expenses.

- learn the ins and outs of your business.

- develop an overall accounting system.

- help develop your business plan and secure any outside financing.

- prepare financial statements when you are applying for a loan.

- prepare regular reports, such as profit and loss statements, ideally using customized forms that reflect the needs of your venture.

- prepare special reports, including, for example: break-even analyses; years-at-a-glance comparisons that can help you identify trends in your business; "client comparisons," comparing your business with similar ones; feasibility studies for using new technology; tax-consequence and cost-reduction evaluations.

- advise you on longer-term business investment or tax strategies.

- advise you on personal financial-planning strategies.

- help set up personnel plans, including retirement savings programs.

Self-employed people may at least want to find a public accountant who is also an enrolled agent in case of an audit.

- work with you, your attorney and other consultants to draft contracts and leases and determine necessary insurance coverage and other business expenses.

- recommend bankers and attorneys who specialize in working with small businesses and the self-employed.

What Flavor?

Should you go with a big firm or a small guy like yourself? Most people starting their own business won't need all the services of a nationally known accounting firm. Usually, most of the initial needs of the newly self-employed can be met by a part-time bookkeeper, or by an accountant who is paid on an hourly basis for assistance and advice. If you need a full-time accountant or the services of a large, full-service accounting firm after your business is established and growing, you can switch to the more expensive assistance then. There's no reason to lay out big bucks at the beginning for services you don't need.

Accountant or CPA?

Should you work with "just" an accountant or with a certified public accountant (CPA)? There are two considerations here:

- **If you expect to create a business with the help of a bank or outside investors,** you may be required to produce certified financial statements; many states require that those statements be prepared by a CPA (an accountant or your state's department of commerce can advise you on this).

- **If you are ever audited,** only an attorney, a CPA or an enrolled agent—a public accountant or a tax practitioner (who may not have an accounting degree or certification) who has met tough IRS standards—may represent you at both the audit and any appeals. Self-employed people who don't need the more sophisticated and often more expensive help of a CPA may at least want to find a public accountant who is also an enrolled agent. You'll find that many are.

Comfort level

No matter what kind of help you get, you should get it from someone with whom you feel comfortable discussing personal financial issues. You'll be sharing all your financial information with your accountant, and talking about money is tough under the best of circumstances; it can be a minor form of torture if you're not at ease with the people advising you.

Attorneys

You know 'em, you don't always love 'em, but in today's litigious environment you can't live without 'em. That's especially true when you're embarking on a business venture. Just look at some of the other chapters in this book: Chapter 7, on protecting your idea; Chapter 11, on what form your business should take; and Chapter 12, on

Questions for Attorneys and Accountants (and Other Experts)

Even though your attorney and accountant are going to be part of your team, you should remember to interview prospects as you would any employee or vendor. Among the questions worth asking:

- **What, exactly, have you done for clients whose businesses are similar** in size or type to mine? Can you give me names of clients I can talk to about your work?

- **How long have you been practicing** in this area of law or accounting?

- **How do you keep up** with tax or legal changes that could affect my business?

- **Who do you turn to** for help with issues outside your area of expertise?

- **What specific services can you provide—** for the money I can afford to pay?

- **What are your fees?** (I've had accountants quote me rates of anywhere from

$40 to $150 an hour and attorneys offer their services for as little as $50 an hour or as much as $390.)

- **How would I pay you**—hourly fees? an annual contract? a contract as well as hourly fees?

- **What can I do to keep your fees to a manageable level?** Are there simple things—organize my files in a particular way, or make copies of all the paperwork I'm giving you, for example—that will reduce the amount of time you need to spend on my business? (Note: Ordinary services can be strikingly high when provided by law firms. It's not unheard of for a law firm to charge 50 cents apiece for the same photocopies that you can make for a dime at a corner copy store.)

naming your business cover issues that can involve major consultations with lawyers. Just about every regulation you must obey, every form you must fill out and every law you must follow will require an attorney's help. The legal profession, in fact, can affect every business decision from hiring your first employee to selling out someday.

Aside from his or her formal legal duties, an attorney can, like the other Good Guys in this chapter, act as advis-

Other Sources of Help

Several kinds of organizations can help you get started and keep moving, including:

Trade & professional associations

Joining an association composed of other businesses in your field will give you an instant network of information and will help you learn how other people in the field—your competitors—are handling their businesses. The organization can be a business, trade or professional association, a local chamber of commerce, or a service organization such as the Jaycees or Kiwanis.

Many trade associations offer newsletters, books and courses to help their members; most also collect financial and business data about all other members of their association, giving you an overall view of the entire industry. (Ways of learning more about your business and industry are also discussed in Chapter 8.)

Consultants

There's an entire industry made up of businesses that specialize in offering general consulting services to small businesses. Subject these folks to the same questions as shown on page 187 to ensure that they're worth their fees—which can be substantial. You'll find small business consultants listed in the Yellow Pages under Management Consultants or Business Consultants.

Service Corps of Retired Executives (SCORE)

A good starting place for anyone looking for outside help is this program of the U.S. Small Business Administration (also mentioned in the first section of this book). In 1994 about 283,000 people tapped the expertise of 13,000 retired businesspeople who volunteered to counsel budding entrepreneurs and business operators.

Many clients come to our volunteer counselors armed simply with an idea for a small business or a product," says SCORE executive director W. Kenneth Yancey, Jr. "We help them focus on business management issues, such as marketing, financing and personnel. Counselors will help entrepreneurs discover whether they have the resources and commitment to make the business succeed or whether their product has a market. In doing that, many times we help potential business owners decide not to go into business for themselves."

Helping people decide that they really don't want to be in business for themselves is, of course, a valuable service. For those who do want to work for themselves, though, SCORE offers not just its couner and teammate. For openers, an attorney well connected in the local business community may know good accountants, bankers and insurance agents. (By now, you see how all these people can be intertwined.) An experienced business attorney has probably seen most of the problems that start-ups encounter and could also help you (eventually) with dilemmas ranging from how to attract investors for expansion to how to collect on bad debts.

selors, who will be of varying expertise and experience, but also a series of SCORE-sponsored business-planning workshops. The workshops, offered at different times nationwide, typically cost $25 or less and can help people focus ideas for their business. It's also possible for entrepreneurs to be introduced to a banker, lawyer or other professional through these workshops or through a counseling session.

For more information, contact the Small Business Administration's district office in your area (check the government, or blue, pages of your local phone book, or call the national SCORE office at 800–634–0245).

Networking and brainstorming groups

These may be advertised only through word of mouth or announcements in your local newspaper. Typically over breakfast or lunch, entrepreneurs share idea generating and problem solving, "war stories" and successes with other people working for themselves. If you can't find such a group, try creating one yourself. It could be an exciting source of advice and support.

The Enterprise Corporation of Pittsburgh

This is a nonprofit corporation (4516 Henry Street, Suite 201, Pittsburgh, PA 15213; 412–578–3481) affiliated with Carnegie Mellon University and the University of Pittsburgh. The corporation can help entrepreneurs develop their business plans and can also recommend legal, accounting and tax advisors. There's no charge for Enterprise's services, although a donation—usually in the form of what the corporation calls "a very small equity position"—is requested if the services add to the success of your venture.

Other entrepreneurship or small business programs

Many universities around the country have instituted these programs, including Baylor (Waco, Tex.), the Massachusetts Institute of Technology, the University of Wisconsin, George Mason University (Fairfax, Va.), and many others. Most of the 56 Small Business Development Centers, counseling services that get funding from the SBA, are located at colleges and universities. Check with the business school of your local or state college and with your nearest SBA office.

*Ask for referrals
to appropriate
professionals from
your family lawyer,
accountant or banker.*

Looking for Your Good Guys

Probably the best way to start looking for people who can help you is to ask other people who are self-employed or running small businesses similar to your own. Ask the owners about their experiences with bankers, lawyers and accountants. Try to get specific referrals. Ask in which areas a recommended professional has been most helpful or least useful, and try to get beyond endorsements based on someone's winning personality.

"If you or members of your family already have a lawyer, accountant or banker for personal matters, you may have a leg up on finding help for your business matters. Even if the family attorney or tax accountant isn't equipped to handle your business needs, these professionals may be able to refer you to colleagues who can. Similarly, the lender to whom you went to when you needed a home loan may not be the right person for a business loan, but you could get a referral to another, more appropriate banker. At least, it can't hurt to ask.

Big or Small?

There seems to be a never-ending debate about whether small businesses should turn to large firms or small ones for their advisers. Here are some factors to consider, in brief:

- **Bigger firms tend to be better known.** If you are trying to establish the credibility of your own firm with lenders or other professionals, you may feel that having consultants from large, established firms on your side will help. But there are, obviously, no guarantees.

- **Bigger firms have a variety of experts and specialists** to focus on any esoteric areas that affect you. On the other hand, a small firm or independent lawyer or accountant specializing in self-employed and small-business clients may be more familiar with your needs on a day-to-day basis.

- **Smaller firms and individual practitioners should, in theory, be able to give you more personal treatment** than a large firm. However, an overworked individual practitioner isn't going to be able to give much personal attention to any of his clients.

- **A smaller firm may care more about your business** than a large, multimillion-dollar firm because your account represents a larger portion of a small firm's total revenues.

- **A smaller firm can often deliver service just as good** as that of a big firm.

Don't see a clear choice? That's because there's no hard-and-fast rule as to what size firm is best for small businesses. Just make sure you're comfortable with the individual who is *directly responsible* for your account and works with you regularly. If you're happy with him or her, you'll probably be happy with the firm as well.

Just make sure you're comfortable with the individual who is directly responsible for your account and works with you regularly.

CHAPTER

15

Staffing Up

When you start working for yourself, your business's organizational chart may be simple: At least to start with, your name will probably appear in all your organizational slots—president, CEO, sales manager and representative, chief cook and bottlewasher, etc.

For many self-employed people, one of the secrets of success is to *not* take on additional staff as they become more established. Many businesspeople go it literally alone, or nearly alone, for their entire careers. Richard Biggs, for example, began an automobile leasing company in 1982, running it successfully on his own into the 1990s. He built his business with no employees or assistants, save one person who fills in for him occasionally when he's away from his Roswell, Ga., office. "The business is me," Biggs says. "I didn't want to take on several employees, add a bunch of overhead, and wind up spending all of my time dealing with people's problems and whatnot when I could use that time efficiently running a business instead."

Technology is also, for better or worse, eliminating the need for operators of small enterprises to hire help. Instead of having someone answer your telephone when you're out, you can buy an answering machine or subscribe to one of the automated answering systems offered by regional telephone companies. Anyone who can type can now turn out clean, error-free letters on a word processor. Optical scanners allow people with personal computers to transfer documents—anything from legal memos to books—directly into the computer system, without typing. Laptop computers make it possible for you to take virtually any written documents with you when traveling and refer to them or modify them on the road. On-line data services permit people to find out what's been written in hundreds of current periodicals, and to get copies of stories of interest, all with the use of a computer and modem and without having to trek to the library.

Even so, technology has not eliminated the need for all workers (something we can all be thankful for), and at some point when you need flesh-and-blood help, you'll have to make some tough decisions.

- **Just how much help do you need and want?** Do you want someone to take on the tasks you don't like or aren't good at? Or are you looking for enough people to do all the work involved in running the business? In that case, you'd be a manager, or "just" a manager. Do you want that, or do you want to be heavily involved in the daily work of the business?

- **What can you afford?** Do you have the money for full-time help, part-time help or short-term contractors? On the other hand, can you afford not to hire the help that you need?

You could try to get along doing everything on your own. Then, you could wind up putting in 16-hour days, seven days a week. Do you want that? If you do find yourself regularly working 100-hour weeks, you're probably getting a solid sign that you need some help. Either that, or you *don't* need friends, a good family life, hobbies or sleep. Your business might survive for a while with that approach, but you're likely to burn out over time—and that could be the death of your business. (See also Chapter 26, "Managing Yourself and Managing Others.")

If you anticipate seeking financing, it's a good idea to decide early on how much staff you'll be hiring and when.

Can you afford not to hire the help you need?

Where a lack of time intersects with a lack of desire or knowledge, you're most likely to benefit from hiring someone.

Staff salaries will be part of the drain on your cash flow, and potential lenders or investors will want to know what payroll obligations you're going to have. (Tactics for getting start-up funds are discussed in Chapter 17.)

Assess Your Needs

Even if you won't require outside money, it still makes sense to think hard about how much help you'll really need when you first start your business. Try this simple self-assessment. (If you have lots of experience in your choice of business, this exercise will probably be easy for you. If you're a relative novice, you'll have to pick other, more-experienced people's brains to get the information you need.)

First, do your best to identify all the tasks involved in starting and running your venture. Estimate how much time each will take, in hours, days or weeks. You can list them together in categories such as administrative, sales, purchasing, production, whatever you think fits *your* business. Then, highlight those tasks that you would—or wouldn't—enjoy doing yourself.

Obviously, if the time needed to operate your business exceeds the time you can spend working, you're going to need some help. Where a lack of time intersects with a lack of desire or knowledge (specialized skills or technical expertise), you're most likely to benefit from hiring someone.

When Will It Pay to Hire Someone?

No one wants to spend money hiring someone who is going to cost more than he's worth—that is, someone who is not going to help increase your profits by at least as much as he is paid.

Sometimes, it's easy to figure out whether it pays to hire someone. Let's say you're manufacturing beach blankets that you sell to retail shops for $8 apiece. Of the $8 you charge, $4 is profit for your company.

Now, let's say you think you could sell a lot more blankets if you had someone working for you whose job was to do nothing but sell blankets to retailers. So you hire a sales representative who will cost you $28,000 a year, including the salary, taxes and benefits you'll have to pay. (Let's also assume, for the sake of simplicity, that the additional employee doesn't add anything to your overall manufacturing or overhead costs beyond his or her salary and benefits.)

If your rep is able to sell at least 7,000 more blankets a year than would otherwise have been sold, he will have increased your profits by $28,000 (7,000 blankets multiplied by $4 in profit per blanket.) Beach Blanket Bingo! Your new hire has earned for you as much as you're paying him. Any blankets he sells over that 7,000 threshold represents additional profits for you.

Unfortunately, most hiring decisions are not so cut-and-dried. When hiring most support staff, you won't be able to establish a direct costs-benefits relationship. Instead, you'll have to think about whether this person will be "worth" it to you in terms of the time you save and the duties you can delegate. If an administrative assistant doesn't produce any additional revenue for you but relieves you of duties you find unbearably boring and releases you to do the things that make the business a success, then that person may well be worth hiring. Sometimes you have to spend money to make money; spending money on help with routine matters can free you to make money by producing or selling your product or service.

You have to make the decision. One thing that can help: Return to the beginning of this book (at least mentally if not physically) and consider again what it is you do and don't like in work and in business. If you can afford to hire someone to do the work you don't enjoy, you will probably be happier, and more successful, in your business.

The Real Cost of Help

You'll have the usual options available to you in terms of paying your help: hourly wages, flat fee per project, salary, base salary plus commission, commission only, and bonuses based on profit. But you can't stop after determining how much you'll pay that person directly. Among the other monetary costs of staffing up:

Spending money on help with routine matters can free you to make money by producing or selling your product or service.

Social security taxes

Formally known as FICA (Federal Insurance Contributions Act) taxes, these are paid in equal amounts by employers and full- or part-time employees (as opposed to independent contractors, who pay their own FICA taxes). In 1995, these taxes would have cost you an additional 7.65% of the first $61,200 of salary you pay to an employee, and 1.45% of any additional pay for the medicare portion of social security. (Rates and maximums may change.)

Workers' compensation and unemployment taxes

You don't just pay for employment, you also pay for *un*employment—federal and state unemployment taxes, as well as workers' compensation taxes. The amount of these taxes can vary from state to state; talk with your accountant or tax planner about them.

Employee benefits

Are you going to give your employees an annual paid vacation? How about health insurance? Tuition benefits? Life insurance? A parking allowance? Company benefit plans range from the nonexistent to the gold-plated. Obviously, a generous benefits plan is going to be very attractive to potential employees. Just as obviously, such a plan may be impractical for a start-up. You'll have to decide just how much you are willing and able to spend on benefits for employees. (The U.S. Chamber of Commerce, by the way, estimates that employee benefits packages are worth more than one-third of the amount that established companies spend on salaries; that is, the benefits package for someone earning $30,000 is likely, on average, to be valued at more than $10,000.)

Other overhead

Your employees may need office space, telephones, parking spaces, typewriters, computers, stationery, pens...the list goes on and on. Again, try to consider the *total* cost of additional help when you make your hiring decisions.

Alternatives: Part-Time, Contract and No-Cost

Even if you do need to bring other people on board, you don't necessarily have to put classified advertisements in the newspaper and set about hiring full-time help. There's more than one way for a start-up to staff up.

Among your options:

Part-time help

Especially in the early stages of your venture, you may not need to employ anybody on a full-time basis. A part-time secretary might be sufficient, for example. Since one of your goals as a start-up is to keep your initial costs low, it makes sense to err on the side of caution and hire people part-time if you aren't sure that there will be enough work to justify full-time staff, salary and benefits packages.

In fact, most jobs can be assigned on a part-time basis as easily as on a full-time one. If the work load later turns out to be more than a part-timer can handle, you can expand the job as needed or bring on additional help. You'll find that people interested in part-time work are probably also interested in flexible schedules.

College students can be an excellent source of part-time help. They may also be available to you as interns for work related to their course of study. These can be either paid positions, in terms of money or school credits, or unpaid. Check with the most likely academic department at your local college or university, but keep in mind that some schools frown on unpaid internships.

You have other options besides students, too. There are plenty of people out there who have skills, professional backgrounds and lots of experience who don't want to work full time. They include parents with young children, retirees and people who want to devote some of their time to other interests—an avocation, going back to school, or even starting a business. With luck, you'll find someone who is more interested in being useful and practicing their skills than in earning "big bucks."

With luck, you'll find someone who is more interested in being useful and practicing their skills than in earning "big bucks."

Contract or free-lance help

Starting up often entails sporadic needs for help. For example, if you're trying to build your client list, you might need someone who can write effective sales brochures and letters to prospective clients. But once you've secured those clients, your need for an on-staff writer or sales assistant will disappear. Similarly, you may need someone to set up an effective computerized filing system, but you will be able to handle the routine filing and maintenance yourself afterward.

Enter the contractor. For most jobs and professions, there are people—small-business people like yourself, in fact—who hire themselves out on a contract or free-lance basis. They have a service they can provide, in the form of their specialized labor or knowledge. Those people give you tremendous flexibility: You can hire them by the job, when you need them, and keep your overall expenses as low as possible. You don't even have to pay the employment taxes and benefits that you would incur with employees, because independent contractors are responsible for their own taxes and benefits.

Many of the lawyers, accountants and other professionals providing specialized services for specific fees are, in effect, free-lancers and contractors, although they usually don't describe themselves that way.

Just calling someone an independent contractor when they are, in effect, an employee—say, to avoid having to the employer's portion of his or her social security taxes—won't cut it if the arrangement comes under IRS scrutiny. Ask yourself these questions if you're unsure of someone's status:

Where to Advertise

• •

Other options worth considering include:

- Listing an opening with the employment service of the trade association that represents your business.

- Advertising in specialized journals or other such publications.

- Letting friends and associates know you're looking for names of potential employees.

- Posting notices at local colleges and universities. Virtually every school has a job placement or career services office for its soon-to-be, recent and not-so-recent graduates. These can be good places to list jobs even if you're not hiring during the May-June graduation season.

- **How much control do you have over when, where and how the person works?** The more control you have, the less likely he or she is an independent contractor.

- **How much risk for loss does the worker have?** An independent contractor is as likely to suffer loss as profit by association with your enterprise. An employee would probably incur no risk.

- **How often and for how long has the person worked for you?** The more frequently and the longer the person works for you, the more likely he or she is your employee.

Family and friends

Don't overlook this option if you have only an occasional need for help. Ask your loved ones to pitch in when stuffing envelopes once a month, handing out brochures at a mall or sporting event, cleaning up after a deadline, or manning a table at the county fair or neighborhood festival. Try to convince them it's fun. Tell them they'll have your undying gratitude. If your sincere thanks aren't enough incentive, try pizza and cold drinks.

Need Help Finding Help?

If you decide you're going to need help, there's no shortage of paths to finding workers. One of the most obvious ways, of course, is to advertise in the classified section of your local newspaper. Be forewarned, though: Ads for general office help that are placed in metropolitan newspapers can easily generate more than 200 responses; you could wind up wishing you'd hired someone just to help you hire someone! The burden can seem even bigger if you're only looking for people to work on a short-term or part-time basis.

Employment Agencies

Employment agencies offer relief—for a fee, of course. Ideally, they can provide you with ready-to-go

Classified ads for general office help can generate more responses than you want to deal with.

workers. The agency writes the classified ads, takes in ré-sumés, weeds out and interviews prospects, tests people for any special skills (typing speed, ability to take dicta-tion) that are required, and sends you someone who fits your needs. In fact, agencies usually have lists of part-time and short-term workers they're familiar with, and "temp" agencies specialize in this. So the secretary, file clerk or re-ceptionist an agency sends you has probably not been specifically hired to work for you but is instead someone the agency sends to a series of clients as they call in for short-term help.

You will probably pay a premium for this service—anywhere from 50% to 150% more than the going rate for the job being filled. But that can actually be a small price to pay if you're in a crunch. It's reassuring to know that you can pick up a telephone and have qualified people at your door the next day.

For the start-up, agencies are perhaps most helpful in supplying short-term or temporary help. You can also turn to an agency if you need full-time help. But if you're work-ing for yourself and need full-time help, you could benefit from doing the interviewing and hiring yourself:

- **In the process of reviewing résumés and talking with ap-plicants,** you can also discover new things about what you want in an employee or what needs to be done in your own business.

- **You'll save the fee that an agency would charge** for plac-ing a full-time employee with you—anywhere from several hundred to several thousand dollars.

- **And, by eliminating the middleman, you'll see all your prospects and nab someone you think is just right—** someone the agency might have eliminated. By nature, many agencies must use a sort of fill-in-the-blanks ap-proach, matching résumés to job description. You can be more intuitive, take risks and find that certain someone who won't be limited by her job description.

(continued on page 202)

Moral and Legal Responsibilities in Hiring

There are some basic laws, both codified and moral, to remember as you go about any hiring—or firing. They all boil down, in principle, to one thing: You shouldn't eliminate an applicant from consideration for a job opening just because there's something you don't like about that person that has nothing to do with the job. If you discriminate, you could be sued. In practice, there are limits to these laws, primarily affecting small business, especially start-ups. Many states also have laws concerning discrimination in the workplace (look in the blue pages of your phone book under state government, employment discrimination agency, human rights commission, or department of labor).

- **You should not refuse to hire people based on their race, sex or anything else not related to their ability to perform a job.** Title VII of the Civil Rights Act of 1964 prohibits employment discrimination based on race, color, religion, sex, national origin or pregnancy. Businesses with fewer than 15 employees are not bound by Title VII. Many states also have antidiscrimination laws.

- **You should not discriminate by refusing to hire people based on their age.** The Age Discrimination in Employment Act of 1967 protects older Americans from unfair treatment in hiring and firing. Businesses with fewer than 20 employees (and employment agencies with fewer than 25 employees) aren't bound by ADEA.

- **You should not discriminate by refusing to hire people who have disabilities.** The Rehabilitation Act of 1973 applies to any employer who receives federal financial assistance. The Americans with Disabilities Act bans discrimination in hiring among all businesses with more than 15 employees. Under ADA, a disability is a substantial physical or mental impairment that limits one or more major life activities such as walking, breathing, hearing, seeing or learning. ADA covers Acquired Immune Deficiency Syndrome (AIDS) and HIV infection.

For more information on ADA and how it is applied, you can request a copy of the *ADA Technical Assistance Manual* from the Equal Employment Opportunity Commission (first copy free, $25 per copy thereafter; EEOC Publications Office, P.O. Box 12549, Cinncinnati, OH 45212; 800–669–3362). This office can provide information about other antidiscrimination regulations, as well.

A good way to keep discrimination laws in mind is to look at them written from another perspective—the perspective of workers who want to know what they can do if employers discriminate against them. One of the most useful books I've found is *Your Rights in the Workplace,* by Dan Lacey (Nolo Press).

Choosing a second in command—whether a near-partner or an office assistant—can require some unexpected calculations.

Who to Hire

There's no hard-and-fast rule about who to hire for any particular job. Your initial instinct may be to hire the most qualified people for every opening, but if you hire someone who's overqualified, he or she is likely to begin looking for new challenges, and a new job, within just a few months.

Many self-employed people find they want to have an employee—even if they have only one employee—who is capable of keeping the business going on his or her own. That can free an owner for vacations, marketing trips, conferences, whatever. Choosing this second in command—whether he becomes a near-partner or is simply a very capable office assistant—can require some unexpected calculations. Business consultant Joe Mancuso, in his book *How To Start, Finance, and Manage Your Own Small Business* (Simon and Schuster), develops a matrix for selecting such a "first mate." This top assistant, he says, can be a combination of either energetic/stupid, energetic/bright, lazy/stupid or lazy/bright.

Obviously, you can eliminate the aides who are stupid...but Mancuso also eliminates from consideration someone who is energetic and bright—characteristics that make this potential aide too much like the typical entrepreneur and too likely to want to run the show himself. Mancuso's top choice for an assistant is one who is bright but lazy. "He works well with the entrepreneur and doesn't try to surpass his energies," says Mancuso.

Organizing Your Help

Whenever you hire someone, you'll want to define clearly what you expect from them. For example, if you're going to need a secretary, you will know pretty much what that secretary will be expected to do, no matter who you eventually hire. Same thing if you'll be needing sales representatives, designers, waiters, truck drivers or other staff. Chances are that you will know exactly what you want because you've already done it yourself.

Don't just carry that knowledge around in your head, though. Put it down on paper. It could take the form of job descriptions and an organizational chart or it could be more of a narrative description. Either way, explain the different tasks that the business has to complete (dealing with customers, ordering supplies, selling product, producing goods or services, keeping tax records, greeting clients, cleaning offices, depositing checks) and show who is responsible for each task (you, your partner, one of your professional advisers, an assistant or other employees).

Usually, tasks are grouped together by what they have in common, and those groupings eventually become job "slots." For example, the tasks of answering the telephone, greeting clients, opening mail and typing letters can be logically grouped together and become the responsibility of someone filling the job slot as your assistant.

The beauty of this exercise is that it will give you a snapshot of your organization. It will reflect how you choose to organize your business, whether as a traditional hierarchy (for example, the pyramid approach with you at the top), a team approach with equally responsible team members, or some other form that you think suits your enterprise. It will show who's doing what and why, who's doing too much or too little, who is or should be communicating with whom, where and how your staff resources could be redistributed, where you need to add extra help, and more. As your business changes, so must your document. That process will give you the opportunity to reassess your staffing needs and your "organization." Keep copies of the various renditions over the years, and you'll have a history of the life of your business.

Documenting your organization on paper gives you the chance to assess who's doing what, how much and why.

Setting Up Shop

In the initial stages of working for yourself, you can probably get by with no expenditures for staff. It is possible in some cases to decide that you'll do a job right by doing it yourself. Of course, this will mean doing *lots* of jobs by yourself, but at this point in the book you already know that.

"It's less likely that you can get by without putting any money into the equipment, office space, and paperwork required to start your business. Even the simplest businesses are going to put some money into start-up expenses; complicated or large-scale manufacturing or retailing businesses can require thousands, even hundreds of thousands, of dollars' worth of capital investment. Now is the time to think of these up-front costs and factor them into an estimate of how much money you'll need to open your doors. (More in-depth information on the nuts and bolts of shopping for and negotiating the prices of your start-up needs is provided in Chapter 21, "Getting Organized.")

A Case of Spinning Down Costs

Dale Plummer and Mary Wellemeyer considered, and reconsidered, those costs when starting their yarn mill in Norwich, Conn. They'd often heard people complain that it had become harder and harder to find high-quality, all-wool knitting yarn as the textile industry declined and mills moved toward acrylics. They knew they wanted to use natural materials to create quality yarns. But quality could be costly: A modern spinning machine could cost $250,000; the total investment in new machinery for a small mill could easily top $1 million. And that didn't even include the cost of the building that would house the operation, or the expense of initial employee salaries, utilities, licenses and other necessities.

Plummer and Wellemeyer didn't have, and couldn't raise, that kind of money. But they knew that in the textile business, old equipment could pack a lot of bang for the buck. So when another New England mill closed down, they seized the moment and bought the machinery they needed—winder, spinning frame, picker and other heavy machinery, some of it dating from the 1920s, none of it less than 30 years old, but all of it serviceable. They negotiated a favorable lease on an aging but sturdy building that had been designed to house heavy industrial equipment. They hired a half-dozen employees, including people with decades of experience in the woolen industry.

By focusing on alternatives to buying new equipment, Plummer and Wellemeyer were able to slash the initial costs involved in working for themselves. Their total start-up costs were still daunting ("the lower six figures," Plummer said) but manageable. Quinnehticut Woolen Co., with its old-time spelling of the state name and attention to quality, was selling its yarns to more than 300 retail stores within a few years of opening its doors. "It's a lot of work and a lot of money to risk, but we know it can pay off," says Plummer.

Plummer and Wellemeyer looked hard for ways to cut what most people would consider high start-up costs. The cost of setting up shop doesn't have to be daunting, however. See the accompanying box for an outline of what it cost me to set up shop.

> ## *Help With the Regulations*
> ●
>
> For information and advice about local, state and federal regulations and licensing requirements, call your **local SBA-affiliated small-business development center** (described in Chapter 8).
>
> SBDCs vary in the services they provide in this regard, from a list of the types of licenses and contact information to individual counseling and help in obtaining necessary permits.
>
> The Maryland SBDC, for example, publishes a *Guide to Business Regulations in Maryland* ($25), which covers zoning, taxes, licenses, regulations and everything you need to know to meet local, state and federal requirements.
>
> Contact your local or regional SBA office (check the government listings or blue pages) or call the SBA Office of SBDCs at 202–205–6766.

General Up-front Costs

Your own up-front expenses will depend on the type of business you're starting, its size, where it's located and other factors. Here's a list of some of the expenses and details that you should be considering at this point. Remember, not all of these items will apply to every start-up:

License and Permits

If you're starting a business, chances are some government agency, somewhere, is going to regulate you. It's likely that you're going to have to apply for, and pay for, a license to do business. Depending on what type of business you're running and where you're located, you might get by with a straightforward business permit. On the other hand, if you're planning to open a large restaurant and nightclub in a mostly residential area, you could need a business license, a zoning variance, a permit to serve food, a liquor license, a health permit, a fire safety permit, and, as they

Small Time: A One-Person Start-up

Here's what it cost me when I started my first business as an independent editorial consultant:

Office rent: $0

I started my business out of my home, setting aside one room exclusively for use as my office. When I needed to meet with clients, I would arrange to see them at their offices or at restaurants.

Personal computer: $1,950

I needed the computer, plus the disks, cables, word-processing programs and other accessories included in the price, to write and rewrite the texts I'd be handling for my clients.

Printer: $550

All that writing and rewriting wouldn't have been much good without a way to transfer it from computer to paper, now would it?

Desk and chair: $300

The desk, for my computer; the chair, for me; both on sale at a nearby independent store specializing in what is loosely defined as "home office furniture."

Filing cabinet: $60

Two-drawer, from a secondhand furniture store.

say on late-night TV, much, much more. Costs of licenses can range from around $100 for a business license to several thousand dollars for a license to serve liquor.

Now is the time to check out the types and costs of licenses you'll need. If you don't have the proper licenses when you start out, you could wind up paying penalties on top of the license costs. You may be able to get the information you need about licenses by talking with your accountant or attorney or by contacting local government offices. Look for headings such as "Licensing and Regulation" or "License and Permits" in your local government telephone listings. Or call city hall, get the number of the person or department handling business licenses, and ask what kind of license or fee is required of someone starting the kind of business you're considering. Another good one-stop source of information is the small business development center (SBDC) nearest you (see the box on page 205).

And don't forget the feds. The federal government has a hand in regulating businesses including interstate commerce, drug manufacturing, meat-product prepara-

Computer paper and ribbons

$70 for a box of 2,500 sheets of continuous-feed paper; $90 for a dozen printer ribbons. Here's an example of how even non-technology-based items can fall in price once there's enough competition: When I started that business, you could get computer paper and ribbons only at computer stores. Now every office-supply store carries these items, which have become as commonplace as the typewriter ribbons and bond paper of previous decades. Today I pay about $16 for the same box of paper and about $30 for the ribbons.

Stationery: $35

For business cards.

Other office supplies: $22

Those included: cork bulletin board, $5; business-card holder, $2; desk lamp, $7; stapler, $3; 12 file-cabinet hanging folders, $5. All were purchased at yard sales. Other miscellaneous office supplies—push pins, notebooks, rubber bands—were just sort of lying around my house, waiting to be used.

Total Cost: $3,077

Not the cheapest start-up in history, but a modest one, to be sure.

tion and investment counseling. Every year, the government publishes thousands of pages of small-print regulations, many of which require businesses to conduct or pass tests on everything from product safety to pollution emissions. Obviously, the vast majority of these regulations won't apply to your little operation, but it will be worth consulting with your attorney to find out which ones do. You may also get information on applicable regulations from a trade group representing businesses like your own, from other businesses like yours, and from the U.S. Small Business Administration. (See also the discussion of SBA's SCORE program in Chapter 14.)

Federal Identification Numbers

If you operate as a sole proprietor and don't hire anyone, you can continue to be known to the federal and state governments by the same number that they have always used to track you—your social security number. But if you operate as a corporation or partnership, or if you hire employees, you'll need to identify your business on tax forms and licenses with a federal employer identification number. Once you do that (by filing Form SS-4, *Application for Employer Identification Number,* with the IRS), you'll begin receiving quarterly and year-end payroll tax return forms. The good news: There is no charge for getting a federal employer identification number.

Rent and Utilities

It's not just the first month's rent you have to take into account. There's also the security deposit and the additional month's rent that may be required as an up-front payment. You'll probably have to pay a deposit to get the electricity, gas and water turned on.

Getting Your Site Shipshape

If you're moving into a modern office in a well-maintained building that already has the features and configurations you need, great: The up-front costs of getting your business location into the shape you want will be minimal.

On the other hand, you may need to lay out some money up front if your business space simply *must* be renovated or modernized—renovations that can range from slapping on a coat of fresh paint to moving interior walls. That presumes that your lease or other contract doesn't require the landlord to pay for such renovations. Figure out these costs now, because you'll have to write the checks before you see your first customer. And don't forget the cost of establishing adequate security, whether a simple alarm system or guard service.

Signs

This isn't such a big deal if you're in a nonretail business. If you have a mall location, the size and type of sign is likely to be determined by mall rules. And local laws may govern the type, style and size of sign you can use. Otherwise, you'll have lots of flexibility and could wind up spending a great deal on a sign that brings in customers. Your zoning board should be able to give you information on "signage" regulations, as should a local merchants' association and, in areas where businesses are near residences, the neighborhood association.

Telephone Service

At the least, you'll have to pay to have service turned on. Depending on the size and type of your business, you might need to have two or more telephone lines installed. Conceivably, you could have one line for your computer modem, one line for your fax machine, and at least one line for yourself. Perhaps you would also want a two-line telephone. This is a more expensive option that would allow you, for example, to speak without interruption with one caller while another leaves a message on your answering machine. People starting businesses that require several telephone lines might even need to ante up the

Local laws may govern the type, style and size of sign you can use.

money for their own business phone system. Features such as call waiting or forwarding, or voice-mail service, may be desirable, too. (The features and prices of telephone equipment and systems change rapidly; you can get up-to-date information by contacting your telephone company and telephone equipment companies; each should be listed in the Yellow Pages. Ask for business services.)

One surprise to get out of the way now: Find out how business phone charges differ from personal phone charges. Many phone companies charge businesses significantly more than individuals for such basic services as local telephone calls.

Gerberg, Cartoonists & Writers Syndicate

Equipment

Filing cabinets, desks, chairs, answering machines, pagers, display stands, cash registers, calculators, computers, copiers, lamps, tools and other hardware, heavy equipment, delivery vehicles—the list of what you could wind up needing depends on your particular business. In any case, you'll have to do some comparison shopping and figure the up-front cost of buying new or used equipment or leasing everything you need for your opening day.

A fax machine is practically a standard piece of business office equipment. You can link it with telephones, copiers and computers. (A "fax board" added to a computer allows you to send files from your computer to someone else's fax machine and to receive faxed transmissions, but it doesn't do you much good if you have to send material from sources other than your computer files.)

Office Supplies

Besides the obvious pens and paper clips, this category can also include such mundane but important details as coffeemakers, small refrigerators and microwave ovens that employees (and you) can use to store and heat lunches.

Property Insurance

If you're leasing your space, you may have to insure its interior—the contents and any improvements. (Leases are covered more fully in Chapter 21.) And you'll want to insure your own property—equipment, supplies, inventory—against theft, fire or other loss. Rates on business property insurance will vary depending on the type of equipment, the location of your business, and the insurer and exact policy you're purchasing. Again, you'll have to do some comparison shopping. Start with the company with whom you have homeowners or renters insurance (some companies offer discounts to customers who purchase more than one kind of policy from them), and then get quotes from competitors as well.

Business and Liability Insurance

In today's litigation-happy society, you will probably want insurance to protect you and your business against lawsuits. Nothing can put a heavier damper on your grand opening than to have a customer step across your threshold, trip, fall, and grab his neck in agony. Anyone who will have customers or clients coming to a business site would be well-advised to have liability insurance; you could be sued even if someone is just walking by your storefront and falls on a cracked sidewalk. Insurance companies can fully inform you about business and liability insurance options.

Business Checking Account and Credit Cards

A relatively minor expense in most cases, but again, something to plan on. A business checking account may cost more than a personal checking account, especially if you're writing lots of checks on the business account. The costs of business credit cards are comparable to those of personal credit cards, but business cards may offer higher

Anyone who will have customers or clients coming to a business site would be well-advised to have liability insurance.

credit limits, more features, and better record keeping. Sole proprietors can even satisfy and simplify their business credit card needs by setting aside one of their bankcards and using it solely for business purposes. (Setting aside one card for business will make it easier for you to keep track of your business charges and will enable you to deduct the cost of that card as a business expense.)

For more specific information about setting up your office or shop, see Chapter 21.

Early Financing, From Seed to Start-up

Money is the engine oil of business—nothing can start without some of it, and nothing can continue to run without it. Run out of oil and your engine will seize up or grind to a fatal halt. Run out of money and—well, you get the idea. Sweat equity will take you just so far.

Most people instinctively know that getting the money together can be a real stumbling block to starting a business. Those who don't soon find out. In fact, they probably find out how hard it is to get money for a new venture the first time they go to a bank and casually inquire about getting a loan to start a business.

Obstacles to getting money can stop you before you get started. But—and this is important—"getting it" is the wrong thing on which to focus initially. Instead, look first at how much money you really need to start your business. Better yet, focus on how *little* money you need to start your business. Then you can think about where the money is going to come from.

Many people do this without even realizing it. If you pursue an avocation without giving up an existing full-time or part-time job, you're probably not thinking in terms of "getting start-up capital." Instead, you're simply working for yourself—consulting or gardening or designing—and minimizing your expenses by working out of your home using the supplies and equipment and tools you already have. That's just fine. Eventually, as your business grows or as you pursue it full time rather than part time, you'll be confronting the expenses of expansion and the need to replace the personal cash flow that was generated by a regular job and paycheck.

What You Need for Business

There are all sorts of formulas for determining the amount of money you need to start your business. In *How to Set Up Your Own Small Business,* author and small-business consultant Max Fallek recommends that you first figure out your direct start-up costs—initial equipment and supplies. Then calculate what you think you'll need to cover early expenses if you anticipate spending more than you'll take in during the first few months—and add an extra 50%. Tally the three figures for your start-up sum. This approach works best if you have a contract or two in hand and can definitely anticipate *some* income during your first few months in business.

"...but on the bright side, you might get a spot on 'America's Funniest Credit Applications.'"

From the Wall Street Journal—Permission, Cartoon Features Syndicate

Let's say you're starting a snowplowing and lawn-care business. You figure you'll need $7,500 for start-up costs (lawn mowers, grass baggers, rakes, shovels, snowblowers, snowplow attachment, fertilizers, office equipment). You also anticipate that your early operating expenses (supplies, advertising, insurance, and so on) will outpace your revenues (based on contracts with an office park and a local townhouse development) by as much as $2,500 before you begin turning a regular monthly profit. (Different aspects of start-up considerations and expenses are covered in Chapters 10, 15, 16 and 21.) In that case, Fallek recommends planning a start-up budget of $11,250:

- $7,500 for direct start-up costs.

- $2,500 for anticipated early revenue shortfalls.

- $1,250, representing a 50% "margin" on the $2,500 anticipated early shortfall.

Fallek's idea is a good one: Plan on needing more money than you think you're going to need. You can't predict what sort of costly, unexpected problems are going to crop up when you start your business. All you can predict is that there *will* be unexpected problems. Extra money in your savings or checking account can spell the difference between making it through an early rocky period and having to give up because your financial cushion was just a little thinner than required to support your venture.

What You and Yours Need to Live

I have my own formula for calculating how much money you will need to begin your venture. It assumes that you won't generate *any* income for a few months and accounts not only for the cost of your business but also for the cost of supporting yourself and your family. After all, you may be willing to eat canned pork and beans until your first client pays up, but what will your family be willing to do? Here's how this approach works:

Step 1

Add up all your "preopening" costs. That means everything you'll need to spend money on before you can honestly say you're ready to start taking on clients or producing goods or selling a product. You may need to rent space, buy equipment and supplies, get licenses and so on.

Step 2

Increase that theoretical amount by 50%. Sorry, but you are bound to inadvertently leave some stuff off your

You may be willing to eat canned pork and beans until your first client pays up, but what will your family be willing to do?

If you start with your Worst-Case Start-Up Cost Scenario, anything that works out better than expected will fill you with encouragement.

list, or underestimate your initial costs. Besides, people tend to underestimate how much *time* they need to start their business—and extra time frequently translates into extra expenses.

There is one way you're permitted to skip this step: If you've already made all the purchases you list in Step 1. If you've done that, you don't need a theoretical pre-opening budget—you've spent it!

Step 3

Figure out three months' worth of your fixed business expenses. This is what your business will cost even if you earn *no* money from it. Include such monthly costs as rent, utilities, advertising and insurance.

Step 4

Figure how much personal income you must generate to support yourself and your family for the first six months of your venture. Go back to the early chapters of this book, where we first discussed your personal financial profile. Add up your family's needs over six months (this presumes you've already pared living expenses as much as is reasonable). Subtract any income you or other members of your household will continue to earn from sources other than your venture and also subtract any savings you can draw on. The difference is another start-up expense.

Step 5

The total of Steps 2, 3 and 4 represents your Worst-case Start-up Cost Scenario. That's the most money you need to start your business. It also represents your *financial comfort level*—not only how much money you have to put into your business but also how much you need so you can live and pay your personal bills in those early months.

If you start from this point, anything that works out better than expected will fill you with encouragement. Better to plan for the worst and be pleasantly surprised than to be overly optimistic and have to scramble the first time something doesn't pan out exactly as planned.

The Psychology of Money

There's no complicated math behind these equations and numbers. By setting aside three months of business expenses against the possibility that you won't generate any revenues for a quarter-year, and by ensuring that you've either saved or will have access to six months' worth of living expenses, you're giving yourself a psychological as well as a financial insurance policy. I've seen people who wanted to work for themselves, who even tried, but who started with very little in the way of a financial cushion—also known as Money in the Bank. Since they had so little to fall back on, they were, from Day 1 of their effort, literally counting the number of days they could continue being self-employed before they'd have to give up. That's no way to start working for yourself. Knowing that it *won't* be a financial disaster if you bring in no money for a month or two will help you to avoid unnecessary panic and to focus on the often gradual process of building a revenue base.

The total amount of money you need for psychological and financial security during your start-up may seem daunting. But remember that this is usually a *worst-case* estimate. You probably won't need the sum you've come up with here. If you take or continue to hold a part-time or full-time job, or have the financial help of a working spouse or other family member, you may find there is no difference between your start-up needs and your financial comfort level; your and your family's income and savings could be enough to permit you to start your business and realize no profits in the initial months. And, in the course of going back to the first section of this book, you may find more ways in which you could, at least temporarily, live on less money than you're used to.

Finally, continuing technological advances and cost cuts in the basic items that many of us need to work for ourselves make it possible to start up for a rel-

Knowing that it won't be a financial disaster if you bring in no money for a month or two will help you to avoid unnecessary panic.

For most people, home-equity loans are among the cheapest ways to borrow money.

atively modest sum—less than you may have thought. Computers with all the firepower many small offices need can now be had for less than $1,500, including software and a printer. Entire offices can be set up for less than people used to pay for a top-of-the-line IBM Selectric typewriter. The second time I bought a printer for my computer, I got one that was four times as fast as my old one, produced better-quality documents, and cost 40% less than the technological dinosaur I formerly used. (You'll find more on setting up shop in Chapters 16 and 21.)

If You Need More Money

If the money you have at hand isn't sufficient, you could borrow what you need. When comparing the possibilities, be sure to consider the cost of borrowing, the date you have to start paying it back, and the amount of your monthly or other payment. Obviously, the ideal scenario for any self-employed person includes the lowest interest rate, lowest fees, least minimum payment and longest delay in beginning repayment. Where can you borrow money for your business? Among the possibilities:

Your Own Resources

Loans based on your own resources include your home, insurance, credit unions, credit cards and retirement plans.

Your home

Second mortgages and home-equity loans are popular ways for homeowners to borrow money, particularly since mortgage interest on your residence is one of the few remaining types of personal interest that you can deduct from your taxable income.

For most people, these loans are among the cheapest ways to borrow money. They can be either fixed- or adjustable-rate loans, and the maximum amount is based on the equity you have in your home. Home-equity loans, also called home-equity credit lines, differ from traditional second mortgages in that they can function like a revolving line of credit. Once approved for a loan, you may borrow part or all of that amount whenever you choose, pay it off, and borrow again as needed up to your credit limit.

The interest rates and fees you'll have to pay for these loans vary from market to market and from lender to lender, so it pays to shop around. Always remember, though, that these loans are secured by your house. If you're unable to repay a second mortgage or home-equity loan, you could wind up losing your home.

Insurance

Many people can get loans against the cash value of their life insurance policies. Even if the interest rates on such loans seem comparable to other kinds of consumer loans, usually in the range of 6% to 8%, they may cost more than that in the final analysis. That's because the insurer may require that you give up some of the dividends that your policy would otherwise earn. The insurer sets aside cash value equal to your loan as collateral and pays, say, only 6%, instead of its usual 8%, on that amount. You have to add the lost 2% to the cost of your loan.

Depending on the policy, you could also be charged a variable rate that fluctuates with market conditions. You probably won't be obligated to make immediate payments, but interest will accrue. Remember that life insurance is death protection—if you die with loans against the policy, your survivors' benefits will be reduced by the outstanding amount of your loans, including interest.

Credit unions

If you belong to a credit union, you may be able to get a loan from it—often at a rate lower than that offered by banks or savings and loan associations. A mem-

There's no shortage of stories about people who have used their credit cards to start their businesses. Sure, it's easy, but watch those interest rates.

ber who has established a good banking and borrowing relationship with a credit union will probably find it more receptive than other kinds of lenders to new-business needs.

Credit Cards

There's no shortage of stories about people who started their businesses by taking out cash advances on their credit cards or by using their cards to purchase equipment and goods. The best thing about this method of financing: It's quick and easy. The worst thing: The typical interest rate on cash advances and accumulated purchases is 16% to 22% annually, although some so-called low-interest credit cards charge 13% or less on purchases.

Your credit card company may require you to repay only a small amount of your balance—or none at all—each month. That's bound to be appealing when your cash flow is tight. But remember that with interest charges continuing to accrue, your balance can really pile up over time.

If your credit card offers a grace period, you could take advantage of it. It works like this: If your card has a zero balance before you make a purchase, you will typically have 25 to 30 days from the date you receive your bill before you'll be assessed any interest. If you pay the balance within that time, you get, in effect, an interest-free short-term loan. You can maximize this advantage if you use the credit card just after the beginning of a new billing cycle. That will give you an additional three to four weeks as well as the grace period before any interest accrues.

Retirement plans

It is possible to withdraw money from retirement plans, including company plans, individual retirement accounts and Keogh plans. However, you'll have to pay taxes on the amount withdrawn and a 10% penalty for money pulled out before the age of 59½. So, for example, if you pulled $5,000 out of a fully deductible IRA at age 40, you would probably be slapped with a $500 penalty. Plus, the full $5,000 would be included in your income for the year and taxed in your top tax bracket. Besides being willing to bear the financial penalty, you have to ask yourself whether you really want to touch money you've earmarked for your retirement. If you do, then there's one way you can remove funds from your IRA early without penalty.

You can withdraw the money in roughly equal payments tied to your life expectancy. The money pulled out of the fund would still be taxed, except to the extent that it is a return of nondeductible contributions. And you must stick with the lifetime payout schedule for at least five consecutive years *and* until you're at least 59½. For example, if you opt for early withdrawal at age 50, you will need to continue taking payouts until age 59½, or if you begin at age 56, until age age 61. If you violate either of the requirements for early withdrawal, the 10% penalty would be applied retroactively to your pre-59½ withdrawals.

To estimate the minimum amount you can take out each year, divide the total amount in your IRA by the remaining years of your life expectancy (published in IRS Publication 590, *Individual Retirement Arrangements).* The actual amount will be larger, however. That's because the IRS will allow you to factor in a "reasonable" interest rate when figuring the penalty-free payouts; it assumes that the untouched balance will continue growing inside the IRA. (The IRS publishes a federal long-term interest rate each month, although other rates could be acceptable, too.)

Here's how the rule works: Say that you are 55 and, according to the IRS's table, you should live for 28.6 years. Assume that you have $100,000 in your IRA accounts. If you divided that amount by 29 years, you would get only about $3,500 a year. But if you project that your IRA investments will continue to earn 10% a year, the annual penalty-free payout would rise to nearly $10,000.

Is it worth paying the penalty to withdraw funds early from your IRA or Keogh? Can you use the loophole?

Gifts of money can be an advantage to both you and the giver, provided you meet certain tax rules.

Check with your accountant or financial planner before pulling any money out of retirement plans.

Resources of Family and Friends

Before you start asking those who are close to you for money, consider how entering into a business relationship can affect your personal relationships.

Gifts

Be sure that any money you're *given* really is a *gift* and that a loved one doesn't expect you to pay it back. Gifts of money can be an advantage to both you and the giver, provided you meet certain tax rules. Anyone can give any number of individuals up to $10,000 a year each without incurring the federal gift tax. It might seem strange, but this tax applies to the giver, not the recipient. For example, a mother could give the full $10,000 to her daughter and $10,000 to her son-in-law, and the father could do the same, giving a total of $40,000 in one year without incurring the tax. The parents get the advantage of removing $40,000 worth of gift property from their taxable estate.

Loans

Be sure that any loan is a *business* transaction: You should have a written agreement that defines all terms of the loan, including the amount being borrowed, the interest rate and the time within which the loan must be repaid. You and whoever is loaning you money should agree on a fair interest rate, preferably one that is at least equal to current market rates.

Are Your Suppliers Interested?

For another alternative source of financing, consider the businesses that will supply your business—that is, people or organizations for whom you will be a customer. It's sometimes possible to get the equivalent of a loan from someone who sees you as a potential long-term client. For example, someone starting a newsletter or magazine could negotiate a couple of months' worth of free typesetting or paper; if you're renting office space in a weak market, you could get the first three or four months (or more) free in exchange for agreeing to a lease of two or three years.

Do you have something of value that the bank will be happy to take from you if you can't repay your loan?

The Traditional Sources

Banks, as they say, are where the money is. But before you start thinking about what you're going to do with the money a bank or other financial institution will lend you, consider the following *inescapable truth:* You can't get a bank loan for a new business unless you have something of value that the bank will be happy to take from you if you can't repay your loan.

That's a real mouthful. Put another way, you have to have *collateral* in order to get a bank loan for a small-business start-up.

Bankers have no idea if your business will succeed or fail. What's more, they often have no great incentive to make a loan to a small start-up like yourself. After all, a banker basically has to fill out the same forms, conduct the same kinds of interviews, review the same documents and in many cases spend close to the same amount of time on a $5,000 loan as on a $500,000 loan. So why should the banker spend a lot of time and effort on your modest needs?

Bankers also tend to be cautious, at least with smaller loans to individuals and small businesses. Although you'd never know it by looking at some of the bank loans to other nations and real estate companies that have become black holes for lenders, bankers are essentially conservative business-people who want to realize a decent profit for their institutions while taking on minimal risk of losses. They are not philanthropists. And they read the business statistics—they know that most small businesses fail within a few years. All this predisposes them to refuse loans to any start-ups, even those like your own, even if you are convinced you're going to be wildly successful. These tendencies are likely to be aggravated in a difficult economic climate.

Those lenders who do make loans to small business-es generally make them only to businesses that have already been operating for several years and have a *track record*—at least a few years of profits, increasing revenues and assets that convince the bank that this business is indeed viable. In some instances, loans may be made to start-ups with outstanding business plans (see Chapter 6).

"Empower me!"

Stevens, Cartoonists & Writers Syndicate

But the attitude of many banks toward small business loans is well summarized in a Bank of America booklet called *Business Financing* (now out of print). The bank's publication states: "Most lenders want to see that you have a successful track record in the same sort of business." And later: "Loan approval rests on confidence in your repayment ability, which is indicated by your firm's profitability, your management expertise and your personal record."

So, when you're starting up, you probably won't be getting a loan from a bank. Unless...Unless you have something more than a great business idea. Unless you have something that the bank would accept as collateral on the loan—something of value, something concrete, something *tangible*.

Something like a car that's worth more than the amount you want to borrow. Or stocks, or antiques, or your house. Or some other asset that, in combination with a bank-determined depreciated value for what you'll purchase with the loan, will be worth as much as the amount of the loan.

Then you can get a bank loan. But then you're personally guaranteeing the loan. The risks become exponential. If your business fails and you cannot repay the loan, you won't lose just the business. You could also lose everything you offered as collateral.

In fact, the loan in this case will be made not to your business but to you, and you are the one who is liable for repayment. This personal backing may be required no matter what legal form your business takes. A bank might even drive this point home by requiring you to take out a life insurance policy naming the bank as beneficiary, thus covering the lender against the ultimate reversal of fortune.

The Government—Local, State, Federal

You've probably seen more than one story about all the money the government makes available to people who want to start businesses. There is *some* money available, but some of the best advice on getting government loans is succinctly stated in *Nolo's Small Business Start-Up: How to Write A Business Plan* (Nolo Press). Author Mike McKeever writes, "The hardest thing about getting money from the government is finding out which program can help you. The second hardest thing is finding out who in that agency can make a decision for or against your proposal. Compared to these two, filling out the forms is easy."

The U.S. Small Business Administration (SBA) is probably the government agency most often thought of as a source of loan money for start-up businesses. However, the SBA usually doesn't *make* loans; most of the time it only *guarantees* participating banks that a loan will be repaid if your business goes belly-up. So you'll have to go through the same application and paperwork process for an SBA-guaranteed loan as you would for a regular bank loan. The SBA's programs and funding for those programs change from year to year; a program you heard about a year or two ago may no longer be in effect by the time you apply for it. Most SBA loan and loan-guarantee

Getting money from the government is no less difficult than getting it from a bank, but for different reasons.

programs have been geared toward existing viable businesses rather than new ventures. There have also been periodic efforts to abolish the SBA altogether, although Congress has resisted those efforts. In short, it is possible to get money through the SBA, but you shouldn't consider this your first option for start-up financing.

Many other agencies either guarantee loans or make loans or grants to small businesses. That doesn't mean these other programs are going to do *you* any good, however. For example, the Department of Agriculture administers something called National Wool Act Payments to encourage the domestic production of wool; the Department of Commerce has money for fisheries development and "utilization" (new product) research. The money exists; whether it exists for you is less certain.

It doesn't hurt to check on sources of government money—so long as you recognize that this kind of assistance is far from a sure thing.

Thanks for the Money...Here's my Company

There's another way that some businesses can raise money. It's called *equity financing,* and it involves selling a part of your business—or an interest in it—to an investor. Getting an investor to put money into your business sounds enticing. For one thing, having someone put his or her money behind you is bound to give you a psycho-

---

Government Resources

• •

Among the places to get information on any government programs are: your local congressional offices, state or local business development or economic development offices, and local lenders who participate in the U.S. Small Business Administration's loan guarantee program.

- For information about federal aid programs, try the *Catalog of Federal Domestic Assistance,* published by the U.S. Government Printing Office (try your local library or call 202–512–1800; $50).

- Another source of information on both state and federal aid: *Government Giveaways for Entrepreneurs,* by Matthew Lesko (Information U.S.A. Inc.; 800–UNCLE–SAM; $33.95). Lesko has made a career (and a successful small business) of packaging information on sources of government help—what you can get, and especially where and how to get it—in easy-to-read and accessible formats.

logical boost: "If *he* thinks this is such a good idea, then maybe it really *is* a good idea!" For another, there's the raw appeal of somebody's contributing hard currency to your efforts: It's wonderful to imagine your start-up worries magically disappearing when your fairy godmother shows up with a hefty bankroll.

However, few start-ups are candidates for such investors. Whatever their name, individuals and companies that invest in businesses are likely to require that you give them much the same financial information and background that would be requested by a lender—if not more. And investors are most likely to put their money into ongoing concerns—not fresh start-ups with lots of dreams but no track record.

Many of these investors focus their efforts on businesses they feel can grow into companies with annual sales in the tens of millions. It's when a start-up becomes a big enough company to be taken public and sold to general shareholders that venture capitalists can sell out and realize truly big bucks. Venture capitalists also often try to gain control of more than 50% of a business with their investment so that they can have the power to approve or veto all significant company decisions. That means if the investors aren't happy with the job you're doing, you can be replaced. Giving away that much control is not likely to appeal to people who start a business so they can work for themselves.

Flavors of Investors

• •

Investors go by several names, including:

Venture capitalists, or angels, or venture capital clubs. These are individuals, firms or groups of people who can invest anywhere from tens of thousands to millions of dollars in new companies.

Small Business Investment Companies (SBICs). There are several hundred of these companies, which are privately run but licensed, regulated and funded by the Small Business Administration. (You can get more information about SBICs by contacting the National Association of Small Business Investment Companies, 1199 N. Fairfax Street, #200, Alexandria, VA 22314; 703–683–1601.)

Investment bankers. Instead of making their money only on the loans they make to businesses, investment bankers can also purchase a portion of a business and the right to part of its future profits, growth and proceeds from any eventual sale of the entire business.

You will need to take the initiative and prepare your own proposal, designing it to sell your idea effectively and to spell out your financial plans and dreams.

Making Your Proposal

When you're ready to look for outside financing, your first task is to write a proposal that sells the source of funds on your concept. If you're applying for a loan, this will be called a *loan proposal;* if you're looking for equity financing, it will be an *investment prospectus.* There are also all sorts of hybrids of these two financing plans—loans that can be converted to partial ownership of a business, equity investments that a business owner can later buy back at a mutually agreed price, and so on.

All lenders have their own loan forms that you'll have to fill out. But you will need to take the initiative and prepare your own proposal, designing it to sell your idea effectively and to spell out your financial plans and dreams.

There are any number of ways to write this document, but these simple guidelines will make any proposal better:

Be brief.

Many lenders will spend no more than 10 minutes initially reviewing your proposal to determine whether it merits serious attention. If your key points and plans are not clearly presented and immediately identifiable, lenders and investors will probably pass up your idea.

Be straight.

Your proposal should be realistic and honest. Don't wildly inflate estimates of how profitable you expect your venture to be.

Be detached.

To the extent possible, try to step back from your great idea and put on the hat of the skeptical potential investor or lender. Beat him or her to the punch by asking yourself, "What are the risks involved in this project?" Then acknowledge potential problems and explain why they will not affect your venture's viability.

If you're looking for money from a lender or investor, you should consult with some of the "good guys" in Chapter 14—your accountant, your attorney, other businesspeople, even your banker. Bankers interested in making a loan will be willing to help you develop your loan proposal; even if they're not interested, they could still give you some tips and possibly point you toward other sources of start-up capital.

The complexity of any proposal or loan application will usually increase with the complexity of the business or the amount of the loan being requested.

The Essentials

From the most simple to the most complex, all loan proposals will probably include the following:

A description of your business

This can include a personal statement outlining your background and qualifications for starting and running this business.

A clear statement of the amount of money requested and how you will use it

Be specific: If you need operating capital, for example, you will want to break that down into amounts needed for payroll, insurance, office supplies and your other expenses.

A projected income statement

Also known as a profit and loss statement. In its simplest form, this is composed of two lists or columns. On one sheet you have all the sources of revenue you expect for your first year in business—everything you'll receive from selling your goods or services. On another you have all your business expenses—the amount you spend on purchasing your ingredients or materials or inventory, for example, plus payroll, rent, insurance, supplies, utilities, credit card charges—in short, everything your business spends money on. Subtract your projected expenses from your projected revenues and you have your projected profit or loss.

This may sound a little familiar, and in fact it is—you looked at this from a different angle when calculating your worst-case scenario of how much money you need to start your business. Now, however, you don't want to be making worst-case estimates. You want, if not best-case, at least realistic estimates of your profit potential to help convince a lender that you've considered all aspects of the start-up and that you have a high probability of success.

Does it sound as if pinning down hard-and-fast revenue estimates can be about as easy as nailing pudding to a wall? That's right. What you, with the help of your accountant, are doing here is taking your best shot at making sincere, informed, educated guesses. Trying to predict the future is a tricky business—even if you have a track record on which to base those predictions.

A projected balance sheet

This is another two-list form. One list or column is a breakdown of all your business assets: cash on hand; checking account funds; inventory and goods in stock; furniture, fixtures and equipment; and other things that the business owns free and clear. The other list summarizes liabilities—money you'll owe after receiving a loan, money owed to others from whom you've borrowed, balances due to suppliers, and so on—and something that accountants usually call *owners' (or share-holders') equity* or *net worth* —that is, the portion of business assets owned by you and other investors. In a neat little accounting trick, a business's assets always equal

---

More on Equity Financing
• •

Among the books that discuss equity invest-ment options in greater detail:

- *Up-Front Financing: The Entrepreneur's Guide,* by A. David Silver (John Wiley & Sons).

- *The Entrepreneur's Guide To Raising Venture Capi-tal,* by Greenberg Consulting and Craig T. Norback (Liberty Hall Press).

the amount of its liabilities plus its net worth—which means that, in practical terms, the difference between your business liabilities list and your business assets list goes on the line called "net worth."

The projected balance sheet provides potential lenders with a snapshot look at what the business owns (which could be used as collateral in a loan) and at what the business will owe, both of which are key in determining how much money is needed to start the venture. Projected balance sheets help lenders determine how much money they want to commit to your venture.

Funds (other than potential bank loan) to be invested in the business

This one's easy: How much of your own money is going into this venture? *The more you're putting in, the more evident your commitment to the business.*

Suggested repayment terms

The lender will decide what size loan you get, at what interest rate and for how long. But you can still suggest a length of time for the loan and indicate whether you would prefer to make steady equal payments on the balance or a large "balloon" payment at the end of the term. Steady repayments impose a constant financial discipline on you, but a balloon payment gives you longer use of more of the money you're borrowing, and it could be a good deal so long as you can pay or refinance that balloon when it comes due. At least you'll be showing that you've thought ahead about repayment, and who knows—maybe you'll get more favorable terms on the deal.

Your own personal financial statement

This will come right from your financial self-analysis, covered in Chapter 4, and it includes personal assets, debts, and credit and personal references. Your personal financial statement will be useful if you wind up having

People who buy, sell, or invest in businesses turns to all sorts of ratios that are used to analyze the health of a business.

to personally guarantee a loan; a strong personal financial statement also, obviously, will be looked on with some favor by any lender.

Ratios "R" Us

In the course of figuring out how much money your business needs, you'll probably come across talk about "financial ratios" or "ratio analysis." Lenders may compute ratios when determining whether to make a loan; people who buy, sell, or invest in businesses turn to all sorts of ratios that are used to analyze the health of a business, including:

The break-even ratio

This ratio in particular is useful for almost anyone planning to work for herself. It can tell you, before you ever deal with your first customer, how much revenue or sales volume you need to at least pay your expenses.

This is, in fact, a more useful analysis for start-ups than is calculating how much your business *could* make if it *could* achieve a particular arbitrary sales volume. Sales predictions and projections can, to some extent, be little more than wishful thinking or figures of convenience. Any estimates of future sales, especially with a start-up that has no track record, must be looked at skeptically; far better to figure out at what level of sales your business will break even.

Lenders may compute your break-even ratio to determine whether your start-up idea is viable—whether you're charging enough for your product and will sell enough to cover your costs and pay back any loans. You could make your computation of the ratio part of your proposal.

More tools for understanding

Among the other ratios that lenders and businesses use (and that might be useful to you down the road):

(continued on page 234)

When Will You Break Even?

There's more than one way to determine a break-even point, but here's a relatively simple method that works well for start-ups. To do this analysis, you'll need to know the average cost that you pay to buy or create whatever you're selling, the average price that you charge for what you sell, and the fixed costs that you have to pay no matter how much or how little you sell.

Here's how to find your break-even point ratio:

1. Calculate the average amount it costs you to produce or buy what you sell. If you create costume jewelry and spend $5,000 to make 500 pieces of jewelry, then your average cost is $10 per piece.

2. Calculate the average amount you charge. This one's easy. For the purposes of this example, let's say you charge an average of $40 per item.

3. Add up all the fixed costs discussed earlier in this chapter—the rent, advertising, utilities and other expenses that you have to pay no matter how little you sell. Let's say you're doing this as a sideline to your full-time job, so you don't pay yourself a salary and your fixed costs are $5,000 a year.

4. Now plug all that into this formula:

$$\text{Break Even} = \frac{\text{Fixed Costs}}{1 - \dfrac{\text{Your average cost of product}}{\text{Average price you charge for product}}}$$

Plug in the numbers you get:

$$\text{Break Even} = \frac{5,000}{1 - \dfrac{10}{40}} = \frac{5,000}{1 - .25} = \frac{5,000}{.75} = \$6,667$$

That figure—$6,667—is the amount of sales you must ring up to break even. To convert that into the number of pieces you must sell, just divide that dollar amount by the average price charged. In this case, $6,667 divided by 40 equals 167 pieces of jewelry to break even. With the 168th sale, you'll begin to show a profit.

If you're a consultant, your product is your own time and expertise, for which you'll probably charge by the hour. If you divide the amount of your fixed expenses by your average hourly rate, you can figure out the number of hours you'll need to work before you break even.

- **The current ratio** (current assets divided by current liabilities) measures whether your business can pay its current debts with its current assets, with enough left over for other expenses. A current ratio of 2 to 1 is often considered good.

- **The acid test ratio,** also known as the quick ratio (cash on hand plus money owed to you plus any other "quickly available" funds, all divided by your current liabilities) focuses on your immediate liquidity and tells you whether you could pay off all your current liabilities without selling any product.

- **The return on investment ratio** (net profits divided by total assets invested in the business) measures your profit as a percentage of the amount you've invested. That allows you to compare your return with what you might have earned if you invested in stocks, real estate, or something else besides your own business. For example, if you have a net profit of $5,000 on a business in which you've invested $50,000, your return on investment is .10, or 10%. This does not include salary you pay out to yourself.

Learning the Equations

• •

For more information about ratios and what they mean to you and your business, you can turn to your accountant.

You can also buy one of the many computer business software packages that allow you to make "what-if" calculations, where a change in one part of a business expenses-and-revenues equation is automatically reflected through every financial equation affecting the business.

You can take a business accounting class at your local university or community college.

Or you can consult: *Basic Accounting for the Small Business,* by Clive G. Cornish (published by the Self-Counsel Press.)

There are many other ratios, including those for return on assets, net profit margin, inventory turnover, and on and on. Most ratios are relevant to some businesses but not others, and most ratios come into play only after a business has some track record on which to base the numbers that go into those computations. (For more on financial analysis, see Chapter 24.)

The Lure of Franchising

The lure of franchising is relatively easy to understand. By buying a franchise, you can, ideally, begin your first day of business with an established and recognized name, a respected product, a proven market, and a time-tested method of drawing and keeping customers. Sounds pretty good when contrasted with the uncertainties of starting from scratch, doesn't it?

There's another side to the coin, of course. Simply put, the franchise may not be that great. There's no guarantee that any particular franchise will make money, just as there's no guarantee that any other business start-up will succeed. And while franchises are generally considered less risky than other start-ups, they also give you less autonomy and freedom. You're still your own boss when you run a franchise, but to some degree you also have another boss—the company that sold you the franchise.

This chapter addresses special factors that you should consider if you think you may want to purchase a franchise.

Franchising Defined

We've all been customers of one franchise or another. Every time we walk into a Burger King, or a Minuteman Press, or a Midas Muffler & Brake Shop, or a Jiffy Lube (to name just four), we're walking into a franchised business. We may not realize just how many different types of franchises are out there. It's not all fast-food and copy shops—among the other businesses that are franchised are Kid to Kid, a chain of stores that buys and sells used clothing for toddlers; Mad Science Group, a home-based business that

When you buy a franchise, your relationship with the franchise company is just beginning.

introduces kids to the fun of science through after-school and party programs; and many real estate brokerages, including Century 21. There are more than half a million franchise businesses across the United States, and they account for 40% of all retail sales nationally.

The U.S. Department of Commerce has defined franchising as "a form of licensing by which the owner (the franchisor) of a product, service or method obtains distribution through affiliated dealers (the franchisees)." In plainer English, that means that you (the franchisee) buy the right to a particular business from another company (the franchisor). At a minimum, the rights you buy allow you to use a well-known name or trademark or a product that is popular with consumers. As a franchisee, you could receive little or no guidance on how to actually run your business. Or you could find yourself at the other end of the spectrum, entering into a contract covering virtually every aspect of a business operation. Franchisors may dictate not only what you'll be selling but also your business location, marketing strategy, operating hours, hiring policies, quality-control procedures, management system, and so on. When you buy a business outright, as discussed in the next chapter, your relationship with the previous owner tends to end with the sale. When you buy a franchise, your relationship with the franchise company is just beginning.

Are You a Franchise Candidate?

Before you get into the nitty-gritty of investigating franchise opportunities, you should look at your own strengths, weaknesses and interests, and consider how they would relate to running a franchise. For the most part, this process is similar to the one recommended for all potential entrepreneurs in the first few chapters of this book. A couple of other questions to ask yourself:

What types of franchise businesses do you have an interest in and the aptitude for?

Sure, the franchisor will probably train you in the franchise business, but it usually won't hurt for you to have some prior background in the field. Working in a hotel can, in theory, prepare you for any job in the hospitality industry, but you could have trouble jumping from the hotel job to running a restaurant franchise if you weren't directly involved in managing the hotel's restaurant.

Do you mind being a boss with a boss?

Many entrepreneurs want to make their own rules, but many franchisors have a strict set of guidelines that must be followed. If you're comfortable with the idea of following someone else's guidelines in exchange for being able to use a successful system to sell a profitable product, then franchising may be for you. But if you want to not only own the dance hall but also be able to call the tunes, then franchising probably won't be right for you.

Franchise Costs

You'll typically pay a one-time fee and a share of all future profits or revenues to buy a franchise. You may also have to pay for initial training costs, on-site start-up assistance, and promotion charges and advertising fees. Some franchisors charge you for centralized bookkeeping services, too. For your fee, you might also get help in selecting a site and negotiating a lease, promoting your business, training employees, and using the franchisor's proven sales methods.

Your costs don't end with the franchise fee. As with other businesses, you could also need additional capital to cover equipment costs, a mortgage or lease, construction of the shop interior, supplies and utilities, and cash reserves to meet personal expenses until the business generates enough money for you to draw a salary.

The exact franchise fee and other start-up costs vary widely, depending on how lucrative or how established the franchise is. Some franchises are available for only a few thousand dollars. Then again, you probably won't be getting a franchise from McDonald's—widely considered the

Your costs don't end with the franchise fee.

You may, in fact, have to spend several months researching companies on your own to fill in gaps not covered by the UFOC.

most successful and profitable of franchises—unless you can pony up at least a few hundred thousand dollars and possibly more than a cool half million.

Obviously, you'll want to get all fees—initial and one-time as well as recurring and annual—spelled out, so you know exactly how much money you'll be paying out to the company for the right to run your business.

Checking Out the Franchisor

Before you buy an existing business, you have to check out the business's current operations. Similarly, you'll want to minimize the risks associated with buying a franchise by checking out the franchisor in advance. The federal government helps you a little with this task by re-quiring franchisor companies to give prospective fran-chisees a disclosure document. Usually, you'll get the

Questions to Ask Franchisors

- **How many franchises do you have?**

- **For how long** have you been granting franchises?

- **What is the failure rate** of your franchises?

- **How many franchisees sell their fran-chises** to new owners each year? (A fran-chisee who sells a money-losing operation to a new owner may not be counted as a failure.)

- **How many new franchises** are being added annually? Where are they located?

- **How much money** will I have to put into the franchise? What's the initial fee? The royalty schedule? Other expenses needed to open the franchise? Expenses needed to keep the franchise running?

- **How well is the product or service sell-ing?** What are the average sales levels of existing franchises?

- **Is there a training program?** What is cov-ered? How long and intensive is the pro-gram? Are training costs covered in the franchise fee?

- **Exactly what kind of assistance** do you give your franchisees? Do you charge for that assistance? If so, how much?

- **Do you give new franchisees exclusive rights** to the territory in which they op-erate? Exactly what are the boundaries of that territory?

- **If you retain the right to add new fran-chises** in a territory, do existing fran-chisees get the first chance to buy those new franchises?

Uniform Franchise Offering Circular (UFOC), which covers information in 22 categories, including:

- the history of the franchise company;

- its fees, royalties and other costs;

- the background of its principals;

- any bankruptcy history;

- any litigation against the principals or the company;

- the duration of the franchise agreement;

- and the franchisor's financial statements.

In some cases, a company will send you a Federal Trade Commission disclosure document, which contains the same information as that found in the UFOC.

Unfortunately, the UFOC is not the be-all and end-all of information for most prospective franchisees. You may, in fact, have to spend several months researching compa-

- **Might my territory be shrunk** if the population in the area increases? If a market grows, the franchisor may want to put another revenue- and fee-generating business in the area.

- **Do you find the site** and negotiate the lease or purchase?

- **Do you provide building plans or specifications?** Do you arrange for any needed contractors? Are these costs included in the franchise fee?

- **Do I have to stay open during specific hours and days?**

- **What goods and services do you make available** for me to buy or lease? Do I have to buy or lease those items? Can I buy or lease the items elsewhere? (Note: Mandatory sales can be a profit center for franchisors—and a real cash drain for franchisees.)

- **Do I have any flexibility in pricing** the product, or must I follow your price guides or orders?

- **When can I terminate** a franchise contract? What would it cost to terminate?

- **Must I sign a noncompete clause?** That is, if I want to sell the franchise and start my own business selling a similar product or service in the same area, can I?

- **What can you do for me** that I cannot do for myself?

nies on your own to fill in gaps not covered by the UFOC. Among the areas you'll want to check out:

Market and Concept

The official brochures of a franchisor are just fine, and they can be helpful. But you need to understand a company's market and its business concept yourself before you invest.

One way of doing that is to approach an existing franchise from the viewpoint of a customer. That's what Mike Ryan did before he became a franchisee with Steak-Out, a Huntsville, Ala. based company trying to do for char-broiled steak and chicken dinners what Domino's did for pizzas. The company's franchisees specialize in home delivery of steak and chicken dinners, complete with baked potatoes, salads and even after-dinner mints.

Ryan traveled to Huntsville to see the Steak-Out concept in action, placing a dozen orders from different locations over a three-day period. The franchise never failed to satisfy him with its service and quality. After meeting with the couple who had begun the franchise, he signed on for three of his own outlets in Atlanta.

Even with his understanding of the business, though, Ryan underestimated one factor: the difficulty of penetrating a big-city market. "Atlanta is such a huge market with so much competition in fast food, it really takes a lot of dollars to properly promote a new business to consumers," he says. Although the stores were profitable, they didn't generate the kind of additional revenues Ryan needed to expand and open additional outlets—and what he really wanted was to oversee lots of restaurants, not just two or three. Eventually, even though the franchises were money-makers, Ryan sold each of the three stores to individual owner-operators.

Strong Management

A great concept is only part of the formula for a successful franchise. You'll also want a franchisor who has a stable financial history. The UFOC and FTC disclosure statements, which provide information on bankruptcies of the franchisor, can help you determine just how financially stable the management is (more on current financial health below).

Good franchise management often has hands-on experience in the business being franchised. If the franchisor is currently operating the business being franchised, it can pay you to work with him or her, even if only briefly and without pay. Seeing how a franchisor operates the business day-to-day can be invaluable.

Not every franchisor continues to operate an individual outlet after his or her franchising operation takes off, but you can still get a sense of how the franchisor interacts with franchisees by spending a day or two at the company's headquarters. While you're there, you could even go over the entire UFOC or FTC statements with the franchisor's principals. There's no guarantee that you'll be certain

More Assistance

Other published sources of information about franchising include:

- *Investigate Before Investing* ($6 plus shipping and handling) and *Franchise Opportunities Guide* ($15 plus shipping and handling), published by the International Franchise Association (1350 New York Ave., N.W., Suite 900, Washington, DC 20005; 202–628–8000, or 800–543–1038 for mail orders).

- *Franchise Annual,* published yearly by Info Franchise News (728 Center St., P.O. Box 550, Lewiston, NY 14092; 716–754–4669; $39.95). This directory lists more than 5,000 franchisors.

- *Franchise Opportunities Handbook* (Superintendent of Documents, U.S. Government Printing Office, P.O. Box 371954, Pittsburgh, PA 15250; $21) is published

by the U.S. Department of Commerce, which compiles this compendium of information on investigating and buying franchises. The bulk of the book is devoted to listings of franchisors, including descriptions, how long the franchisors have been in business, money needed for a franchise, training provided and other information.

- *Evaluating Franchise Opportunities* is published by the Small Business Administration (free; contact your local SBA office to order by mail; see also page 22).

- *Kiplinger's Personal Finance Magazine, The Wall Street Journal, The New York Times, Money* and other publications carry advertisements for franchise opportunities.

about the skills of the management team after visiting the headquarters or spending some time working in the business, but you'll have far more useful information about the business than if you skipped these steps.

Government Watchdogs

● ●

The Federal Trade Commission (6th and Pennsylvania Ave., N.W., Washington, DC 20580; 202–326–3128 or 202–326–3220) and at least 15 states administer laws governing franchises and provide information about franchisors and the franchise business.

- **For assistance at the federal level,** contact the FTC. The second phone number listed above offers a variety of recorded information, including how to reach the state offices described above and how to obtain copies of any complaints on file against the franchise you're considering. It also offers the option of speaking with an attorney.

- **To find out whether your state regulates franchisors,** contact your state's department of business registration, commerce or corporations; securities commission; office of the attorney general; or secretary of state.

Financial Health

Financial statements that a franchisor provides in the UFOC should be carefully reviewed to determine whether the franchisor is in good financial shape. You should have an accountant who is familiar with franchise financing go over the financial structure, source of earnings, amount of indebtedness, credit status and any other financial information that's relevant.

A franchisor's source of earnings can be especially telling to any prospective buyer. If the franchisor's profits are mostly from selling franchises and collecting up-front fees, it may not be as focused on promoting the franchisees' continued success as you would like. A successful franchisor who gets most of his revenues from franchisees' sales royalties may have a greater incentive to see those franchisees succeed.

Franchisor's Earnings Claims

A franchisor may make earnings claims for new outlets. That's fine so long as you understand the basis for the earnings claims. Any projections are based on a broad set of assumptions about costs, prices and overall business conditions. Incorrect assumptions translate to incorrect estimates. For example, you should be able to look at the earnings claims and ask yourself (or the franchisor) how the estimates would be affected if your energy costs were 10% higher than estimated or if business at the new franchise site was 15% less than anticipated.

One good way to determine whether a franchisor's claims are valid is to ask what percentage of the current franchisees have had profits or incomes that equaled or exceeded the amount claimed, and how many franchisees did that well during their first year of operation. Other franchisees' first-year results are important for you because your initial experiences are more likely to mimic those than any later performances. Of course, it can pay to have your own accountant check any theoretical profit and loss statements as well.

Franchisor's Master Plan

A franchisor should have a master plan—a blueprint for how fast it wants to grow and where it wants to place new franchises. For your purposes, the best franchisors will

More Financial Information on Franchises

Publicly held

If the franchise company that you're interested in is publicly held, you can get financial data from the company's annual report, and you may be able to get information on any company from Wall Street analysts who track the company's stock.

- *Nelson's Directory of Investment Research,* an annual directory available at libraries or through investment advisers, lists research analysts and their specialties by firm. Its monthly supplement identifies current research reports written by those analysts.

- Another way to locate the right analyst is to check with the trade association most closely related to the product or service that the franchise sells.

Privately held

If the franchise company is privately held, you may obtain a credit report from Dun and Bradstreet. The online computer service, Dialog, also regularly features D&B's Financial Records, which is compiled from D&B's credit reports.

Information on both

On-line services—including Dialog, CompuServe, Prodigy, Dow Jones News/Retrieval—offer financial profiles of public and private companies.

probably be those who plan to expand slowly and who focus their efforts within a limited region. That's because the franchisor will be more likely to be able to help you on short notice and less likely to have its resources stretched too thinly over too many franchisees.

Current Franchisees

Franchisees may be the only source of real numbers that accurately show what you can expect to earn. Franchisors' earnings projections—if you can get them—can be subject to dozens of variables. Franchisees can and will speak from experience about whether the parent company is:

- **keeping its promises** of support, assistance in marketing, continuing training, or other services covered in the franchise agreement.

- **effectively using a national advertising fee,** if charged (which is often 2% to 4% of the franchisee's monthly gross sales).

Questions to Ask Franchisees

- **What was your line of work before** you purchased the franchise?

- **What goods or services does the franchisor supply?** Are the franchisor's prices competitive?

- **Do you have an exclusive territory?** If so, how large is that territory? Do you have first option to purchase new franchises in your territory?

- **How much have you invested** in your business?

- **Were the start-up costs and working capital requirements** stated by the company on target?

- **What's your gross?** Your profit? How much do you take as a salary?

- **When did you begin to break even?** If you haven't broken even, when do you expect to?

- **How many hours a week do you work?**

- **Do you like what you're doing?**

- **Do you think the franchisor has kept its promises?**

- **If you had it to do again,** would you still buy the franchise?

- **forcing franchisees to compete with one another** by opening outlets too close to one another.

Franchisees aren't likely to hide any problems they're having with the parent company.

You can get the names and addresses of franchisees in your area, including those that have sold their units or have gone bankrupt, from the UFOC. Call as many as you can, and visit at least a few. Be sure to ask whether running the business has differed from the picture the franchisor painted for the operator before he or she signed on the dotted line.

Obviously, deciding whether to buy a franchise is a complicated process. Review any contracts with your attorney, and have an accountant who is familiar with the franchising industry analyze all financial statements. If you don't agree with the terms, conditions and controls of a franchise agreement, you may want to get it modified or decide not to enter into the agreement.

Has running the business differed from the picture the franchisor painted for the operator before he or she signed on the dotted line?

Multilevel Marketing

Another way of working for yourself without starting from scratch involves joining a multilevel marketing (MLM) system. In multilevel marketing, you work as an independent distributor for a company, selling the company's products but also recruiting other people to sell for the company. Your profits come both through the commissions and bonuses you earn on your own sales and through profits you earn on sales made by the people you recruit. Those people, called your "downline," usually represent your opportunity to make real money. After all, you can sell only so much yourself, but if you recruit lots of other people to sell the company's product, and receive a percentage of *their* sales, you could make a lot more money.

The structure of a multilevel marketing system is pyramid-shaped, with all the people you've recruited under you, and all the people *they've* recruited under you and them, and so on. Remember, this means that someone above you is profiting from your sales, and from your downline sales.

Hundreds of companies use multilevel marketing networks to sell products and services ranging from baskets and pantyhose to home-security systems and long-distance telephone services. The overwhelming majority of people who work at MLM do so on a part-time basis.

Start-up kits for all kinds of direct selling, including MLM, cost an average of $70 to $110. That low start-up cost is one of the big lures of MLM systems. Compensation plans vary, but in the most common kind, the so-called stair-step, you get commissions on your own sales, and after you recruit a minimum number of distributors (usually three to five) and reach a minimum sales volume, you get a share of their commissions, too. You can also earn a commission on sales by distributors recruited by *your* recruits (another step down the pyramid) and so on down the line for three or more steps or generations, depending on the company.

Pressure to keep lots of distributors under you means you have to continually recruit new ones. That pressure can be quite high; the turnover rate among distributors tops 80% annually at some companies. But if you maintain a certain level of sales and a certain number of distributors, you may be able to earn even larger commissions on every sale. That can lead to a unique self-trap: Some multilevel marketers are so tempted by those larger commissions or bonuses that they buy the company's product themselves, figuring that it will just sit in their inventory until they can sell it. If they can't sell the product, they can wind up with a garage full of cosmetics or nutritional products, for example. In the worst cases, people have filed for bankruptcy after failing to maintain their downline of sales reps or to sell the products they had purchased.

Developing your downline doesn't necessarily end with recruiting (and recruiting and recruiting) new people. Many states require you to actively manage your downline by training, motivating and staying in touch with them. These duties are normally part of your deal with the company, too.

A Direct Sales Resource

● ●

The Direct Selling Association (1666 K St., N.W., Suite 1010, Washington, DC 20006–2808; 202–293–5760) represents and serves more than 125 companies involved in direct sales, including multilevel marketing companies, such as Amway, NuSkin and Shaklee, and more-traditionally organized companies, such as Avon and Tupperware.

- Membership requires a yearlong investigation by the association's legal department of a company's contracts, recruiting and training aids, track record, reputation, and compliance with federal and state regulations.

- The association stands ready to assist in the relationships between its member companies, their distributors and their customers.

- You can contact the association to learn whether a company you're considering is a member in good standing and to obtain a list of members (including their telephone numbers and the products they sell) and a copy of the association's code of ethics.

How Much Can You Make?

Top salespeople in MLM companies can earn more than $100,000 a year in commissions and bonuses from their own sales and those of their downlines. However, Jeffrey Babener, a lawyer in Portland, Ore., whose law firm represents direct-selling companies headquartered throughout the U.S. and abroad, says $300 to $1,000 a month is a more reasonable expectation. It often takes a long time—sometimes years—to build a solid business. Distributors usually must turn in their proceeds to their company, which in turn issues commissions and bonuses. Many MLM companies encourage distributors to work at MLM part-time rather than to give up a full-time job too soon. That's not a bad idea.

One of the problems with MLM is that it can be a victim of its own success. If too many people think a product

Scoping Out an MLM: Questions to Ask

The product

- **Is the product of good quality and competitively priced?** Would you buy it if you were not selling it?

- **Does the company guarantee customer satisfaction?** Is there a money-back guarantee if a customer is not happy? Does that money come out of your pocket or the company's?

- **How much (if any) of the product do you have to keep in inventory?** The less, the better.

- **Is there a company policy of repurchasing inventory that you are unable to sell?** The Direct Selling Association recommends a 90% buy-back policy, minus any commissions or bonuses that have already been paid on the merchandise.

Stay away from companies that require or pressure you to buy a lot of merchandise when joining their program.

The company

- **How much will the company charge you to join?**

- **How long has the company been in business?** New MLM companies have relatively short lives; one that has made it past three or four years is likely to be around for a while.

- **Is the franchise company on financially sound ground?**

or service is a great idea, an area may become innundated with salespeople. When that happens too many salespeople are chasing too few customers and everyone is hurt.

The pressure to keep selling products and recruiting new salespeople can also take its toll. "Your friends and relatives start running for the hills whenever you approach them after you've become a dreaded MLMer," was the message sent by one correspondent on a Prodigy Services computer bulletin board.

Getting More Information

If you're thinking of signing up with a MLM company, make sure that you get any promises in writing and that all literature and other information comes directly from company headquarters, not from an overly enthusiastic salesperson who gives you an overly optimistic assessment

- **What is the company's public image?** Some companies' images are so bad that marketers don't tell prospects who they work for until well into the sales pitch.

- **How do other distributors feel about the company** and about the people who have recruited them (also known as their "uplines")? Talk with as many distributors as you can, especially those who are in the same upline that you would be joining.

- **Does the company offer training?** Is there a fee? An MLM company offers less regimentation than a franchise, but you may receive far less support.

- **Are there any limits on the number of distributors** the company allows in an area? Fewer distributors in an area can mean less competition for you

The compensation plan

- **How many levels of downline distributors** can earn you bonuses and commissions? What are the commissions at each level?

- **How long does it typically take to get payment from the company?**

- **How difficult is it to reach and maintain advanced status levels** or other incentive levels where you can receive bonuses and larger commissions?

- **What extra expenses will you have to allow for?** Do you need to attend national sales conventions at your own expense if you want to qualify for bonuses and incentives?

of your prospects. You can always call a company's head-quarters and ask for information yourself. If anyone makes any representations about income, find out what percentage of distributors make the amount being quoted over what period, and ask how long it took them to work their way up to that level.

Buying a Business

Kay Austin-Holmes felt she'd reached a dead end in her job as a marketing director. So, determined to find a new job, she walked into B.J.'s Word Processing to have her résumé redone and professionally printed. An hour later, she was on a new career path, though not one she had intended: She had tentatively agreed to purchase the shop.

"The owner had been losing money ever since she turned the day-to-day operations over to a manager instead of overseeing the shop herself, had gotten involved in other projects, and just wanted to get out," Austin-Holmes remembers. "She'd had the business up for sale for a year, but all anybody ever saw was that she had these old, out-of-date word processors that had cost her $17,000, and that after two years in business she was more than $20,000 in debt."

Austin-Holmes, though, saw an ongoing business with potential—a low-overhead operation, with a long list of clients, that could succeed with hands-on management. She also saw that most of the owner's debt stemmed from those expensive word processors, not from day-to-day operations. "In literally 20 minutes, I agreed to buy her word-processing machinery and her desks and chairs and refrigerator and a client list of 2,000 people—her entire business—for $3,500," the Los Angeles resident said. The seller kept responsibility for the business's debts. "There was nothing wrong with the business; it just needed to be watched over every day by someone who had a direct interest in its success," says Austin-Holmes. After buying the business, Austin-Holmes renegotiated her lease, getting the landlord to clip

Experiments—including the expense of failed experiments—have all been conducted by someone else.

the monthly rent from $640 to $600, and renamed the firm "B.J.'s Professional Image Business Centre."

Austin-Holmes and an on-call crew of independent contractors now turn out financial statements, legal reports, professional résumés, brochures, synopses of books and scripts, and other documents requiring editorial expertise. Her start-up costs were relatively low because the previous owner had bought all the equipment for the business and Austin-Holmes was buying it from her at a truly deep discount. Her business generates a profit, "and I was still able to use those word processors for a couple of years," she laughs.

We're not recommending that you fly into a business purchase as quickly as Austin-Holmes did. But when the business and purchase terms are right, buying a business that's already up and running is one of the easiest ways to start working for yourself.

Why Buy?

Among the potential advantages of buying a business:

- **You're buying customers.** You can immediately tap into an active and loyal clientele—a built-in base of customers who will, you hope, continue to use your product or service as long as you continue to keep them happy.

- **You're buying a known product or service.**

- **You're buying all the past efforts** that went into making the business successful. Experiments with pricing, location, products and/or services, and marketing (including the expense of failed experiments) have all been conducted by someone else. You can build on those efforts once you're in control. Kay Austin-Holmes, for example, took a basic word-processing business and expanded it to include such editorial services as preparing script synopses and consulting on business brochures—new services that might appeal to customers the business already had.

- **You're buying the reputation** of the business, also known as goodwill. In the case of a business providing a good product or service to satisfied customers or clients, goodwill can be worth a lot.

- **You may be buying a built-in work force** of employees who already know the business. Training employees can be expensive; when you buy an existing business you may have staff who are ready to go from day one.

- **You may buy the business for less money** than you would spend to start it yourself.

Ask your banker, attorney and accountant for leads.

Getting Started

You may, like Austin-Holmes, meet up serendipitously with the business you'd like to buy. Or, you can look for leads through the following sources:

Newspaper ads

Read the "Business Opportunities" section of your local papers, *The Wall Street Journal* and the Sunday *New York Times*. Also check trade journals and contact the trade association that represents the kind of business(es) you're interested in. Check back issues as well; the price of a business you're interested in may be falling, tipping you off that an owner is eager to sell and open to further negotiation.

You can also run your own "Business Wanted" ad in trade journals or local or national newspapers.

Your advisers

Ask your banker, attorney and accountant for leads or information about potential purchase opportunities. Other professional firms that work with small businesses, suppliers and local business groups are all part of an informal network that is often the first to hear that an owner wants to call it quits.

Finding a Broker

You can find business brokers through other businesspeople, your local *Yellow Pages,* and the International Business Brokers Association, located in Concord, Mass. (508–369–2490).

Business brokers

Brokers can take information about the kind of business you're looking for, then try to match you with appropriate possibilities (see the accompanying box). You can expect to be charged an hourly rate or a percentage of the price of the business you purchase. Ask potential brokers for the names of three or four buyers who purchased businesses listed by the broker; then ask those buyers whether the venture worked out as billed by the broker, how they were treated by the broker, and whether they would use the same broker to buy another business. Remember that brokers work on commissions paid by the seller, much as real estate brokers do, and thus tend to represent the interests of the seller. Some business brokers, however, work as buyers' agents.

Doing the Homework

Once you've found a business that interests you, you have to figure out if, and why, you actually want to buy it. Shopping for a business demands all the careful planning required when starting from scratch, and it also calls for wending your way through the history of the seller's decisions and mistakes.

Why Is the Seller Selling?

There's a saying that when you buy a used car you're buying someone else's headache. That's sometimes true for secondhand businesses, too. So start by answering the most obvious question: Why is the present owner trying to sell? Among the possibilities:

The business is a money-loser.

Or, it isn't profitable enough for the present owner. These reasons don't necessarily rule the business out for you. It may be badly managed, or the owner may be taking out too much in salary, or economic conditions affecting the business may be about to turn around.

The owner has personal reasons.

Perhaps the owner wants to retire or is in ill health. This also doesn't rule out the business, especially if those personal reasons have nothing to do with the success of the business. A motivated owner and a successful business are a good combination for a potential buyer.

An ill wind blows.

Simply put, the seller may know something you don't. Maybe the market is saturated and profit margins are about to collapse. Maybe a major revenue-producing contract for the business is expiring and won't be renewed. Maybe the business is going to take a heavy hit from new competition (many small retailers have found the going much tougher after a big discount operation like Wal-Mart has opened nearby). These are the kinds of problems that can transform a going concern into a bad investment.

It should be obvious that buying a business can be tricky and that it can be difficult to determine whether the owner's reason for selling is a reason for you *not* to buy. All of this means moving very cautiously when you consider buying a business.

What to Ask the Owner

Among the questions to ask the owner of a business you're considering buying:

- **What did you work at before** this business?

- **Do you like** what you've been doing?

- **How many hours a week** do you work?

- **How much have you invested** in your business?

- **What's your gross?** Your profit?

- **How much do you take** as a salary?

- **Where do you purchase** your goods or services? Have you used these vendors for a long time? Have you compared prices recently from competing suppliers?

- **Is your lease transferable?**

- **What kinds of business taxes or licenses** do you pay? How often do licenses need to be renewed?

- **What do you intend to do** after selling this business?

- **If you had it to do again,** would you still have gone into this business? What did you do right? What do you wish you had done differently?

Finding an Appraiser

The American Society of Appraisers (535 Herndon Parkway, Suite 150, Herndon, VA 22070; 703–478–2228 or 800–272–8258) can provide a list of business appraisers. Call or write the society for more information.

Those Who Can Help

You could start by talking informally with people who know a little something about the business and its current operations: its customers, employees and suppliers of goods and services. Is the operation run well? Are customers loyal? Is the quality of the goods or services constant? Are bills paid on time? The answers to those questions can alert you to some problems, and may also show you ways of making a business more profitable.

As when you start a business, you'll also need to turn to the experts: your lawyer, accountant, banker, and other people who can help you scrutinize the company and give you some insight into it. (The roles of these experts are discussed more fully in Chapter 14, "The Good Guys.") Local chambers of commerce may be able to give you information about general business conditions in your area; professional associations are sources of information about business practices and profitability in different industries. (Sources of information about different types of businesses are also discussed in Chapter 5, and ways of researching a business's market and prospects are covered in Chapter 8.)

Besides drafting any sales contract, a good lawyer can also make you aware of what you need to know about the business. He can help interpret existing leases for equipment or property, contracts for deeds, pending lawsuits, and any other agreements into which the business has already entered.

Your accountant can examine the business's financial records and help determine whether the business is on sound footing, easily stabilized footing, or sandy footing that could be washed away by an incoming tide of red ink (see the box on page 257). For more insight into the business's financial standing, you'll want to see bank and credit references, too.

An appraiser specializing in business appraisals can help you determine the value of an existing business (see the box at left).

All that help isn't cheap. An appraiser's thorough analysis of a business can cost several thousand dollars; attorneys can command $300 an hour or more.

You may also be able to get some help and guidance by contacting the nearest district office of the U.S. Small Business Administration, listed in the government, or blue, pages of your phone book. The SBA's Service Corps of Retired Executives (SCORE), also mentioned in other chapters in this book, may be able to give you further insight into the workings of a particular business or industry (see especially page 188).

Any time you or your advisers see red flags, be prepared to investigate further or to drop the business from consideration if necessary. Causes for concern include: severe or increasing losses, unpaid tax liabilities, unsettled lawsuits against the company, expensive or otherwise unfavorable long-term contracts with suppliers or employees, and long-term leases at far above current market rates.

If a seller refuses to open up all the books, just walk away. And don't take the seller's word that the books you're

Looking at the Books

Robert F. Klueger, a corporate and tax attorney and author of *Buying and Selling a Business: A Step-By-Step Guide* (John Wiley & Sons), provides a detailed guide for reviewing a firm's books. He includes among the records that should be reviewed by you or your experts to determine the financial health of a business:

- **Income statements and balance sheets** from the previous three to five years. Income statements show income and expenses; balance sheets show assets and liabilities as of a particular date, a sort of financial snapshot.

- **Income-tax returns** from the previous three to five years.

- **Any loan agreements.**

- **Any current contracts** with major customers or suppliers.

- **Any patents or trademarks** used by the business. You want to be sure the business owns what it uses and to learn whether any valuable patents are about to expire. Klueger points out that if a patent expires, other businesses could jump in and sell what may have been an exclusive product or service for far less than what the business had previously charged.

- **Records of accounts receivable and accounts payable.**

- **Any outstanding litigation.**

- **Any insurance policies.**

- **Any contracts** with unions or employees.

- **Any leases** for real estate or equipment.

- **Records of the age and condition** of any buildings or equipment.

*Once you've
researched the
business, you need to
outline its future with
a written plan.*

being shown aren't the "real" books because some profits have been skimmed from the till and away from the eyes of the IRS. You shouldn't pay for undocumented profits—and, of course, you should know that it is illegal to do business this way yourself.

Put It in Writing

Once you've researched the business, you need to outline its future with a written plan. This plan is your blueprint, summing up everything you've learned about the venture and its market, its competitors, its profitability, its location, and its projected future costs, sales and profits. Again, these are the same things you have to look at when you consider starting your business from scratch. (If you've skipped directly to this chapter, go back to Chapter 6, which will give you an overview for a plan of action and all the aspects of starting a business that you need to consider.) Putting everything on paper will help you understand just what you're getting into and will prepare you well for future challenges if the deal goes through.

Negotiating the Deal

If your accountant and other experts give you the nod, you're ready to negotiate. One attractive reason to buy an existing business is that you may be able to get it for less money than you would spend to start from scratch. In some cases, you can take over a business simply by assuming responsibility for its debts because the owner is doing all he can do to get out from under. That can be a good deal so long as the potential profitability of the business outweighs and can soon erase the debts. In other cases, you may be able to use the assets of the business as collateral for loans that are made to purchase the business. That can be more attractive than having to pledge your personal assets for a loan.

Formulas abound for determining the "right" price and vary according to the category of business involved—retail, wholesale, service, consulting or manufacturing—

and even within those groupings. Among the ways a business's worth may be determined:

Book Value of Assets

Calculating the value of a business's assets and deducting that from the business's liabilities is one of the simplest ways of coming up with its value. However, it can be simplistic. As Michael Coltman points out in *Buying and Selling A Small Business* (Self-Counsel Press), the book value of an asset (cost minus the amount by which it's depreciated) may not reflect its actual market, or resale, value. You could wind up paying more for something than it's worth in the used-goods marketplace. Office equipment, particularly computer equipment, can rapidly become outdated. Even the book value of the land owned by a business can be overstated if the local commercial real estate market has sagged markedly.

The Cost of Replacing the Business

This values the business based on what it would cost to replace its physical assets (any useful buildings and equipment), minus a reasonable amount for depreciation, plus the current value of its land, inventory and other assets.

But the value of a business depends on lots of things besides the cost of building and buying the business's structure and assets. This method tells you nothing about the business's profit potential or economic viability—key issues for any purchaser.

Expected Business Earnings

A better way of determining what you might pay for a business is to base any purchase price on the earnings you expect the business to produce. Under one common pricing method, the price should not exceed four to five times the anticipated after-tax annual earnings of the business. You should be able to come up with a tentative figure for anticipated earnings based on the financial his-

A better way of determining what you might pay for a business is to base any purchase price on the earnings you expect the business to produce.

tory review, outlined earlier in this chapter.

Let's say you estimate that the business's annual profit after all expenses (including your salary) will be

$30,000. If you want to recover the purchase price of the business in four to five years, then you'll want to pay no more than $120,000 to $150,000 (four to five times the anticipated annual earnings of $30,000). Of course, this price is just a starting point and would be adjusted to reflect any liabilities you're assuming, general market trends and other factors affecting the desirability of the business.

One of those factors is an intangible asset: *goodwill.* Sellers almost always want to get compensation for goodwill, which represents the effort they've poured into building the reputation of the business and developing a loyal customer base. However, for your purposes, the value of goodwill should be limited to the amount of profit the business earns in excess of what the average business of its type earns. If a seller wants to be paid for goodwill, let him or her try to prove that the business's profits have indeed been higher than average for that type and size of business.

Clearly, there's potential for a lot of back-and-forth haggling in establishing a purchase price. You'll have to be looking not only at the financial figures as you understand them and as they're explained to you by your accountant and appraiser but also at the situation of the individual business owner—how much he or she wants to sell the business, where there might be some flexibility on price, and so on.

Financing the Purchase

Once you've settled on a price, you need to have a way of paying for the business. This is one area where buying a business can have some clear advantages over starting from scratch.

It's usually easier to get financing to buy an existing business than to start a new one. With an existing business you often have hard assets—equipment, inventories, buildings, real estate—to use as collateral for a loan from a bank.

The seller of the business can also be a great source of financing. With seller financing, the seller makes a loan to you so you can purchase the business. If you don't pay back the loan, of course, the seller—now lender—could take back control of the business. Arnold S. Goldstein, author of *Starting On a Shoestring: Building a Business Without a Bankroll,* (John Wiley & Sons) says that sellers often resist financing the sale of their businesses initially, but that they typically will agree to finance anywhere from 30% to 80% of the purchase price, often at a lower interest rate than you could get through a bank.

Before you leap at seller financing, though, ask yourself whether it's a good deal or a last resort that you're turning to because a bank has a good reason for denying financing—a reason you should take to heart before committing yourself financially.

Other sources of money include the usual cast of characters: family members, individual investors and, occasionally, state or federal loan programs. (Ways and means to finance your business are discussed more fully in Chapter 17.)

A Good Contract

Details of any financing arrangement will be covered in the *contract* for the purchase. These agreements can be very complex and you'll want to have a lawyer drafting the documents. Any contract should have a list of the assets you're buying and the liabilities you're assuming, and it should include warranty provisions that assure you clear

Before you leap at seller financing, ask yourself whether it's a good deal or a last resort.

Once the deal is done, it's time for you to dedicate yourself to your business with the same single-mindedness that you would bring to starting up from scratch.

title to the business and protect you against any legal problems that have not been disclosed or that could arise in the future based on what the business did in the past.

The contract could also include provisions preventing the seller from going into competition against you within a certain geographic distance of the business or for a stated number of years.

Your accountant should also review any purchase contract to make sure it lets you take full advantage of any tax breaks for expenses incurred in purchasing a business and its assets.

Wrap Up the Loose Ends

Here are a few things you should do before closing on the sale:

- **Have your attorney form any required legal entities.** If you're forming a corporation for the purpose of buying the business, you'll want to form it before buying the business so the corporation, not you, will be the owner. (See Chapter 11 for more on the legal form of your business.)

- **Make the rounds of the seller's principal suppliers and customers.** You want to make a transition as smooth as possible, with no surprises for you or them.

- **Meet with key employees.** Try to tell them, to the extent possible or practical, the direction in which you want to take the business.

Buying a business means buying past decisions and, in some cases, past mistakes. Go in with your eyes open, your financial and legal bases covered, and your mind satisfied that you got the best deal you could get. Now, all you have to do is dedicate yourself to your business with the same single-mindedness that you would bring to starting up from scratch.

Getting Organized

Rolando Beramendi doesn't claim to be a detail-oriented person. "All the forms you need to fill out, all the things you need to buy!" he says, remembering what went into starting his food-importing business. "I went nuts trying to keep track of it all at the beginning. Every time I turned around there was something else we needed to buy or take care of."

For many small-business people, getting organized can be the full-time job they have to complete before beginning the full-time job of running the business. Here's a guide to some of the elements you may want to consider as you get ready for your first day.

Licenses and Permits

Not every division of local government will have licensing or permit requirements for you to meet before you start your venture. But any division *could.* The specific licenses you'll need will depend on the business you're running—a bookstore, for example, won't need a food and beverage license. Keep in mind that running a business from home won't necessarily free you from these legalities.

So start at the lowest level of government—typically with your municipal court clerk or business licensing office—and work your way up through county and state levels to find out what permits or licenses, if any, you need for your business. Starting with the most "localized" government is best because smaller offices will be able to guide you to larger entities when necessary. Your attorney

Getting organized can be a full-time job before beginning the full-time job of running your business.

should also be able to tell you what licenses you'll need and help you to get them. (For other sources of help with licenses and regulations, see Chapter 16.)

Negotiating and Signing a Lease

If you need work space outside your home, consider leasing instead of buying business space. You'll tie up less of your start-up funds, and that's a major advantage for most businesses (an issue discussed in Chapter 9). The true benefit of any lease, though, depends upon its terms.

What to Look For

Among the things you should look for when leasing any property:

A building that is well-maintained and in good condition

Your lease should specify what happens (for example, what your rights are, and what reductions in rent will be made by the landlord) if the space you're leasing isn't ready by the move-in date.

A clear explanation of the common areas you'll be able to use

Common areas include parking spaces, driveways, loading docks, hallways, elevators, storage and dumpsters.

The right to renew your lease when it expires

With an option to renew, you can extend your lease beyond the original term, but you don't have to. The option can also specify what the new rent would be, so you can do some longer-term planning knowing what you'd be paying for your space. If you don't have an option, your landlord could toss you out of your space when your lease is up, or increase your rent to the point where you couldn't afford to stay.

An explanation of what building services your rent covers

These may include electricity, heating, ventilation, air-conditioning, cleaning, garbage removal, recycling pickup, maintenance and security.

Commercial space often doesn't include round-the-clock heating and air-conditioning; office buildings, for example, typically cut back or eliminate air-conditioning at night and on weekends. Be sure you know what you're getting, especially if you or your equipment will be working non-standard hours. Computers, for example, may not operate in extremes of heat or cold.

Check on what kind of security service the landlord provides. You'll want to be confident that you and your employees or clients will have easy access to your office and that people who have no business being there won't. Inquire about escort service to your car after hours or whether management provides parking-lot security, especially after dark.

The right to make improvements to your space

Besides the right to make improvements to your space, you'll want the right to remove any improvements when you leave. Otherwise, anything—air conditioners,

Checking Out a Building

Ultimately, you'll have to visit and inspect any space you're considering leasing (or buying). Among the things you'll want to find out:

- The age of the building.
- The condition of all mechanical systems, including electrical, plumbing, and heating/air-conditioning.
- The extent of any necessary remodeling.
- Access to the building: Are the doors large enough to easily bring in fixtures or items you'll be selling? Is the building accessible to people with disabilities?
- Availability of public bathrooms.
- Availability of storage or warehouse space.
- Type of security system (door locks, fire and smoke alarms, burglar alarms).
- Type and amount of insurance on the property.

It's important to understand what you're responsible for under each type of lease you are considering.

built-in desks, shelving—that you attach to the space could wind up belonging to your landlord.

Calculating Your Rent

There are several ways to determine rent:

- **With a flat payment** (or gross lease), you pay the same monthly rent over the term of the lease, and the landlord is responsible for all expenses of operating the building.

- **In a net lease,** you also pay for at least some of the real estate taxes on the property.

- **With a net-net lease,** you add property insurance to your costs.

- **In a net-net-net lease** (typical of leases for industrial property), you are responsible for virtually all building expenses—property taxes, insurance, repairs, and so on.

- **A percentage lease** specifies a fixed monthly rent, plus a percentage of the gross sales of your business. This is most commonly found in leases to retail businesses, especially in malls and shopping centers; you should try to specify that the percentage apply only to sales above a relatively high amount and that there be a cap on the total rent you can be charged, no matter how high your sales go.

It's important to understand what you're responsible for under each type of lease you are considering, and to know how leases differ when comparing leasing options in different buildings. For example, a net-net-net lease can be a good deal if the rent is low, the building is in excellent shape and property taxes are moderate and stable; it could be a terrible deal if none of those things is true.

What Length of Lease?

Leases can range in length from less than a year to more than 20 years. What length of lease should you look for?

When commercial real estate markets are strengthening, many people advise businesses to sign long-term leases so they won't have to worry about future rent hikes that could drive them out of their property. When markets are weak, the advice is typically to "go short" so you can take advantage of weak rental markets and even negotiate reductions in rent. The only problem is, people have trouble predicting what future rental markets will be like. The best advice is simply to sign the contract that you're most comfortable with, that you can afford, and that gives you the best options for renewing and extending your lease if you want to remain at the same location in later years.

A Cost-Efficient Office Alternative

If you just need an office in which to work and meet with clients, you can opt for a traditional layout in which you have your own entryway, reception area and back offices; or a system in which you have your own leased space but share a common entrance with other businesses. In this *shared arrangement* or *shared office suite,* each tenant typically pays a proportional share for a receptionist, along with additional fees for shared secretarial services, copying machines, fax machines, and so on. Such arrangements can help small start-ups keep their overhead down, while ensuring access to important tools and services. Commercial real estate brokers should be familiar with shared arrangements. The usual leasing considerations will apply.

Signs

One of Susan Dickman's first purchases when she opened her pet-grooming business in Chicago was her sign—a large red-and-yellow creation that spelled out "Groomingtails" in neon. Mack said it helped establish her business right away. "It really stood out—people even came in to tell me how different the neighborhood looked when part of the sign burned out for a few days."

Dickman later shortened the name of her business to "Groomies," but by then she didn't need an expensive new

Shared arrangements can help small start-ups keep their overhead down, while ensuring access to important tools and services.

sign to generate business. "After establishing a reputation, I didn't feel the need for it," Dickman says. "Just a little plaque was very cost-effective for me."

A sign can cost as little as you need to spend on it,—say, under $50—or as much as you want, into the thousands. But look at it as an investment as well as an expenditure. Effective signs will pay for themselves many times over. The best signs are:

Simple

You want the name of your business on your sign so people can find you. You don't need much else—messages or mottos can detract from your name.

Eye-catching

Use designs or colors that stand out and contrast well with the surrounding buildings and signs. Black lettering on a white background is a simple but high-contrast combination.

Readable

It's not enough that potential customers *see* your sign—they have to be able to read it as well. Letters that are four inches high can be read from a distance of about 100 feet; foot-high letters can be deciphered from almost 400 feet away. Typefaces (letter designs) intended to create a mood or to represent a historical or foreign theme, for example, can be very beautiful—but so difficult to read that passersby won't even try.

Sign companies should be able to help you choose the right size and style of lettering for your location as well as help you pick out the materials your sign will be made of and incorporate logos or other artwork into the design.

Getting the Okay

• •

The documents you might have to pay for before opening your business could include:

- Business license.

- Construction permit.

- Occupancy permit.

- Fire inspection certificate.

- Health department license or certificate.

- Food and beverage license.

- Commercial motor vehicle license.

- An inspection certificate from the Occupational Safety and Health Administration (OSHA).

Good sign companies, knowledgeable about local codes and laws governing signs, can also help by arranging for any necessary local sign permits. Tom Brickler, owner of The Neon Shop, a Chicago sign company, says the time and expense of doing that is typically included in the cost of the sign.

Signs, and inclusion in a building directory, may be provided for in your lease. If your business is located in a mall—strip or enclosed—you'll have to deal with its sign regulations. And if you're working out of your home, you probably won't have any sign at all. Zoning regulations often prohibit commercial signs in residential areas, and neighbors usually aren't nuts about signs either. (Even commercial vehicles painted with business names and logos may be verboten.) But you can make sure your house number is easy to see—day and night—from the street if clients or delivery services come to you.

Guidelines for finding a sign company are similar to those you would follow for finding many other types of vendors: Visit the shop and talk about what you need. Ask for references and call other customers or go look at examples of the company's work. Or, if you see a sign you like, ask who made it, then contact that company. You can also find companies listed under "Signs" in your Yellow Pages.

Parking and Landscaping

No matter what kind of business you're starting, you may be required to provide a certain number of parking spaces for your business. The number may depend on the number of part-time or full-time workers that you employ.

Local government offices—the traffic or public safety department is a good place to start—should have relevant parking guidelines, including any special requirements for delivery areas or handicapped parking zones within your private lot area. If you're leasing your space, your landlord may be responsible for providing adequate parking. The landlord may also pay for painting the lines that denote parking spaces. In any case, providing adequate parking for customers, clients and

Local government offices should provide relevant parking guidelines.

A college agricultural or extension service may be able to help you with design and planting suggestions for free.

suppliers is always a good business move.

Be sure any spaces assigned or belonging to your business meet all regulations, including size requirements. It can be tempting to try and squeeze in an extra space by making all of the spaces a little smaller than mandated, but that can be a false economy: People involved in accidents in parking spaces have filed lawsuits claiming that the spaces were not appropriately sized. Companies that paint parking lots should know the standards. Also, any parking area should be well-lit at night and free of garbage or debris.

Landscaping can run the gamut from a couple of windowboxes or a rock pathway, to professionally planted and maintained trees, shrubs and flowers. Good landscaping can make your entire business space more attractive; in the case of a retail business, it can even help draw customers who might otherwise drive or walk right by just another commercial building. Just remember that *maintaining* a professionally designed landscape can be the most expensive part of a landscaping project, with cumulative maintenance costs sometimes exceeding initial outlays after as little as three years.

You can hire a professional landscape contractor to maintain your property, or you can do the work yourself if you're willing to invest in any specialized supplies and equipment you'll need. A college agricultural or extension service may be able to help you with design and planting suggestions for free. If you choose to hire a nursery or professional landscaper, check your Yellow Pages under "Landscaping."

Office Decor

You should find out what a landlord will do for you when you negotiate the terms of a lease. Virtually anything related to the appearance of your space (and its improvements) can be included in negotiations: moving internal walls; installing electrical outlets or additional lighting; raising or lowering ceilings; bringing in and caring for plants; providing carpeting and draperies.

Some basic rules apply to the appearance of any business area. Keep it as clean as possible, even if that means *you* take out the garbage, scrub the bathroom and sweep up the floors once a week. Make sure you have enough filing cabinets—an office full of loose files isn't just inefficient, it's annoying. Don't skimp on lamps—good lighting can go a long way toward creating a cheerful and attractive atmosphere. A coat of white paint can also go a long way to brightening an office.

Of course, you could hire a designer or interior decorator to put together the "look" of your office. But if you're trying to keep your start-up costs as low as possible, you can also look at how other, similar businesses designed their offices, and even ask them to recommend places to shop for furnishings or design help. You can also get some ideas by visiting local furniture show-

"Don't knock it. The copy machine hasn't broken down in a month."

Toos, Cartoonists & Writers Syndicate

rooms and by looking at office-design magazines. Don't neglect used-furniture shops or classified ads for second-hand furniture; used items sell for a fraction of the cost of new, even if they're only marginally worn. And if you are buying new furniture, don't limit yourself to "business furniture stores." Often, something that says "business" on it costs more than something similar that says "home." A $50 card table from a department store could work just as well as a $200 computer printer table from a business furniture store. Leasing furniture is an option, too, especially if you can't afford to buy what you have in mind.

In general, try first to come up with something that you're comfortable with and can work in, and then do some comparison shopping that will allow you to keep your start-up costs low without compromising your credibility or appeal with potential clients or customers.

There seems to be no end to the office equipment you could buy, and there will always be something else that you might be able to use.

Obviously, the overall look of your workplace will depend on whom—if anyone—you need to appeal to or impress. The waiting room of an auto service center will probably emphasize utility and comfort, while the conference room of a graphic-design firm will want to display its creativity and design sense. If you are the only person you have to satisfy, then this is your opportunity to create the work environment that you've always imagined.

Office Equipment

Working for yourself means suddenly realizing that you—not "the guys in purchasing"—are responsible for purchasing and maintaining a variety of equipment that you probably used to take for granted. There seems to be no end to the office equipment you *could* buy, and there will always be something else that you *might* be able to use. Every piece of equipment comes in countless variations to suit every taste and budget. You'll have to check the variations yourself and consider what you can actually use and afford. But here are some thoughts on the office equipment you're most likely to consider in one form or another.

Desk Chair

This may be the most important piece of equipment you'll buy. Chances are you'll spend more time in your chair than anywhere else when working. So make it a good chair that you're comfortable with. Sit in it for a while—20 minutes is not too long—to see how it suits you. If you'll be doing your own typing, sit in a typing position at a desk. Does the curve of the chair back adequately fit and support your back? If your back tires or aches, or if you feel uncomfortable in any other way, move on to another chair.

Other factors

- **Do you want armrests?**

- **Will you want to roll from place to place** in your office, say from computer table to desk?

- **Will you want a spring mechanism** that allows you to lean back (or put your feet up on your desk)?

- **Do you need to adjust the seat height?**

Desks

The standard commercial desk is 60 inches wide, 30 inches deep and 29 inches high. Smaller and larger versions are available. Desks for typing are 27 inches high; don't plan to type at a higher desk because you'll soon find it's not terribly comfortable. That's why you will probably want a separate typing table or computer table, possibly arranged as an L with your desk. Think about the kind of storage, if any, that you'll want beneath your desk—center drawer or side file drawers, for instance.

Filing Cabinets

You'll probably want at least one, with at least two drawers, along with manila folders and hanging files, to make organizing and locating materials easier. Legal-size drawers take more space, but they allow you to file 14-inch-long documents without having to fold them. The question of whether to use lateral or vertical files is mostly one of personal preference.

Shelves

Shelves can hold current projects, books, magazines, supplies, telephone directories, and much more. Shelves can effectively function as a supply closet if need be.

Telephones

If you're going to be a one- or two-person shop initially, a single telephone line may be all you need. If you're transferring information via computer modem or fax machine, you'll probably want to have two phone lines. The choices for telephone service now in-

Shelves can effectively function as a supply closet if need be.

clude single-line, two-line and multiline telephones, and telephone systems that link all the phones of a business into a "network" that can either be installed at your business or operated from regional facilities. How many lines you'll need will vary depending on your business; a consultant working alone may find one speaking line with a call-waiting feature sufficient, whereas a mail-order business may require multiple lines.

Similarly, you can now have your own answering machine for when you're out of the office; pay for a private answering service with operators to take your messages; or use a "voice mail" system provided by your local telephone company that will take messages electronically when you are on the phone or out of the office. These machines and services can help eliminate missing a potential sale and keep you from playing "telephone tag" with your associates. Some businesses choose the live services over the automated ones in the belief that people are more likely to leave a message with a person than with a machine.

How to shop

The technology and hardware of telephone communications change rapidly; *Consumer Reports* magazine periodically compares telephones and telephone answering machines, as does *What to Buy for Business* (see the accompanying box). You also can learn a lot about your telephone options just by going to a store that sells lots of different phones and comparing prices and features. Speak with a business service representative with your

---

Keeping Pace With Office Technology

● ●

An excellent source of information and advice about purchasing office equipment is *What to Buy for Business,* published by What to Buy Inc. (924 Anacapa St., Suite 4G, Santa Barbara, CA 93101; 800–247–2185; $121 for a subscription to ten issues, including any updates; $23 per single issue, plus $3 for shipping and handling). Subtitled *The Independent Consumer Guide to Business Equipment,* this publication accepts no advertising. Each issue covers a major type of office equipment, offering introductory discussion as well as equipment specifications and prices, "Best Buys" and "Bad Buys," and user feedback. What to Buy Inc. publishes frequent updates as changes in technology warrant and occasionally focuses on the specific needs of smaller businesses.

local phone company to get information about business rates and features. In general, start small until you have a clear idea of what your future needs might be. One bit of advice about buying versus renting the telephones themselves: In most cases, it now makes economic sense to buy if you anticipate using the phone for more than two years. (Telephone needs are also discussed in Chapter 16.)

Typewriters

Even in the telecommunications age, many people work for themselves using no fancier equipment than a typewriter, which can come in handy for writing an occasional letter or addressing envelopes. However, if you'll need to store lots of data that can be retrieved quickly, maintain complex bookkeeping or mailing-list systems, keep track of inventory, do financial spreadsheets, or send out several letters, reports and other documents on a regular basis, you'll probably want to consider a...

Computer Resources

● ●

An especially good resource for self-employed folks is *Home Office Computing* (P.O. Box 53561, Boulder, CO 80322–3561; $19.97 per year) a monthly that deals in lay terms with the issues affecting people who work out of their homes. Much of the information in this magazine is useful to start-ups whether your business is home-based or not.

For the most current information on personal computers generally, your best bet is to check the computer magazines sold at your local newsstand.

Personal Computer

Depending on the nature of your business, this may be the single most important piece of equipment that you'll buy. Computers prices have fallen to the point that a computer, monitor (screen) and printer can be had for less than $1,000. A modem, either internally added or externally attached to your computer, will allow your computer to exchange information with other computers. A "fax board," added internally, will allow you to send material from your computer to someone else's fax machine. Both can cost less than $100. That's the hardware of the system. You'll also need to budget for software that you'll need for such functions as word processing, communications, accounting or other spreadsheet applications, graphics, inventory control, project planning and scheduling.

Despite falling prices, don't skimp today while awaiting tomorrow's bargain. If a PC will be essential to your business, this is the time to push the limits of your budget. Buy cutting-edge equipment with more speed and memory than you can use now. That will allow you to keep up with new versions of your software without having to purchase every new generation of hardware. Remember, you're not buying a home computer, you're buying a business computer.

When shopping, your best choice may not be name-brand hardware made by the market leaders and sold by local computer dealers. Your best deal could be an IBM-compatible machine purchased by mail order from direct-sale manufacturers. Direct-sale manufacturers and large name-brand retailers have been locked in competi-

Tips for Desk Jockeys

If working for yourself means long periods spent at your desk and computer, be sure to take periodic breaks and *move around*. That's a cheap way to avoid fatigue, muscular discomfort and problems like carpal-tunnel syndrome, a painful nerve inflammation in the wrist that can result from using your hands and wrists repetitively.

But the positioning of your body, your desk and your chair will also be important. The Human Factors Society, an ergonomists' group, offers these practical tips:

- **The home row of your keyboard** should be at elbow height when your fingers rest on the keys.

- **The desk surface for writing** should also be at elbow height.

- **Adjust your chair height** as needed.

- **The top of your computer screen** should be no higher than eye level.

- **Seat cushioning** should be 1½ to 2 inches deep.

- **Sit back in your chair and lean against the backrest.** The front end of the chair shouldn't rise up and press against the backs of your legs, nor should your feet lift off the floor. If you can't adjust the chair, use a footstool to avoid cutting off the circulation behind your knees.

- **Consider such gadgets as** lumbar pillows for extra back support, document holders that mount next to your computer screen, task lighting that directs light at your hard copy and keeps glare off the monitor, and screen hoods to cut down on glare.

tion, with each type of vendor claiming superior product quality and service. Many direct-sale manufacturers do provide consistent and responsive service and support—presuming that you're technically proficient and comfortable enough to, say, install your software yourself, do any troubleshooting over the phone, or remove a defective memory card yourself for replacement. If you want or need more hand-holding, you may want to visit a local computer retailer.

And while you're at it

For help with shopping for and setting up a computer system that meets your business needs, you should develop a working relationship with a computer consultant. Even if you are computer literate, you won't always have time to do it yourself. You'll want someone who can help you add to your system, streamline it, and develop computer security measures as needed. And you'll definitely want someone on call in case of a system failure or other emergency. Talking with other self-employed people is a great way to get a referral to a freelance systems manager.

For other sources of information on hardware and software, see the box on page 275.

Fax Machines and Copiers

These have also plummeted in price in recent years. Fax machines are now used regularly by anyone who wants to send or receive printed materials in minutes for the price of a telephone call. Copiers—especially so-called desktop or personal copiers—have also infiltrated an increasing number of offices. Before you invest in either of these products, though, figure out how often you'll need them initially. If you're not making lots of copies regularly, the corner copy shop will still be a good deal. Many copy shops also have fax machines. They may charge as little as $1 per page to send or receive a document. (Some have been known to charge as much as $5 for the first page and $2 a page thereafter. It wouldn't take long to justify purchasing your own fax machine at that rate.)

Keeping Costs Down

Again, there's no reason you have to buy all new office equipment. Used desks and other furniture, typewriters, filing cabinets, and even computers can be perfectly good. If you do buy used electronics, try to purchase them from a business that will guarantee them for at least 90 days. To find good deals on used goods, check your newspaper's classified ads and auction pages. Many cities now have locally published advertising tabloids stuffed with classifieds of goods and services for sale. Look in the Yellow Pages under the category of equipment you want. You can even call some retail stores—slightly damaged goods may be deeply discounted at a central warehouse, and the business's own cabinets and other supplies may be sold for pennies on the dollar when a remodeling is contemplated.

Extended Service Contracts

What will you do if something goes wrong with a

Questions Worth Asking About Office Equipment

- **Do I really need** this equipment?

- **Which features** are my primary incentives for buying the equipment?

- **Can I afford the equipment?** Will the equipment "pay" in terms of increased productivity or efficiency or ease and pleasure in conducting the business?

- **Can I afford not to have the equipment?** Will my clients, suppliers and others whose business paths cross mine interpret my failure to have this equipment as a lack of professionalism or seriousness in my business?

- **Is there a cheaper way** to get the same service or options that the equipment of-

fers? (A 20-line central switchboard system may be nice, but if you don't anticipate having more than a couple of employees it's probably unnecessary.)

- **Would last year's models do fine?** Could I get the features I need without buying the latest and most powerful hardware?

- **How much space** is the equipment going to take? Do I have the space?

- **Would it be cheaper to lease** the equipment? Is the technology changing so quickly that it makes more sense to lease? Would I be better off renting the equipment until I've used it enough to know whether I should invest in a purchase?

piece of office equipment? A computer or printer that goes on the fritz can spell disaster for a small business. And in any case, not having access to something you normally rely on will be inconvenient.

Many people now pay for *service contracts* or *extended service plans* to protect themselves from technological breakdown. These agreements are usually designed to provide more coverage and—yes—service than a factory or manufacturer's warranty. Service contracts may provide for regular inspection, cleaning or maintenance; priority handling of your problem when something does go wrong; and guaranteed replacement of your ailing equipment with a free loaner machine if repairs cannot be done within a day.

The terms, costs and coverages offered will vary depending on the contract, so it can pay to shop around. Also remember that different types of equipment are subject to different levels of use, abuse and failure. These differences will also be reflected in the prices you're quoted for service contracts. Some small-business people

- **How "fast" is the equipment?** How many pages per minute does the copier copy, or the printer print, or the fax machine send? How quickly does the computer process information or run programs? You'll have to "test-drive" the computer or talk to your consultant or read up on the product to figure that out.

- **How fast do I need** the equipment to be?

- **Do I need the latest thing because it is going to become the standard** that everyone expects? In computers, for example, some software programs run only on the latest or most powerful PCs; in contrast, laser printers are considered the "standard" in some circles, but many businesses continue to operate just fine with older technologies.

- **How am I going to learn** to use the equipment? Will the company selling the equipment provide training if necessary?

- **How long will this equipment last?**

- **How reliable** is the equipment? What will I do if something goes wrong?

- **How long it will be before this equipment is outmoded?**

- **What additional services** do I want with the equipment? If I'm buying a computer, do I want a service maintenance contract? If I'm getting telephone lines installed, do I want access to call waiting, call forwarding, conference calling, and other services?

believe that service contracts on office copiers are particularly good investments.

Your Filing System

There's no best way to set up a filing system. What's important is that the system be one that you—or whoever else uses it—can easily understand and follow, so a minimal amount of time is spent looking for information that you just know is "around here somewhere."

The system also should be one that can expand as your business generates more paperwork. It may be all right initially to have just a single folder labeled "Expenses," but as time goes on you'll find yourself breaking that down into separate categories for supplies, office equipment, consulting fees, wages, utilities, and so on. The key with a filing system, as with your business hours, is that it be *consistent* — the same rules and practices for filing papers should be followed every day.

A few ways to set up your filing system:

The Portable Office

People used to complain about being "chained to a desk." With advances in business technology, people who are constantly working need no longer be chained to a desk—they can instead be chained to a job or business no matter *where* they are.

Of course, these high-tech developments are also tremendously helpful to people who are working for themselves. Here's just some of the business equipment that used to be thought of as confined to an office but that is now portable enough to be tossed in a car and taken on the road, effectively allowing (or forcing) you to take your office wherever you go:

- Personal computers.
- Computer printers.
- Fax machines.
- Copying machines.
- Mobile or cellular telephones.
- Video recorders.
- Dictation equipment.

Alphabetical filing

This is relatively simple. Just put your papers in alphabetical order according to the topic of the file—"Jones Account" or "Lease," for example. You'll have to remember, of course, whether you filed "Jones Account" under "J" or "A."

Subject filing

You can file papers alphabetically by categories—for example, "Clients," "Expenses"—and within those categories file alphabetically by subject. "Jones Account" would go within the Clients file, "Lease" within the Expenses file.

Date filing

Maintain two files, one containing copies of everything you generate—bills, invoices, letters—by date, and another containing the letters, bills, and other papers you receive every day and decide to keep.

Many businesses maintain more than one filing system, combining date files with a separate alphabetical file, for example. Larger businesses also use number-

Control Your Paperwork

A good source of information and ideas on how to set up and maintain filing systems—without drowning in them—is *Taming the Paper Tiger,* by Barbara Hemphill (Kiplinger Books), which shows you how to organize *all* the paper in your life.

Odds and Ends

Among the assorted supplies that you won't be able to grab from the company's supply closet anymore:

- A telephone card file like a Rolodex.
- Pens and pencils.
- Pencil sharpener.
- Clock.
- In and out-boxes for current papers and projects.
- Paper.
- Paper clips.
- Rubber bands.
- Scissors.
- Cork bulletin board.
- Push pins.
- Stapler.
- Staple remover.
- Adhesive note pads.

A handy idea: A small postage scale costs less than $15 and will save you trips to the post office, thus saving money over the long haul; you'll be able to affix the correct postage to envelopes instead of putting on extra stamps "just in case."

based systems for handling thousands of files. Again, the key is to have a system that you're comfortable with and that you'll always use.

Filing Equipment

Files can be kept in anything from a couple of plastic milk crates to multithousand-dollar motorized filing systems that bring the files to you (like the overhead hanging systems that dry cleaners use to bring the clothes around to the front of the shop).

Among the most common filing cabinets are vertical files (two-drawer or four-drawer versions), in which individual folders are filed from front to back; lateral cabinets, in which the folders are filed sideways; and open-shelf units, in which folders are again filed sideways but without any drawers to pull out (or to hide the files from view).

Again, the main factor in deciding what type of filing equipment you use is personal preference, along with the logistics of what will fit in the space you have available. Two-door "legal-size" vertical filing cabinets are wide enough to file 8 x 14-inch papers without having to fold them. "Full-suspension" cabinets, which essentially means the file drawers are placed on wheels on tracks, will easily slide open and shut, no matter how many files you cram in.

For more information on the multitude of office filing systems that are available, ask for catalogs from any large office-supply or furnishings company. These catalogs will also help you locate shelving and storage systems, whether elegant or industrial-strength.

Paper You Must Save

• •

You can get additional information on how long to keep records by writing to the IRS for Publication 334, *Tax Guide For Small Business*, or by talking with your accountant or attorney. In the meantime, you should keep:

- **All tax records**—receipts, calendars, logs, the works—should be retained for at least three years from the date for filing your taxes for the year in question. That means that all records for the 1994 tax return, filed on April 15, 1995, should be saved until April 15, 1998.

- **Payroll and personnel records** should also be kept for at least three years.

- **Shipping records** should be kept for at least two years.

- **All contracts** should be kept indefinitely.

Some small-business people now keep their telephone-number records in one of the portable electronic "calendars" or "telephone books" that have gained popularity in recent years, and they may also keep phone numbers in computer files.

Property and Liability Insurance

Your business can be threatened by any number of random disasters. It could be gutted by fire, destroying your entire inventory. A customer could slip on a slick spot on the floor and fall, then sue you for the costs of medical care and rehabilitation. Thieves could steal valuable equipment.

Accidents happen. That's why you need two main types of insurance for your business:

Property Insurance

This covers your building, equipment, inventory and other property. You can insure against fire, windstorms, burglary, vandalism, explosions and other disasters with property insurance policies. If you rent and are not responsible for insurance on the building, you can get policies that cover only your business property.

There are two general types of property insurance:

- **Replacement-cost** coverage reimburses you for the cost of new buildings, supplies, equipment, and so on.

- **Actual-value** insurance reimburses claims based on the estimated depreciated value of the property that you've lost.

Obviously, replacement-cost insurance will carry higher annual premiums than actual-value coverage—you'll want to compare prices and benefits and decide which level of coverage and cost you prefer.

If you have an office in your home, your homeowners policy might cover your business equipment, or you might need to add a rider to the policy. Contact your insurance company to find out what you should do.

If you rent and are not responsible for insurance on the building, you can get policies that cover only your business property.

Liability Insurance

This protects you against claims for damages to other people for which you might be held financially responsible. For example, the customer who slips on your floor could bring a negligence suit. If a product or service you sell injures someone—if, for example, you have an electrical contracting firm and your work causes a fire in the client's building—liability insurance could protect you against an ensuing lawsuit.

You may not need additional liability insurance if you're working out of your home; never have anyone come to your home for a business meeting, delivery or other purpose; don't produce a product or service that could in any way be construed as harming a client or someone else; and already have liability coverage as part of your homeowners' policy. Then again, you *still* may need it. Again, check with your insurer.

Other Types of Insurance

Depending on your business, you could require:

- **Motor vehicle insurance,** which will usually cover damage to your vehicle as well as liability coverage for damage caused by the driver of your car to other autos and people;

- **Workers' compensation,** which protects employees from medical costs and lost income due to on-the-job injuries and protects you from employee lawsuits over on-the-job injuries (which your state may require); and

- **Business interruption insurance,** which helps protect you if a disaster like a fire temporarily closes down your operation. This coverage can include such fixed expenses as salaries to key employees, taxes and interest, along with making up at least part of the revenues you'd lose while your business was temporarily closed.

Full-line insurance companies can give you more information about these policies and tell you if your existing insurance—your auto insurance, for example—should be modified to include coverage for business-related use of your car.

It can pay to check with at least a few insurers before you buy. Compare rates and make sure you're aware of any conditions or exclusions. As always, the goal is to get the most coverage for the least money.

Minding Your Own Business

If you're working for yourself for the first time, you're bound to encounter situations that you hadn't thought of and won't be prepared to deal with. However, you can minimize such occasions if you take the time early in your venture to make basic decisions about how you're going to operate on a day-to-day basis.

These "ground rules" may not come into play much at first, especially if, like many start-ups, you are initially a one-person shop. However, developing some standard policies now—about such elementary issues as when you'll be open for business or which delivery services you'll use—will prove useful as your business starts to grow.

Here are some basic areas of day-to-day operations that you can make decisions about now. Some, like how to handle cash transactions, are most relevant to retail businesses, but virtually every business will, at some point, need policies for dealing with all of these issues:

Operating and Office Hours

Perhaps the most important thing about operating hours for anyone working for themselves is that the hours be *consistent*. Potential customers find it tremendously confusing and frustrating not to know when (or if) you're open for business or available to discuss projects. Here's what happens when customers have to call you all the time to find out whether you're available: They go to someone more reliable, and they stop coming to you.

If you're in a mall, the mall management will probably dictate your hours of operation. Otherwise, think about your customers and their needs. When are they most likely to want to do business with you? Would weekend or early evening hours help them? How about early morning hours? Long hours can provide a competitive advantage. Even traditional businesses are trying to adjust their schedules to accommodate their customers. Columbus, Ohio-based Banc One, one of the leading regional banks in the U.S., has kept some of its offices open evenings, Saturdays, and even Sundays to better serve its customers whose work schedules conflict with standard banking hours.

Consistent hours don't necessarily translate into seven-day-a-week operations. A Southern California tire chain, 4 Day Tire Stores, is open 43 hours a week—but the hours are from 8:30 A.M. to 8 P.M. Wednesday through Friday and from 8:30 A.M. to 5 P.M. on Saturdays. The chain has identified these as the hours that are best for its customers and, not incidentally, most profitable for the business.

Once you've established your regular hours, plan to have at least one other person available to help whenever you're dealing with customers or clients. It is possible to get by with just yourself on the scene, but one-person shops can mean long waits for service, and potential customers may simply leave when they see a long line and only one person helping customers. (Employee hiring is discussed in Chapter 15.)

What's Overtime?

One other thing about hours: If someone working for you puts in more than 40 hours a week, he or she will probably be entitled to overtime pay—one and a half times regular hourly pay—for the time that exceeds 40 hours.

The Fair Labor Standards Act exempts people the government defines as executives, administrators, professionals and outside salespeople from this provision.

For detailed information on federal regulations governing employer-employee relations, write or call: Wage and Hour Division, Fair Labor Standards, U.S. Department of Labor, 200 Constitution Ave., N.W., Room S3502, Washington, DC 20210; 202–219–7043.

Handling Cash

If you're in a business dealing with the general public (and sometimes even if you're not), you'll need a system for handling cash so that you can avoid any confusion on the part of employees, customers or yourself. (For information about handling checks and credit cards, see Chapter 23.)

Small-business "systems" for handling cash can range from an open cash box to a state-of-the-art piece of hardware that not only gives change but also automatically records what has been purchased, tracks inventory and even enters prices (if it's linked to scanners that read product bar codes).

You may not need such a high-powered piece of equipment. But if you're running any sort of retail operation, you'll at least want a register that prints out customer receipts and also keeps a record of your daily sales for you. These "double tape" systems are common on cash registers sold today.

The Logistics

Here are some quick tips for handling cash.

Start the day with an adequate supply of change.
You can get rolls of pennies, nickels, dimes and quarters from your bank; you might want to set a regular time of day or week when you go to the bank to do this.

Don't keep large amounts of cash on the premises.
Many business owners (or their trusted assistants) take a quick run to the bank whenever the amount of excess cash on hand (that is, cash not needed in the ordinary course of running the business) tops a certain amount—say, $500 for a small retailer.

**If you are usually paid by check,
don't let the checks accumulate for long.**
Aside from the possibility that you might misplace a bundle of checks, you're losing interest on that money until it is deposited in your account.

Avoid letting employees make change for themselves.

Here's a simple rule: If an employee wants to change his $20 bill, for example, into smaller denominations, have him ask you or another authorized employee to make the change. This protects your employee from falling under suspicion of taking money from the cash register.

Ring up sales first, then bag the items.

Keeping the two steps of a sale separate will help you avoid confusion. There's nothing potentially worse than starting to ring up a sale, turning to bag an item, getting distracted…and leaving the cash register door open until you give your customer her change. An open register can simply be too tempting a target for some people. Always keep your cash drawer closed when it isn't in use.

Mention sales totals, and the amount of money you've been given, to your customer.

If you're given $10 for a $3.50 purchase, say, "That's $3.50 out of $10" as you ring up the purchase. This will help you and the customer remember how much money you've been given. It will also help avoid the kind of unpleasantness that can develop if you're handed a $10 bill that the customer thought was a $20.

Double-protect yourself against a customer claiming you were given a larger bill.

A customer might say that he or she gave you $50 instead of $20, for example. Put the cash you were handed on the front portion of the register and leave it there until you've counted out the change. *Then* put the money in the register.

Count out change aloud.

Start from the cost of the sale, and add to the amount that the customer gave you. For example, for the $3.50 sale in which you're given $10, count out "$3.50, $4, $5, $10," as you take the change out of the register. Count it out again when giving it to the customer.

Put coins in the customer's hand first, followed by paper money.

That keeps the change from sliding off the bills, forcing you and your customer to chase after it.

Shipping and Receiving

Shipping may bring to mind tractor-trailers or transoceanic containers, but it's really just another way of saying making deliveries. This can be as simple as delivering an item yourself (in which case you may want to add a delivery charge). Many self-employed people also turn to local messenger services, the U.S. Postal Service, United Parcel Service (UPS), or any of the many companies that specialize in next-day delivery.

The "standard" fees for delivery services are often negotiable. Local messenger services will discount to regular customers; even the major overnight delivery companies discount 50% or more to large customers.

All the services above (even, in some cases, the Postal Service) will pick up packages at your place of business. They may add a small pickup fee, for example, $5 per pickup regardless of the number of packages you're sending or $5 for a week's worth of pickups if you have an established account.

The message is plain: Use any quoted prices as a base and negotiate downward from there. You're likely to get the best price if you agree to give all of your business, or all of a certain type of shipping business (overnight service, for example, or all packages over ten pounds) to one company. Most companies will send you monthly summaries of

Keep on Trucking

If you're producing, buying or selling large quantities of goods, you may need to work with a common carrier—a trucking firm—on an occasional or regular basis.

You'll find companies listed in your Yellow Pages under "Trucking," "Transportation," "Delivery" or "Moving."

You can also hire a transportation broker who will locate and negotiate with carriers for you. For a list of brokers in your area, contact: The Transportation Brokers Conference of America (5845 Richmond Hwy., Suite 750, Alexandria, VA 22303; 703–329–1894).

shipments, and you can also keep track of shipments by logging them in your daily calendar or expense book.

Rules for Receiving

The flip side of delivering is receiving, and the rules here are fairly simple:

- **Always count the number of cartons,** packages or envelopes and make sure it squares with the number for which you are signing.

- **Always note any visible damage** to packages on the delivery receipt.

- **Always contact the supplier immediately** if any goods have been damaged.

- **And always keep your own record of shipments received** by noting them on a standard form—either a preprinted "Receiving Record" form or your own notebook or computer form.

Pickup at Home

A couple of quick tips if you're working out of your house or functioning as a sole proprietor:

Getting express delivery pickups by private companies is usually fairly easy. Often, you don't even have to be present when the pickup is made. With Federal Express, for example, once you open an account, you can establish a daily pickup schedule and just leave the packages outside your front door.

You'll make your life easier if you take the time to set up an account with whichever company you'll be using often; the company can bill you directly or bill your credit card.

A Few Words About Mail Service

U.S. postal rates have increased to the point where, for people who have already invested in facsimile machines, it's often cheaper to send a one-page letter within the U.S. by fax than by the mail.

It is possible to save some money on Postal Service rates by taking advantage of presort discounts. These are available to senders of large amounts of mail—typically a minimum of 500 pieces—who take the time to sort their mailing by ZIP code before taking it to the post office. There are also smaller discounts available for using the full nine-digit—rather than the five-digit—ZIP code. Third-class bulk mail can also be a big money-saver when you're sending out large numbers of identical brochures, catalogs or other materials and time is not of the essence. Bulk mail requires presorting by ZIP code and mailing a minimum of 200 pieces or 50 pounds. Compare Postal Service rates and service with those offered by UPS to see which can give you the better deal on small packages. The rules, regulations and savings on different types of discount mailings change regularly; contact your local post office for details and ask to speak with someone familiar with services for business mailers.

One other tip: Invest a few bucks in rubber stamps that say "First Class," "Do Not Fold or Bend," "Fragile", and whatever else may apply to the mail you'll be generating. These stamps will save you a lot of time otherwise spent in handwriting instructions and notes on envelopes and packages.

Security and Theft

For anyone who hires employees, "internal theft," also known as employee theft, can be a worrisome and tricky problem. The best general way to avoid having an employee theft problem is, of course, to hire only top-notch people—something that can be easier said than done. Checking references is always a good idea. Having more than one person on duty at all times also helps, because each person acts as an automatic check on the other, especially if *you* are the second person.

External theft—theft of money, equipment or merchandise by patrons or others—is also a concern for many

---

For More Postal Information

• •

U.S. Postal Service Business Centers are a source of one-on-one help for small-business mailers, providing information, acting as a liaison between you and the various divisions of the Postal Service, helping you choose appropriate services for your needs, and setting up business-reply mail accounts. The Postal Service maintains centers in most major U.S. cities; to locate the one nearest you, call your local post office.

• You can also request a free copy of the *Small Business Direct Mail Guide* from the U.S. Postal Service Marketing Department (P.O. Box 7899, Mount Prospect, IL 60056–7899).

• If bulk mailing is an important component of your venture, you may want to request a free monthly update of mailing rate and class information published by the Postal Service. Ask for *Memo to Mailers* (U.S. Postal Service, National Customer Support Center, 6060 Primacy Pkwy., Suite 101, Memphis, TN 38188–0001).

businesses. Theft deterrence can include everything from the surveillance-oriented (computerized cash registers that track every transaction, hidden cameras, security guards and undercover personnel) to the reward-oriented (profit-sharing plans that give each employee a sense of ownership and interest in the company's well-being). Positive reinforcement can also include employee discounts and year-end bonuses if losses are kept below a certain level.

Most start-ups with few employees won't need a full-blown internal security program; however, if you are interested in developing such a program, you can contact private security consultants (look in your Yellow Pages under "Security Control" or "Security Systems Consultants"). Your local chamber of commerce may have information or seminars on reducing theft loss; local police departments also can be sources of advice.

Theft Protection

• •

Concern among businesses about theft, both within the business and from outside, is so widespread that the Council of Better Business Bureaus publishes an entire book dedicated to detecting, preventing and coping with all kinds of theft.

To get a copy of *How to Protect Your Business,* send a check for $14.95, plus $2 for shipping and handling, to the Council of Better Business Bureaus Inc., Attn.: Publications Dept., 4200 Wilson Blvd., Suite 800, Arlington, VA 22203.

Establishing Procedures

Operating procedures invariably differ from one business to another and change as a business grows. It's important to: write down exactly what your procedures are, be consistent in following them, and build a pattern that can be used to show why you did something when you did it or why you changed a procedure.

Keeping an office handbook (three-ring binder) on hand for anyone's reference and updating it as policies change can be very helpful.

The box on page 294 lists some other areas for which you'll want to have well-defined rules or procedures even if you're working alone. Addressing these issues early on will keep you from having to always reinvent the wheel.

To Smoke or Not to Smoke

Smoking—and a business's policy concerning it—is a serious matter today. If you simply don't want people to smoke in your workplace, put up a No Smoking sign. Even if you don't mind having people light up in your presence, you may still have to adopt a formal policy on smoking. Many state and local laws prohibit or restrict smoking in certain public areas and places of business. Most restaurants have set aside specific areas as "smoking" and "nonsmoking," in response to either customer demand or legislative order. Even businesses that you may have once thought of as "smoke-filled" are changing their ways—some bowling alleys, for example, prohibit smoking around the lanes themselves. Remember, your own policy can be more restrictive than the local smoking regulations, but it can't be less restrictive. Check with your city hall, county health department or chamber of commerce for information on local smoking regulations. If you maintain a smoke-free workplace, mention that to your insurance

Write Your Own Rules

Rules may be the very thing you want to get away from, but you can only benefit by thinking about:

- Billing clients.
- Filing paperwork.
- Taking telephone messages.
- Answering correspondence.
- Ordering supplies and equipment.
- Hiring help of any kind.
- Delegating authority (assigning someone to be in charge when you're not available).
- Establishing staff responsibilities (who does what).

- Taking vacations.
- Handling staff pay raises, sick leaves, lunch breaks and other benefits.
- Handling employee terminations (why and how).
- Getting permission and recording expenses for business travel.
- Using the telephone for nonbusiness purposes.
- Allowing (or not allowing) employees or clients to carry food into your workplace.
- Allowing (or not allowing) employees or clients to bring pets into your workplace.

agent when negotiating business coverage and see whether she will factor that into your rate. If you purchase health insurance for yourself or any employees, inquire about discounts for coverage of nonsmokers.

Odds and Ends

Just for good measure, a few other problems that you might never encounter but should think about now:

Employees call in sick

It does happen. How will you cope when you or a key employee becomes ill? One suggestion: Line up temporary services in advance. Temp agencies are no longer just for short-term secretarial help. You can now hire accountants, writers, manual laborers, and even lawyers through temp agencies.

The power goes out

Have some small personal backup system, even if it's as simple as Coleman lanterns and candles for lighting and a battery-powered calculator so you can keep making sales.

Personal-computer users should have a system for ensuring that a power outage doesn't wipe out hours of work. If necessary, back up your files at the end of every day. If you were unable to use your PC for some period of time, a battery-run laptop computer could come in pretty handy.

Martin, Cartoonists & Writers Syndicate

Fire breaks out

You absolutely should have fire extinguishers on the premises. Depending on where you're located, you or your landlord may be required to install a sprinker system as well. And all employees should be aware of where emergency exits are and what to do in case of a fire or other crisis. Exit doors and escape routes should be clearly marked.

Customers leave valuables

Simple: Have a designated lost-and-found area, whether it's a spare office or a shoebox in your desk drawer. Try to call the client if you know or can identify the owner of the lost goods—there's nothing like an honest business that takes a few seconds for this kind of personal service to keep customers coming back.

Someone gets hurt

Have a first-aid kit available—and know what's in it and how to use it; keep a list of emergency phone numbers posted in an easy-to-see location.

A business vehicle breaks down

Know where you can turn for short-term rental of a car, delivery van, or whatever motorized mode of transportation if yours has taken ill.

When a Client Is Unhappy

Sooner or later every business in every field picks up a displeased customer, or two, or three. If you're a consultant, you may want to establish a policy about reworking part or all of a project for a client (see the discussion of preparing an estimate in Chapter 23). If you're a retailer, it will help if you clearly post your return policy—how long from the date of sale returns are permitted, whether you'll give cash refunds, store credit or exchanges, and so on.

In general, and to whatever extent possible, *all* businesses should have a policy of trying to solve the customer's problem. Here's one approach:

- **Ask what exactly is wrong, and what exactly the customer would like you to do.** That's what consultants and providers of services, who often cannot fall back on a written "returns policy," usually have to do. As often as not, the suggestion will be a reasonable one that you can honor.

- **Deal with complaints quickly and adequately.** By so doing, you can transform unhappy customers into some of your most loyal customers. After all, you've proven to them that you will correct problems—something they can't be certain other businesses will do. Remember, too, unhappy customers whose complaint you haven't satisfactorily dealt with will pass the word along—and along—and the damage can mushroom with the negative word of mouth.

- **Recognize that there will be some clients whom you will never please, no matter how hard you try.** The appropriate solution may be to tell such customers that you don't have the product or service that they need, and if you can, refer them to someone else who does. In that case, you're still solving the problem—yours as well as theirs.

- **Use each occasion as an opportunity to learn** how you can improve your product or service and reduce the number of complaints you'll see in the future.

Billing
and Credit

Through the early stages of starting your own business, you're likely to be concerned about *getting* credit—getting whatever money you need, using your personal credit history to help convince suppliers that you can be trusted to pay your debts and are worthy of being allowed to order goods on credit, and building up your business credit by paying bills when due.

But sooner or later, you're likely to find yourself also concerned about *giving* credit—allowing those who buy from you to pay with something other than cash. This chapter deals with the basic billing and credit issues that many new businesses must confront right at the beginning of their operations.

Billing

Billing may seem like a nonissue: You offer goods or services for sale; the customer pays for an item and walks away with it. End of discussion.

But getting paid isn't always that simple. Consultants, gardeners, accountants, attorneys, programmers, florists, home-improvement contractors and many other self-employed people can't just stamp a price on an item, and they don't necessarily receive their money upon purchase. Instead, they usually have to bill their clients for the services they've rendered.

Doing this means, in effect, allowing your customers to pay their bills in full at the end of a week or a month or some other billing cycle—say, at the end of a project—rather than at the exact moment of purchase. For example, I usually bill my clients when completing a job or portion of a job, with payment expected within 30 days. I'll admit, though, that I don't do this out of concern for the comfort of my clients or because I don't mind not getting paid for several weeks. I do it because it's not typical for clients in my field to pay in advance, and it's not practical to expect clients thousands of miles away to write me a check the moment they receive work from me.

Two techniques will make the billing process much easier for both you and your client:

An estimate ensures that both you and the client have clearly understood the nature of the work.

Prepare An Estimate

Be as accurate as you can, including the cost of your labor and any supplies or expenses that you will pass on to the client. Use the estimate as an opportunity to reiterate, in writing, a description of the good or service that the client has requested; that way, both you and the client can be sure that you have clearly understood the nature of the work. Include the estimated date of completion for the project (and for any intermediate steps). Depending on the work you're doing, the customer may expect a certain amount of revision or follow-up work gratis, and you may want to offer it. But above and beyond that—say, after a certain stage in the project, such as an accepted design, or after a certain number of hours—you may wish to charge an hourly fee, perhaps less than your usual. Also note the terms of payment, such as those discussed below. And, finally, request approval of the estimate by your client. This could take the form of a copy of the estimate initialed and returned to you. If you're working with other businesses, it could be a purchase order authorizing your work. Adapt these steps to your circumstances and your clients' needs.

Charge a Deposit

This will improve your cash flow and protect you from customers who are still shopping around even as you reserve a slot in your schedule for them or begin working on their project. A serious and able client shouldn't object.

Make clear under what terms the deposit is refundable—if at all. For example, if your customer must reserve a date for your services, you might ask for final confirmation of the event no later than two weeks beforehand.

The Bill Itself

There's no such thing as a standard billing statement, although many different types of billing forms can be found at your local office supply store. Methods of billing vary from profession to profession, region to region and business to business. In general, though, any bill you give a customer should include:

- **your business name and address,** and the name and address of the person or company being billed;

- **the date and nature of the work performed** or the item purchased;

- **the goods or services received** and the amount charged for each item or service;

- **the total amount due,** after adding any taxes and subtracting any deposits or other payment received;

- **a message to indicate that you're waiting for your money**—"Please Pay Now" or "Due Within 10 Days of Bill Date," for example.

A bill could also state a penalty for late payment, for example "1.5% penalty on balance due after 30 days." (Check with your attorney to make sure that any interest you contemplate charging is not in violation of state or federal laws covering maximum consumer interest charges.)

Second Billings

As noted earlier, the length of time between when you send a bill and when you can expect payment varies *widely*. Similarly, the span between when you send a bill and when you follow up with a second notice can also vary depending on the individual circumstances. However, 30 days is often considered a reasonable time in which to expect payment. If you don't receive payment within that time, send out a second bill. This time, you could add a handwritten note or stamp the bill "Late" or "Past Due" for emphasis.

If you still don't receive payment, you'll have to be more insistent, with, for example, a third letter requesting payment and a final letter informing the client that you will have to pursue other avenues of receiving what you are due. Always date your letters and include information on the date and nature of the goods provided, the payment you expected, how much you are owed, and a deadline for receiving payment. Save copies of these letters; you will need them if you wind up going to court against your debtor (see the box, below).

What About Accepting Checks?

Sooner or later, most people starting their own businesses have to decide whether they'll accept payment by check. There's nothing wrong with accepting a check, of course; there's a problem only if the check bounces.

The Court of Last Resort

If, after you've sent letters and made the requisite phone calls, it turns out that you truly have a bad debt on your hands, you have two likely options: hire a collection agency, which could cost you from one-third to one-half of the amount that you're owed; or file suit against the debtor in small-claims court, which will take a little of your time and possibly cost you a modest filing fee. In small-claims court you can often present your case without an attorney—in fact, some states specifically bar attorneys from representing people in small claims.

Rules for small-claims court suits vary from state to state—some courts allow attorneys while others do not; the maximum amount you can sue for can be as little as $1,000 or more than $5,000, depending on the state. Contact your local court system for detailed information on filings.

To collect for sums in excess of the maximum allowed by your state small-claims system, you would have to file suit in a higher court. Again, rules vary from state to state and from case to case; you would want to talk with an attorney about your specific claim.

For a guide to the small-claims court system, you can also pick up a copy *Everybody's Guide to Small Claims Court,* by attorney Ralph Warner (Nolo Press).

If a customer does write a bad check, first go to the source to find out why the check bounced.

If you're selling to other businesses or to the government, there's really no issue to confront: It's doubtful that another business or an official agency will pay you with cash or a credit card. But anyone doing business with the general public has to deal with the "Do you accept checks?" question right from the start. Many retailers, including those running bars, restaurants and convenience stores, often simply refuse to accept checks. Many businesses accept checks with proof of identification, such as a valid driver's license. Some businesses try to accept checks on a case-by-case basis. You'll have to make your own decision.

When a Check Is Bad

If a customer does write a bad check, first go to the source to find out why the check bounced. Call or write to the customer (his or her address should be either printed on the check or copied onto it from a driver's license or some other identification) and explain that the check has bounced and you want to redeposit it. If the bounce was unintentional, the customer will probably be both embarrassed and prompt in making the necessary deposit.

What if the customer is not embarrassed and does not promptly cover the check? You might wind up trying to get your money directly from the offending check writer's bank. For example, in Oregon you could ask the bank to issue you a cashier's check—presuming there are sufficient funds in the account on which the check was written. Each bank has its own policies on returning bounced checks, holding bounced checks, and charging fees for bounced checks—and some banks charge a fee to the account of someone who tries to *deposit* a bad check. Ask about your bank's specific policies and fees.

If it turns out that you've got a really bad check on your hands, you'll probably have to turn to the law for relief. See the discussion of small-claims court on page 301.

Avoiding the Problem

One way to safeguard yourself is to maintain a list of your customers who have passed bad checks and haven't made an honest effort to make good on them. Or you could subscribe to an automated equivalent—a check approval/guarantee system. These firms guarantee the checks they authorize, meaning you get your money no matter what and the burden of collecting on any bad checks falls on the authorization company.

Merchants can rent, lease or purchase the necessary computer terminals. (In some cases, they can use terminals previously installed for credit-card authorization.) Cost for the service may include a start-up fee and will vary depending on the nature, location, and volume of your business, and the amounts of the checks you typically receive. Two such firms are Equifax Payment Services and Telecheck. (Call 800–555–1212 and ask for the 800 numbers of their offices closest to you.)

Giving Credit Where Credit Is Due

I had a girlfriend who *always* bought gasoline for her car with a credit card. She didn't care that a gas station charged her extra for using her credit card; she wasn't impressed that she was paying just for the privilege of saying, "Charge it." Her reason: She deducted business-related car expenses and liked always having a record of her purchases; perhaps more important, she often carried little money with her and didn't want to have to worry about having enough cash when pulling into a gas station.

This, in short, illustrates the primary reasons for offering credit to your customers: They like the convenience of credit, they like having a record of their purchases, and they might even choose you over a competitor simply because you offer credit when the competitor does not. And, whether or not it's a wise financial move for the customer, you could benefit from a spontaneous purchase that the customer might not make otherwise.

The convenience of credit *is* an attraction to cus-

By offering credit, you could benefit from a spontaneous purchase that the customer might not make otherwise.

If you're running a small operation, offering credit directly can be an incredible burden.

tomers. However, you have to weigh the increased sales you might realize from letting people "charge it" against the increased costs and paperwork you can incur when you offer that option.

There are a couple of ways of offering your customers credit.

Credit Direct From You

The most direct way to give your customers credit is to offer them a charge account from your business. When they come in and make a purchase, customers qualifying for this privilege can simply "sign" for their bills—that is, acknowledge their purchase (and debt) and agree to pay you at a future date.

In principal, this seems easy—you can just keep track of the purchases of your creditworthy customers on a couple of pieces of paper, in a notebook, or in a computer file, bill them at the end of the month, and receive your payments soon thereafter.

Many businesses do offer their own lines of credit. However, if you're running a small operation, offering credit directly can be an incredible burden. First, you'll have to decide whether to even offer credit to a customer. That means either being willing to personally judge a customer's creditworthiness or actually writing up guidelines for the income, assets or credit history a customer has to have before you will give him or her credit (see the box on page 307).

If you do start giving credit and plan to charge interest on a customer's account, you'll have to let your customers know, in writing, how much credit you'll extend, how long they have to pay it back, what their minimum regular payment will be and how much interest you're going to charge them. You will have to comply with a host of federal laws, including the Federal Truth-in-Lending Act and the Fair Credit Billing Act, which are designed to protect consumers against unfair credit practices. You also have to figure in other costs—additional bookkeeping and accounting time, billing forms, postage, filing—when deciding whether it pays you to offer direct credit.

And, of course, you may simply not be paid. One small Southern florist recalls the customer who couldn't afford to pay the $60 on his "tab" because, among other things, he had had to replace the roof on his home to the tune of $15,000. The florist was at the bottom of his customer's priority list. One such situation may not be a big problem, but more than a few of them could cause a cash-flow crunch. Going to small-claims court for every case probably won't be a cost-effective option.

Credit Card Accounts

Instead of offering direct credit, many businesses allow customers to charge their purchases to widely accepted credit cards such as MasterCard, Visa, Discover and others. By accepting these cards, you can give your customers the convenience of credit without having to bear many of the burdens that come with offering direct credit.

Visa and MasterCard

Both Visa and MasterCard sell their services directly to banks, not to businesses. You'll have to apply to a bank for the right to offer customers the option of paying with these cards. Exact requirements vary from banking institution to institution and even from one start-up to another: A bank might ordinarily require that you be in business for three months before setting you up to accept charges, for example, but might waive that if you have an excellent personal credit history or if the bank is conducting an aggressive campaign to capture more merchant credit accounts. Contact a bank with which you already do business if you're interested in offering your customers a credit card charge option.

Banks or their agents handle most of the paperwork associated with credit sales. Typically, you get approval for a credit card sale (usually through a terminal at your business that telephones in to a central computer system), fill out the credit sales slip, check to make sure the card's expiration date has not passed, and compare the signature on

A bank might ordinarily require that you be in business for three months before setting you up to accept charges, but there are exceptions.

No matter which card you offer, you'll have to pay a fee for the privilege, though those fees can change and may be negotiable.

the card with the customer's signature on the credit charge slip. That's it for your end of the "credit verification" business. The sales are credited to your account when you deposit your sales slips in the bank as you would for a regular bank deposit. In some cases, businesses can now make these deposits electronically as well.

American Express

The American Express system is similar, but you directly contact American Express—not a bank—if you're interested in accepting the card.

The other cards

There are also several other cards, including Discover and Diner's Club. You can get more information on these and other cards by contacting your banker or by calling the card company directly. (If the company does not have a number listed in your local directory, call toll-free information—800–555–1212—for the telephone number; when you contact the card company, ask for merchant services.)

Your cost: Is it worth it?

No matter which card you offer, you'll have to pay a fee for the privilege—often between 2% and 4% of your gross sales charged to Visa or MasterCard, around 4.5% for American Express. Those fees can change and you may be able to negotiate reductions, depending on such factors as how much business you'll be doing, how automated your system will be and how much competition there is in the credit industry. You could also have to pay some sort of start-up or equipment-rental fee as well. Depending on the card and the institution, you could have to open a separate account for your credit charges.

Check with other local small businesses and ask about their experience with credit cards—how many people pay with them, whether the merchants think accepting cards helps their business—before approaching a bank or other institution. It's not cheap to accept credit cards—the 3% cut you pay the card company represents the profit margin of a lot of businesses—and you may want to restrict credit to sales of more than, say, $10 or $15. But it may be worth the cost, in a business where you must offer credit, to avoid being burned by nonpayment.

Halting Credit Problems Before They Occur

By obtaining a credit report you can get an idea of the financial health of a potential customer with whom you anticipate doing a substantial amount of regular business. The larger credit reporting corporations (see the accompanying box), maintain data bases of information on millions of businesses and individuals. They've often been charged with providing information that isn't 100% accurate. But at least it's a start. They may charge a minimum monthly payment or a per-report fee and typically negotiate what they charge you based on your volume of inquiries. Their rates are likely to be prohibitive for a small-business person who has only an occasional need for a credit report. A less-expensive alternative may be smaller, local credit-reporting agencies, many of which tap into the data bases of the "big boys" and may supplement that information.

In either case, you'll be called upon to prove that you are a bona fide business and that you have a "permissible purpose" for requesting a report, such as granting a loan or extending other credit.

For More Information

• •

For information about the national credit-reporting services, write:

- **Equifax** (Information Service Center, Attention: New Accounts, Drop 11–D, P.O. Box 740245, Atlanta, GA 30374; 800–766–3708).

- **Trans Union Corp.** (555 W. Adams Blvd., Chicago, IL 60661; contact your local Trans Union office to subscribe).

- **TRW Information Services** (505 City Pkwy. West; Orange, CA 92668; 714–385–7000).

Bookkeeping and Accounting

An old joke:

The fledgling entrepreneur is in his office, interviewing four accountants to handle his company's books. The first accountant walks in and sits down. The entrepreneur asks, "How much is two plus two?"

"Well, it's four, sir," the accountant replies.

The businessman sends the accountant out, calls in the next candidate, asks the same question.

"Four, of course," says the second accountant.

The same sequence is played out with the third accountant, who is also quickly dismissed. Then the fourth candidate enters the office.

"So, tell me. How much is two plus two?" the entrepreneur demands.

The accountant thinks for a moment. "Well, that all depends," he says. "How much do you *want* it to be?"

Why the Numbers Count

That's one view of accountants and accounting: people using a system to make numbers do what they want them to do. The truth, of course, is that accountants can't change mathematical facts. They can, however, give new or added meaning to old numbers. Good accountants, and a good accounting system, will allow you to maintain tighter control over your new business and to know—not guess—how you're doing financially.

That's important. For one thing, the Internal Revenue Service requires businesses to maintain books or records of their financial doings. You can bet that if you're ever audited by the IRS, the auditor will want to see documentation to support all the revenues and expenses you've reported on your tax forms. And don't discount the likelihood of being audited. If you file a 1040 with a Schedule C, *Profit (or Loss) From Business,* and declare less than $100,000 of income, you are at least twice as likely to be audited as someone filing without a Schedule C.

Kostas, Cartoonists & Writers Syndicate

The documentation is important not just for the government but also for yourself. It is entirely possible for an entrepreneur to lose money, no matter how successfully he sells his product or service, because he isn't keeping proper track of all his expenses.

Documentation will also prove vital if you ever want to sell your business to someone else. No one you would want to do business with is going to lend you money, invest in you or buy you out if you don't have well-kept books.

I once was approached by an individual who was driving himself semi-crazy trying to handle every aspect of a small but growing business on his own. He no longer wanted to deal with suppliers or paperwork or taxes or any other logistics that didn't involve what he enjoyed, which was the act of selling his product. He wanted to essentially *give* me his business—have me assume all control and responsibility for the business, put him on commission as the business's sales agent, and reap any profits for myself. I couldn't seriously consider his proposal, though, because he could never produce a coherent breakdown of where the business's revenues were coming from and where and why the business was spending money. He needed good accounting help and didn't have it.

Accountants are, of course, one of the "good guys" discussed in Chapter 14. This section outlines the kinds of

That's all bookkeeping is, really—a formal, written record of your business's financial transactions.

information and records you should keep so you can make the best use of your accountant. If you decide not to hire an accountant, these records will help give you the basic information you need to be a do-it-yourselfer.

It Begins With Bookkeeping

When you start your business, you'll want to know how you're doing financially—whether you're making or losing money. You'll be tracking how much money you spend in running your business and selling your product or service, as well as how much money you're bringing in from any sales. That's all bookkeeping is, really—a formal, written record of your business's financial transactions. (For some of the "whys" of bookkeeping, see the box on page 312.)

The Two Systems

There are two types of bookkeeping systems:

Single entry

In single-entry bookkeeping, an entry is made in your books for every financial transaction. All of the money coming in to the business from sales goes on the income side of your books; all of the money going out for supplies, rent and other costs of running the business goes on the expenditures side of your books.

A single-entry bookkeeping system is relatively simple to set up. All you need is a book or computer program in which you can record your daily receipts and expenses. Your "books" can, in fact, be just one or two books—a multi-columned, lined pad will serve many people just fine.

At the end of the month (or however often you choose), you can add up the figures for your receipts and expenses and get a quick accounting of how much money your business is bringing in.

A single-entry system poses two disadvantages, though:

- **It gives an incomplete picture of your business;** it doesn't reflect your inventory, equipment, loans, and other assets and liabilities.

- **It doesn't double-check your arithmetic.**

Double entry

Double-entry bookkeeping solves these problems, but it's also more complicated. With double-entry bookkeeping, there are two financial sides to everything your business does. Buying some supplies or equipment? That will be recorded as a "debit" on one side of your financial records, because your business has spent money; however, it will also be noted as a "credit" on the other side of your records, because your business has purchased goods that could now be considered assets or inventory.

Sound confusing? It is. Bernard Kamoroff, a certified public accountant and author of the useful book *Small-Time Operator* (Bell Springs Publishing) says that double-entry bookkeeping "transforms business bookkeeping from a part-time nuisance into a full-time occupation." You can try setting up a single-entry bookkeeping system on your own; however, you'll probably want to leave a double-entry system to the professionals.

One System for Self-Employeds

I use a single-entry bookkeeping system. I have a computer and could use it with a personal finance or spreadsheet software program to keep track of my business revenues and expenses, but I've found it's just as easy for me to do it by hand. Of course, I'm not in retail—my receipts for services performed are relatively few and for fairly large sums.

Here's a modified version of my bookkeeping system. It has three main components:

The journal

This is where I write down everything I do that involves my business. Whether I'm purchasing a 59-cent

You can try setting up a single-entry bookkeeping system on your own, but you'll probably want to leave a double-entry system to the professionals.

box of paper clips or a $500 printer, whether I'm driving to the copy shop or flying to another city, it gets written down in the journal. I use a portable calendar as my journal, noting any relevant information—where the transaction took place, the business purpose, and so on—under the appropriate date.

The ledger

This is where I summarize all those journal entries. I use 11- by 17-inch paper divided into 16 columns, and assign a category—"supplies," "equipment," "postage," "telephone," "income," and so on—to each column. I chronologically list the expenses for each category.

The receipts

After I put an entry into the ledger, I file the documentation for it—the original receipt—in an envelope labeled by category of expense. The most recent receipt

Bookkeeping Tips for the Self-Employed

Establishing a policy of keeping your business records distinct from your personal records (especially if you're in business part-time while employed elsewhere or if you're a sole proprietor) will help you with the bookkeeping and accounting aspects of your venture for as long as you work for yourself. Some tips to keep in mind:

- **Record business-related expenses as they occur.** Don't let papers and receipts pile up for months. Trying to remember why you did what you did months ago can be very difficult.

- **Note the purpose of a business purchase when you make it.** Even something as simple as writing down the reason for the expense on the back of a receipt is very useful.

- **Set one credit card aside for business use only.** That will make it easier for you to remember which expenses are business expenses and which are personal. You might also open a checking account exclusively for business expenses and deposits.

- **Keep track of all expenses and income even if your new venture loses money initially.** That's because the IRS allows you to deduct expenses related to money-losing businesses so long as your venture is indeed a business and not a hobby. The IRS requires that you show a profit in three years out of five to qualify as a business.

goes behind all the others in the envelope, so I also have receipts ordered chronologically by category. I also write down the specific item purchased or reason for the purchase on the check or receipt.

I like this system for a couple of reasons. At the end of the year, I have all my information in place for my accountant to do my taxes. All I have to do is add up all the columns of expenses and income, and give her the final figures, along with a few specific questions about the tax code that I invariably have. Also, with this system I have created a lasting and detailed record of what my business has spent money on, when the money was spent, and why. If I'm audited a year or two later, I won't have to try and remember why a particular transaction took place or how a certain number was arrived at—it will all be there in the form of receipts and journal and ledger entries properly grouped and entered in chronological order.

- **Start paying estimated taxes to the federal government and your state** if you are realizing a profit right off the bat (regardless of whether your business is a sole proprietorship, partnership or corporation). Estimated taxes have to be paid four times a year—in April, June, September and January.

- **The rules for how to calculate your estimated tax payments are tricky,** subject to change, and dependent on how much profit you're making, when you're making it, what you've earned in previous years, and whether and how much tax is being withheld from earnings you may have at other jobs. Talk with your accountant to find out what your estimated tax obligations might be.

- **Talk to your accountant** about the best way of keeping records for tax purposes.

- **People working for themselves may deduct all expenses related to their business ventures**—advertising, licenses, travel, legal fees, equipment, supplies, rent, insurance, travel, and so on—but only if they maintain proper records.

Accounting—A Step Further

An accountant can help you set up a bookkeeping system. He or she can also do your accounting, which is basically a way of consolidating, interpreting and bringing some sense to all those bookkeeping figures.

Remember the loan proposals we discussed in Chapter 17? Part of the problem with getting a loan as a start-up is that you have to give estimates, or projections, of your company's profit-and-loss statement and its balance sheet. By definition, a start-up doesn't have a track record of profits *or* losses, and its balance sheet (its listing of assets and liabilities) may quickly change depending on which sources of start-up funding pan out.

Resources for Running the Numbers

If you're a determined financial do-it-yourselfer or just want to know more about bookkeeping, accounting and taxes, check out these resources:

Publications

- *Your Own Shop: How to Open and Operate a Successful Retail Business,* by Ruth Jacobson (McGraw-Hill).

- Internal Revenue Service Publications (800–829–3676), including: #583, *Taxpayers Starting a Business* (tax strategy), and #334, *Tax Guide for Small Business* (nuts-and-bolts tax information). Ask for both.

- *The Kiplinger Washington Letter* (weekly; $73 per year; 800–544–0155 or 301–853–6590) and *The Kiplinger Tax Letter* (twice a month; $56 per year). These newsletters will help any self-employed person stay on top of changing tax regulations and laws and trends in Washington that affect business owners.

Software

If you're bound and determined to do your taxes yourself, then a tax-preparation software program may be a good investment. These programs can't do all the work for you, but they will provide on-line tax help and written documentation, recalculate the figures when you correct a mistake or try a "what if" scenario, and transfer data among the related forms you'll use to report self-employment income, deductions and taxes. To find the program best for you, read software reviews and ask for recommendations from friends and advisers. Programs to consider (all for $100 or less) include:

- *Kiplinger TaxCut,* by Block Financial Software (IBM and Macintosh; to order call 800–365–1546).

- *TurboTax,* by Intuit (IBM).

- *MacinTax,* by Intuit (Macintosh).

But with good bookkeeping, you or someone who helps you will be able to create a proper profit-and-loss statement. You'll also be able to produce a legitimate balance sheet. Both of these documents will be very helpful if, after your business has a track record, you apply for a business loan.

Professionals are there to help you and, within financial reason, you should let them.

Do-It-Yourself, or Hire Someone?

Should you do your own balance sheet? Perhaps. First, answer this question: If you go out and purchase a $3,000 piece of business equipment, write a business check for $1,000 and charge the remainder to your business credit card, which have you changed: your business's cash assets, its fixed assets, or its liabilities?

Time's up.

Okay. It was a trick question: You've changed *all* of those categories. Your business's cash assets have declined by the $1,000 check you wrote. Your fixed assets have increased by $3,000, the value of the equipment you purchased. (That sum will decrease as the equipment depreciates, or loses its value as a piece of used equipment.) And your liabilities have increased by the $2,000 that you borrowed.

If you didn't know all that as a matter of course—or if you just won't get around to doing this work yourself—maybe you should turn to your accountant. Again, professionals are there to help you and, within financial reason, you should let them. If you really want to take these tasks on yourself, you can pay an accountant to do your first statements, while you watch how the documents are put together, and then try to do it yourself.

But for most start-ups, hiring an accountant will be the way to go. Even if you go out and learn all about proper profit-and-loss statements and balance sheets and even double-entry bookkeeping, there's still one other big piece of paperwork that you, as a start-up, are probably going to want help with the first time you confront it: your business tax return.

Deep in the Heart of Taxes

As pointed out in Chapter 11, the type of return you file and the forms you fill out will vary depending on the legal form of your business (sole proprietorship, partnership or corporation) and on the financial particulars of your own enterprise (for example, whether you have employees, pay benefits or keep inventory). This book isn't the place to show you how to prepare your first business tax return; the resources listed in the box on page 314 will help you in that area. But here's why you might want good tax planning and preparation advice throughout the tax year:

The forms of your life

Let's say that you have the *simplest* form of business—a sole proprietorship with no employees—and that in your first year you buy equipment for your business and establish an office in your home. On that basis, you'll owe and have to learn how to calculate estimated quarterly tax payments (which means sending four checks a year to the IRS instead of one) while being introduced to several tax forms you may not have previously discovered, including:

- **Form 1040** (long form),

- **Schedule C,** "Profit or Loss From Business,"

- **Form 4562,** "Depreciation and Amortization,"

- **Schedule SE,** "Self-Employment Tax,"

- **Form 8829,** "Expenses for Business Use of Your Home," and

- **Form 2210,** "Underpayment of Estimated Tax by Individuals, Estates and Trusts."

An easier way

If you're self-employed, Schedule C-EZ, a shorter version of Schedule C, Profit or Loss from Business, may make filing your taxes a lot easier. You may be able to use the simpler form if:

- **You run only one business.**

- **Your gross earnings are no more than $25,000** and your expenses are no more than $2,000.

- **You don't deduct your home office.**

- **You have no employees.**

- **You have no inventory.**

- **You don't report depreciation and amortization.**

- **You don't report a net loss from your business.**

- **You use the "cash" method of accounting** (you report your income in the year you receive it and your expenses in the year you pay them).

For more information, check with your tax preparer or the IRS at 800–829–1040.

Usually, the same accountant who prepares your taxes can do your other financial summaries. Doing both will give him or her the opportunity to help you maximize your deductions, minimize your taxes and make your business as profitable as it can be.

Controlling Inventory, Supplies and Quality

Whatever you do when you work for yourself, you'll have to buy at least some supplies and maintain some inventory, and you'll have to set standards for the quality of whatever you buy and whatever you sell.

If you're selling your advice or a service, your inventory needs may be modest—a ready supply of paper, report covers, billing forms and other office supplies. If you're a retailer or manufacturer, the amount you spend on finished goods or raw materials could dwarf other expenses. For example, the owner of a small but fully stocked swimwear store says that her inventory of men's and women's suits, goggles, fins, kickboards and other swim paraphernalia at any one time is worth more than $50,000. And in every case, you'll have to balance the need to have enough high-quality inventory with its cost.

Purchasing supplies and merchandise is, says small-business consultant and author Max Fallek, *only* a matter of buying "the right quality, at the right price, from the right source, in the right quantity, at the right time." Easy, right? Not at all. But here are some guidelines to help you as you wrestle with questions of both quality and quantity of product and supplies.

The Quantity Question

There's no clear-cut formula for determining how much inventory you'll need initially. It will depend on how fast your product is turned over, how quickly suppliers can send new goods to you, even the time of year if you're in a seasonal business. If your suppliers can get goods to you fast, you can get by with less inventory, even if you're turning it over quickly. For example, if you're running an ice-cream shop and can get your supplies delivered three times a week, it won't matter if you turn over your inventory every week. You can start with what you think is a week's worth of ice cream and go from there. If you see that you're going to run out, no problem—just order more. But if you're running a furniture store and it takes six months for new orders to be filled, you'll have to either order way in advance; keep inventory in storage as well as on your showroom floor; or use your showroom pieces as models only, requiring customers to order and place a deposit for the pieces they want and alerting them to a wait of so many months (many furniture stores operate this way).

In every case, you'll have to balance the need to have enough high-quality inventory with its cost.

Planning for the Daily Bread

Even in a high-turnover business, maintaining proper inventory and supply levels can be tricky. Shortly after it opened, Marvelous Market, a producer and retailer of breads and pastries in the Washington, D.C. area, baked 300 pounds of bread a day. As demand increased, the store gradually upped its production to 600 pounds a day. Owner Mark Furstenberg, who had worked in several businesses and had also been a journalist before starting Marvelous Market, originally wanted just a small operation. "I wanted to have a neighborhood bread bakery that people would also think of as a food store," Furstenberg says.

Then the bakery was discovered. "Within a couple of weeks, we got this huge amount of publicity—a couple of stories in the *Washington Post*, two television spots, an Associated Press article. We became a fad," Furstenberg says.

The result was chaos, as people lined up to buy the

highly touted loaves coming out of Marvelous Market's ovens. The store was producing as much bread as it could—2,000 pounds a day with virtual round-the-clock operation—but still could not meet the demand. At one point, Furstenberg instituted a rationing program, limiting customers to no more than two loaves per person.

The old guidelines for buying supplies—in this case, the flour and other ingredients used in the breads—had to be revised drastically. Only after opening a larger bakery was Furstenberg able to comfortably meet the daily demand for several thousand pounds of his breads.

Harris, Cartoonists & Writers Syndicate

"Controlling inventory and purchasing is very hard," Furstenberg notes. He maintains a computerized history of sales for each store, as well as a "leftover bread report" for each store and a daily production schedule based on anticipated sales and previous trends. All the recipes are in a computer as well. "We can adjust the quantities of bread that we're going to make and the computer tells us how much we'll need of each ingredient for the week," Furstenberg says. He purchased software ready-made for the baking industry.

Furstenberg keeps track of his business's purchases and expenses, and he has kept records of all transactions from the time he opened the business. Because he tracks weekly purchases and sales, his inventory and purchasing system is geared to having supplies on hand to meet needs for the coming week.

The Stock Count

Every business selling goods (as opposed to services) will need some kind of system for keeping track of inventory being bought and sold. A basic way of doing this is the stock count. This is just what it sounds like—a count of how much stock, or inventory, you have on hand. Stock counts can be done daily, weekly or monthly. At the same time, sales counts should be done. You should reorder when the raw materials or finished goods you have on hand will be used up or sold during the time it takes to get new supplies delivered. For safety's sake, build in a cushion of anywhere from a couple of days on up, depending on the vagaries of your suppliers, to allow for delivery delays that could leave you in the lurch.

Stock counts also apply to service businesses—you need to keep track of your supplies and any goods used in providing, billing, or collecting payment for your services.

Suppliers—Finding Them, Using Them

Every business needs its suppliers, whether what is being supplied is unfinished materials, items ready for sale, or basic office supplies used in the conduct of a full-time or part-time venture.

Here are a few general tips for locating suppliers:

Check your Yellow Pages.
The telephone book is an often-overlooked, under-utilized and incredibly diverse source of information. It's always a good place to start looking for vendors. If you can't find exactly what you want, you might find a related business that will know of the supplier you're looking for. Business-to-business directories, available in many communities from the same publishers as consumer directories, can also help.

You might find a related business that will know of the supplier you're looking for.

Even if you're using one supplier, you should stay in touch with, or at least know of, an alternative source.

Check with your other business contacts.

Once again, business trade associations, industry publications, your chamber of commerce and other businesspeople are also good sources of information and tips. They sometimes offer warnings about vendors to avoid.

Negotiate.

You already know this, but sometimes a little reminder can be helpful: No price or condition is cast in stone. Don't be afraid to ask for discounts based on the amount you're buying, on your willingness to pay promptly, on the fact that you will be a steady customer, or on any other advantage that might sway a vendor.

Have alternatives.

Even if you're using one supplier, you should stay in touch with, or at least know of, an alternative source. After all, you never know when someone is not going to be able to come through for you. Marvelous Market has primary suppliers but also maintains contacts with secondary vendors. "It's possible that a supplier will not have enough of a whole-wheat flour or a multigrain mix, so I have to know about alternatives," says Furstenberg.

The Price of Inventory

When thinking about your approach to inventory, here's an important point to remember: Inventory indirectly costs you money every day. Simply put, any money tied up in inventory is money not available for other business expenses or investments.

Let's say, for example, that you're selling personal computers and you've purchased at wholesale $200,000 worth of computers. You paid for the computers upfront; you're also paying for the space where you store them. Every day that those items sit in your warehouse or out on the floor, you're losing the potential interest that the money spent on them could otherwise be earning.

You may be satisfied if within a year you are able to "turn over" your inventory—that is, to sell all the items that you have and replace them with new ones—and realize a profit of $50,000 after accounting for overhead and other expenses. But by having spent the $200,000 all at once, you've also missed out on $8,000 of potential interest; that's assuming that you would otherwise have invested the money in an interest-bearing account earning 4%.

If you could run your business more efficiently by carrying an inventory worth only $100,000, you would have the other $100,000 available for other expenses or investments. Your "lost" interest would be halved, to $4,000. Clearly, it makes sense to carry only as much inventory as you need—at least if you have to pay for it on delivery—and to turn that inventory over as quickly as possible.

Another alternative: Try to get suppliers to give you 30 or 60 or even 90 days to pay for goods received. That way, your money stays in your accounts longer. Sell your products fast enough and you effectively won't have to pay for goods until you've sold them.

If you have to borrow to pay for your inventory, your cost of inventory will be even greater. Then you're not just losing theoretical interest payments on your money— you're *paying* interest on the wholesale value of your inventory every day it sits in your business. And chances are the interest rate you're paying will be far higher than what you would receive on money you have in the bank.

Operating Just-in-Time

It's tempting to try to keep inventory costs down by stocking just enough inventory, especially when you're starting out and worrying about all your costs. This is not a bad idea. In fact, it's a variation of the "just-in-time" system that swept through industry in the 1980s. Under just-in-time, companies work closely with suppliers to order and receive goods only when the goods are truly needed, thus minimizing the need for storage space, reducing strains on cash flow, and trimming every aspect of overhead associated with having more inventory and supplies on hand than a company knows what to do with.

But don't allow yourself to let inventory costs control

Try to get suppliers to give you 30 or 60 or even 90 days to pay for goods received.

your ability to sell: Not having what people want can kill your relationship with customers. For example, I once wanted to buy a couple of bathing suits at a small sportswear shop. The shop didn't have any in my size, but the manager said she would be happy to order them for me. That seemed great—personal service with a smile. However, it took three weeks for the first suit to arrive; I never even bothered with the second suit. The suits may have taken a long time to arrive because the manufacturer was backed up or because the order wasn't placed properly or because the shipping company fouled up, but none of that made any difference to me, the customer: All I knew, or had to know, was that I couldn't rely on this retailer when I needed a common item in a timely fashion. Needless to say, I haven't ordered anything from that shop since. The moral: Don't let the inventory tail wag the sales dog.

Quality Control

Along with managing and maintaining inventory, you have to manage and maintain quality. The acceptable level of quality depends on what you're selling: You could

A Word About Supplies

For many people starting service businesses, the main form of supplies will be office supplies—paper for a variety of purposes, envelopes, file folders, billing forms, and so on. Businesses buying small quantities used to have limited options on office supplies and price breaks were rare— a stationery store was not going to give a discount for buying five 100-count boxes of envelopes instead of one box.

All that has changed. Several mail-order firms sell discounted office supplies; retailers have opened warehouse-style discount office-supply stores that offer little ambience but lots of cut-rate prices. Smart conventional retailers often have responded by emphasizing the quality of their service. However, if you are going to be a regular customer, a small office-supply retailer will often cut her prices considerably if you ask, and sometimes even if you don't: I've had merchants offer to cut 30% from all their listed prices if I would agree to contact them first with my relatively meager orders.

Great discounts are available to start-ups who shop around. Just a small example: At one store, I can buy 100 business envelopes for $1.99—a fairly typical price. But I can go to another supply store where I regularly shop and purchase 500 envelopes for $2.59.

Shop around. It pays.

be marketing convenience, selection or low price, as well as quality. No matter what your overall marketing strategy, though, a consistently high level of quality can be a very effective selling tool.

Baking Better Bread

Mark Furstenberg had a unique challenge when he started his bakery: He wanted to produce only the highest-quality products. He was working with recipes developed by a nationally recognized chef who had agreed to help him—Nancy Silverton, co-owner of Los Angeles's Campanile Restaurant and La Brea Bakery. In bread baking, everything from the quality of the flour to the humidity of the climate affects the final product. And here was Furstenberg, 3,000 miles away from Silverton, in a different climate, with access to different flours and other ingredients. "If you take a live yeast from one city and start feeding it with different flour and water and air in another location, the character of that starter changes and you must adjust and adapt to those changes to make the recipes work," says Furstenberg. "Many of the breads developed into something distinctly different [from the original versions.]"

To develop and maintain quality control at different locations as he expanded his business, Furstenberg created what he calls baking teams—groups of people who work together and understand each aspect of the baking process. These teams are not wedded to one location and thus can share knowledge and information with the salespeople in each store, while learning the routines and quirks of each retail operation.

Furstenberg also makes as many employees as possible responsible for "quality control"—that is, for producing and selling only excellent breads. "Every sales clerk in the company has the authority to not sell a loaf of bread if it is deficient," he says. "If the bread is good and tastes good, sell it; if there's something wrong with the bread but it still tastes fine, give it away; and if it is not right, then throw it away. It's very hard for a bread to fail without my knowing about it. The bakers tell me if a

Furstenberg makes as many employees as possible responsible for "quality control"— that is, for producing and selling only excellent breads.

Let people who work with you know that the quality of the product or service matters to you, even if an employee is not directly involved in its creation.

bread fails, and we usually figure out why."

Responsibility for quality of execution is pushed down throughout the system and made everyone's concern, while ultimate responsibility for the recipes and products sold remains centralized and part of a carefully tested process. Furstenberg remembers looking at a shelf in one of his stores and seeing a type of bread he had never encountered. When he asked what it was, he was told it was the "new bread" that one of the store's bakers had created by adding dry herbs to some existing dough (a definite no-no for some bread aficionados).

"I went to that cook and I said, 'Look, this is not a free-lance operation. I encourage your creativity, but only if you work with us and we taste your new bread and we test it and improve it if needed until it [is good enough to be included] on our bread list.' "

Ways to Achieve Quality Control

Furstenberg's methods highlight some of the things that can make quality-control programs work for all small start-ups:

Push responsibility from top to bottom.

Quality-control efforts are most effective if they involve everyone. Furstenberg sets the standards for quality in his business, but clerks know that they have a role to play—that they are, in fact, the last and most important link in the quality chain.

Communicate.

Let people who work with you know that the quality of the product or service matters to you, even if an employee is not directly involved in its creation. You may be starting your business with no employees other than a part-time assistant, but your efforts will be enhanced if he or she knows what you're trying to accomplish and what is expected of, and by, the business. Your emphasis on quality will rub off on your assistant's work.

Set standards.

The idea of "quality" is not new or foreign. But it can seem so if people do not know what constitutes a quality product or service. Furstenberg doesn't have to define what a good loaf of bread tastes like; he only has to make clear that any product sold from his bakery has to meet the standards and pass the tests that every other loaf is subjected to.

Define success (and failure).

Employees know what an acceptable product is in Furstenberg's stores—bread that looks right, feels right and tastes right. They might give away a product that doesn't meet all these standards, but they can't take money for it. That sends a clear message about the important relationship between quality and the company's reputation.

Make the quest for quality an everyday fact.

There's no need for "quality rallies" here: The quality system is just part of the daily review of operations. Anytime something is not right, employees and employer talk about it and try to correct the problem before an aberration becomes a habit.

Forget slogans.

It's a lot easier to motivate people through actions and incentives than through slogans. Slogans also can be twisted in wicked ways. At one time McDonnell Douglas, the aircraft manufacturer, was busily promoting its Total Quality Management System (TQMS) while its employees were joking that the initials really stood for "Time to Quit and Move to Seattle"—the home of rival Boeing.

Other Quality Issues

Commitment to quality also applies when you're purchasing materials or services. Lousy supplies will affect the quality of finished products and decrease your client's satisfaction. So will slipshod services that result in incomplete work, missed deadlines or escalating costs.

Once again, you'll need to have stated policies, an

There's no need for "quality rallies" here: The quality system is just part of the daily review of operations.

Of course, your customers will be sure to let you know if what you're selling is acceptable. Listen to them.

understanding of and emphasis on quality throughout your business, and a purchasing system that institutionalizes your commitment. This may mean something as simple as opening boxes as soon as they arrive to make sure they contain what was ordered, or as technical as conducting periodic stress tests on metals used in a manufacturing process.

Your needs, as well as your "specs," will depend on the line of business you're entering. Chances are, you'll know what constitutes a good product or service and can draw up guidelines to ensure that you get or produce it; if you need help and more information, you should also be able to turn to industry trade associations, government regulatory agencies or even your vendors themselves.

Of course, your customers will be sure to let you know if what you're selling is acceptable. They don't need to know all the ins and outs of your business, nor what's realistic or possible for you to provide or accomplish. But they can certainly tell you want they want and expect. Listen to them.

Managing Yourself, Managing Others

This is a story about someone we'll call "Fred Twist the Optimist." Fred has a small remodeling and construction business—basically, himself and whomever he might hire to help out on "rush" jobs or especially difficult projects. He can paint interiors or exteriors, shingle a roof, run electrical wiring, refinish floors, install carpet, demolish or build walls. If he felt like it, Fred could probably build a house all by himself. What's more, he's very good at what he does. Fred Twist the Optimist treats each project as if his name were going to be emblazoned on it. His clients rave about the quality and relative affordability of his work.

But Fred Twist the Optimist has a fatal flaw. He tells his clients whatever they want to hear. Because he's confident of his abilities, and because, like the rest of us, he just plain wants to be liked, his invariable response to questions about a project is, "No problem—I can do that."

That makes clients very happy when they hire him—but not for long. Fred, unfortunately, always underestimates how long it will take him to complete a job. That alienates people who find themselves inconvenienced—say, moved out of their houses while work is being done—for longer than they had planned. And it means Fred puts a lot more of his time and labor into a project than he had planned. So he winds up unhappy about the amount of time he's spent for the money he made, and his client winds up unhappy that the project has taken so much longer to finish than was promised. Bad feelings linger all around.

Since you're the boss, nobody is going to tell you how to deal with distractions.

Entrepreneur, Know Thyself

Our friend Fred is a lousy manager of himself. He likes being self-employed and being his own boss, but because he overestimates his abilities, he winds up feeling harried, underpaid, alienated and unappreciated. Depending on your point of view, Fred is either a poor planner or a fellow who simply tries too hard to please his customers.

Every self-employed person has an Achilles' heel, or even several—things that keep you from enjoying your work, take up more of your time than they should, distract you and interfere with the success of your enterprise.

Since you're the boss, nobody is going to tell you how to deal with distractions. You'll have to resolve that problem on your own. You're also going to be responsible for keeping yourself motivated and on-track. To do that, it will help to go back to the first chapters of this book and to remember, when you feel disconnected from your work, why you want to work for yourself.

Surviving the Distraction Devils

Here's a short list of tips for managing yourself:

Have long-term goals, but take pleasure in today.

Remember, one of the reasons you're working for yourself is because you want to be happier in your personal as well as your professional life. You are your own boss... and there are few things worse than working for a fundamentally unhappy boss.

Set priorities whenever possible.

Separate the tasks you must do today from the ones you *should* do today. The "haves" will invariably constitute a shorter list and help save you from panicking over "all the things I gotta do." And maybe some of those "shoulds" will turn out to be optional projects, which you can choose to either pursue or let fade away.

Don't be afraid to close your office door.

An open-door policy with family, friends, employees and clients is nice, but you should be able to work without interruption.

Manage your telephone.

If you feel like you're spending too much time in nonproductive telephone conversations, restrict your "phone time" to a certain part of the day. Have your secretary—or your answering machine—take messages during critical work periods.

Remember that procrastination wastes time.

True—it takes time and energy to decide how you're going to put something off. If a project seems too overwhelming to begin, see if you can break it into bite-size chunks or maybe delegate it away.

Golden Rules

Try these ideas for getting the most out of your start-up team:

- **Treat everyone the way you would like to be treated.** It sounds simple. Amazing, though, how hard it can be to treat people civilly, respect their intelligence, and ask them questions rather than dish out orders.

- **Be specific with directions.** Let people know exactly what you need and give them sufficient guidance.

- **Try not to spring unpleasant and arbitrary surprises.** In one government office, workers were told two weeks before Christmas that nobody would be allowed to take vacation days the day before or the day after the holiday. You can imagine what that did for morale, especially among those who had purchased nonrefundable airplane tickets.

- **Use positive reinforcement.** Sure, you expect people to do their jobs properly. But why not let them know you appreciate their good work and don't take it for granted? Positive notes and words of encouragement can go a long way toward creating a good work atmosphere.

- **Listen.** You won't always have all the answers. Even if your "staff" consists of one part-time secretary, he or she is going to know things about the job, and about your business, that you don't know. Listen to the opinions of those you work with or turn to for specific tasks. Asking how the work is going lets them know you care about their opinions. And you might learn something. Opening your mind to new knowledge can be one of the most rewarding aspects of working for yourself.

A job—even your own job, even a job that you've created for yourself and that you've always wanted—is just a job.

Don't overload your schedule. It's tempting to take on as much work as possible, to never turn down a job—after all, you don't know when the next call for work will come. It's hard, but resist this temptation. Overloading yourself won't get you repeat references or good customers; it will only lead to frustration and unnecessary stress. Even if you really are Superman or Superwoman in disguise, try to be realistic about what you can do in any given day, week or month.

Life—and business—can be pretty funny.

The writer, editor and medical researcher Norman Cousins was probably the leading advocate of the therapeutic power of laughter; doctors tell us it's a great way to release stress and emotions. Business is serious, but it can also be a hoot. If you don't believe it, start reading the feature article that appears in the middle of the front page of *The Wall Street Journal* every day.

Learn relaxation techniques to relieve stress.

A good place to start is with a book: *The Relaxation Response,* by Dr. Herbert Benson (Avon Books). Exercise can help relieve stress; so can meditation and formal courses in stress reduction or "stress management." The Yellow Pages or your personal physician may direct you to more information.

Find time for your family and friends.

All work and no play does more than make you miserable and possibly lonely—it can make your family unhappy and even reduce them and your friends to mere acquaintances. Yes, your business is important. Yes, professional success is important. But a job—even your own job, even a job that you've created for yourself and that you've always wanted—is just a job. It can't replace the people in your life. Another way to look at this: People are far more important than things, and a job is a thing. Few people at the end of their lives have ever said, "I should have spent more time working."

Open up.

When you make time for people, let them know what's on your mind. Try not to be afraid to share your hopes and especially your fears. You'll be surprised how many people will rally to you and help you *if* they know that you need and appreciate them. If you have trouble expressing the challenges and difficulties of your venture—well, let them read this book.

Once you learn how to relax, practice it.

Everyone has something that helps relieve stress, whether it's a workout, a relaxation exercise, a certain type of music, or recreation with friends or family, or something else enjoyable. Allow yourself that time. It will make you more productive in the long run.

A little humility goes a long way.

Learn to use two of the biggest time-saving phrases in the English language: "I'm sorry," and "I made a mistake."

Recognizing when these phrases are appropriate and being able to say them and mean them will save you a lot of energy that you would otherwise spend trying to justify the unjustifiable. These phrases will also save you time, allow you to ditch an unproductive decision or path in favor of a more effective one—and impress other people no end with your down-to-earth ability to admit that you are not perfect.

These phrases will also provide a great example for the people you work with and want to properly manage and inspire.

Learn to use two of the biggest time-saving phrases in the English language: "I'm sorry," and "I made a mistake."

Managing Means Motivating

The best boss I ever had never did anything *to* his employees. He didn't threaten us or tell us how to do our jobs. He didn't badger us. He didn't use his authority—the power to hire and fire us—as a weapon.

Instead, he did things *for* us. He always told us what his goals were and what our roles were in meeting those goals. He remembered employees' birthdays. He thanked us for jobs well done. When something wasn't getting done, he talked with the employee individually, not to chastise but to ask what needed to be changed to accomplish the task at hand. The guy was a saint. When I realized that I would have to leave my job to pursue a new career path, I felt so bad that I told my boss three months in advance, so he'd have plenty of time to find a replacement.

"You can't call in sick, Harold, you're self-employed."

From the Wall Street Journal—Permission, Cartoon Features Syndicate

This boss was tremendously successful in communicating to us what we were expected to accomplish and in letting us know that he cared not just about our work but also about us as individuals.

That's the perfect combination for successful management: Clearly tell people what you expect, show support for the good work you demand, and let people know that you care about them. This formula can work not only in managing employees but also in your professional relationships with suppliers of goods and services, with freelance or contract workers, with your advisers, and with anyone else whose work affects your work. After all, when was the last time you heard someone talk about how eager she was to go out of her way for an overbearing, unyielding manager or client? It's simple: People who feel valued, appreciated, even loved are more likely to be happy and productive.

Money is also a great motivator. But even if two similar jobs in similar businesses pay similar salaries, the nonfinancial compensation—the emotional benefits—can vary tremendously and can far outweigh any monetary difference. And people who are in a workplace with a good emotional environment are bound to be more highly motivated than those working in the kind of place that leaves employees eager to flee at the end of the workday.

Nothing Stays the Same

Be flexible. Your business, after all, won't be static; it *will* change over time, and you'll need to change with it. The most tried-and-true methods will require at least occasional adjustment. Here are some examples of the kinds of changes you can expect:

- **Even the most steady clients will cut back** or disappear altogether.

- **The market may boom and bust.** You may reach a point where you'll have more clients—for whom money is no object—than you can handle. You may also find yourself left with just a few penny-pinching customers or clients at some point.

- **The idea and the market niche that once belonged to you** may suddenly swarm with competitors.

- **The location that was originally so appealing** may take a turn for the worse, or it may become a hot property— more lucrative for your business, yet still affordable.

- **You may need to hire more help,** or you may find yourself having to let people go—a hard decision for any business owner.

- **Your venture could grow like wildfire,** requiring an investment of resources that you never anticipated.

In working for yourself, as in life, the only constant you can expect is change. Use this book throughout the process to challenge your assumptions and to answer all the important questions.

The most tried-and-true methods will require at least occasional adjustment.

KIPLINGER BOOKS

To order any Kiplinger product, call toll free, 1–800–727–7015 between 9:00 A.M. and 9:00 P.M. Eastern Time, or send your check to: Kiplinger Books and Tapes, P.O. Box 85193, Richmond, VA 23285–5193.

For information on bulk rates or to order in bulk, call Dianne Olsufka at 202–887–6431.

Please send me:

Books	Price		Quantity	Total
Retire & Thrive (paper)	$15.00	C		
Money-Smart Kids (paper)	$12.95	K		
Buying and Selling a Home (paper)	$13.95	T		
Invest Your Way to Wealth (hardcover)	$23.95	G		
Make Your Money Grow (paper)	$14.95	S		
Taming the Paper Tiger (paper)	$11.95	M		
12 Steps to a Worry-Free Retirement (paper)	$14.95	U		
Career Starter (paper)	$10.95	V		
Working for Yourself (paper)	$14.95	N		
Survive & Profit From A Mid-Career Change (paper)	$12.95	D		
Facing 40 (hardcover)	$19.95	R		
Handbook of Personal Law (paper)	$14.95	A		
Cut Your Taxes (paper)	$15.00	E		
Video Guides				
Money-Smart Women	$29.95	W		
Retirement Security	$29.95	I		
Estate Planning	$29.95	Z		
Family Finances	$29.95	J		
Small Business Growth	$29.95	P		
Guide to Mutual Funds	$29.95	Q		
Audios				
Make Your Money Grow (abridged)	$13.00	1		
Invest Your Way to Wealth (abridged)	$15.00	2		
Taming the Paper Tiger (abridged)	$10.00	3		
Money-Smart Kids (abridged)	$13.00	4		

Subtotal	
*Sales Tax	
**Shipping	
Total	

* **Sales Tax:** *DC 5.75%; FL 6%; MD 5%; VA 4.5%*

** **Shipping:** *$3.00 for the first item; 75¢ for each additional item. For Federal Express delivery within 5 business days: $4.00 for the first item; 50¢ for each additional item.*

❑ My check payable to Kiplinger Books is enclosed for $_____.

❑ Charge my: ❑ VISA ❑ MasterCard ❑ American Express ❑ Discover

Card No. ☐☐☐☐☐☐☐☐☐☐☐☐☐☐☐☐

Signature _____

Exp. Date _____ Daytime Phone (_____) _____

Name _____

Company _____

Address _____ Apt. No. _____

City _____ State _____ Zip _____